REVIEW COPY

REVIEW COPY

Development Projects and Critical Theory of Environment

REVIEW COPY

Development Projects and Critical Theory of Environment

Jyotsna Bapat

SAGE Publications
New Delhi ■ Thousand Oaks ■ London

Copyright © Jyotsna Bapat, 2005

All rights reserved. No part of this book may be reproduced or utilized in any form or by any means, electronic or mechanical, including photocopying, recording or by any information storage or retrieval system, without permission in writing from the publisher.

First published in 2005 by

Sage Publications India Pvt Ltd
B-42, Panchsheel Enclave
New Delhi 110 017
www.indiasage.com

Sage Publications Inc   **Sage Publications Ltd**
2455 Teller Road   1 Oliver's Yard, 55 City Road
Thousand Oaks, California 91320   London EC1Y 1SP

Published by Tejeshwar Singh for Sage Publications India Pvt Ltd, phototypeset in 10/12 Nebraska by Prism Graphix, and printed at Chaman Enterprises, New Delhi.

Library of Congress Cataloging-in-Publication Data

Bapat, Jyotsna.
  Development projects and critical theory of environment / Jyotsna Bapat.
      p. cm.
  Includes bibliographical references and index.
  1. Economic development projects—Environmental aspects—India—Case studies. 2. Environmental impact analysis—India. 3. Economic development projects—Social aspects—India—Case studies. I. Title.
  TD195.E25B35   338.9'27—dc22   2005   2005006112

ISBN: 0–7619–3357–3 (Hb)   81–7829–502–4 (India-Hb)

Sage Production Team: Anupma Mehta, Shinjini Chatterjee, O.P. Bhasin and Santosh Rawat

To my family for its dedicated and
unflinching support

Contents

List of Tables   8
Preface   9

One   Introduction   13
Two   Critical Theory of Environment   36
Three   Methodology of Research   70
Four   Environmental Protest, Locality and Modernity   87
Five   National Parks, Land Alienation and Tribal Livelihoods   109
Six   *Aierawat* (The White Elephant) and Other Stories   128
Seven   Cultural Imperatives of Technology Transfer   151
Eight   Limits to Pollution Abatement   172
Nine   Do Ideologies Matter in Urban Transport Projects?   190
Ten   Environmental Struggles, Protest and Survival   216

References   229
Index   237
About the Author   244

List of Tables

8.1	The Nature of Co-operative Societies	175
8.2	Sample Villages and Households along the Tungabhadra River	184
8.3	Perception about Impacts of Pollution	187
9.1	Major Catchment Areas from North to South Bombay Island City	195
9.2	Number of People Assigned to Temporary Tenements	197
9.3	Number of People Assigned to Permanent Tenements	198
9.4	Infrastructure Amenities at Permanent Sites	199
10.1	Strategic Alliances and Outcomes of Projects	227

Preface

For the past decade or so, I have been involved in impact assessment studies related to the social and environmental impacts of development projects. These projects can be broadly categorized as those aimed at bringing about economic growth directly due to industrialization, and indirectly by promoting improvements in rural and urban infrastructure. These include projects related to irrigation dams, electricity, coal, transport and industrial pollution control. In addition, there are projects that claim to be 'green projects' and yet promise to bring about economic growth, like modern amusement parks and eco-tourism development projects through the development of national parks.

The decision to cite these techno-economic development projects is important. These projects are always located in relatively economically underdeveloped regions of relatively developed states. These regions are usually agriculturally underdeveloped, drought-prone areas, with high out-migrations. There is generally no overt resistance to the project by project-affected persons (PAPs) during the initiation stage. Local politicians consciously attempt to create awareness about the ability of the project to bring about economic and industrial growth. People who have out-migrated from these regions see this as a means of returning to their native lands. Even the technocrats and bureaucrats coming from the region believe that the region would gain economically, and therefore gain increased political clout in state politics as a result of the project. Thus, there is a strong positive public opinion related to these techno-economic development projects, in spite of the subsequent emergence of resistance, and sometimes social protest movements, against them.

The specific questions to which I am trying to find answers are:

- Why do local communities resist development projects 'after the fact'?
- Why do these protests against development projects, which are diverse in form and content in different regions, end up making similar moral and ethical claims?
- How should future environmental policies evolve?

At a more pragmatic level, I am motivated by interest in policy. Environmental impact analysis (EIA) has developed as an interdisciplinary methodology to capture the impacts of development projects on physical and socio-cultural-economic environments. Although EIA studies are carried out to measure and predict the impacts of a development project on the ecology and geology of a region, the socio-cultural and economic impacts on human populations affected by the project are specially categorized and measured under the social impact assessment (SIA) studies. This forms a distinct subset of all major EIA studies.

Environmental protest movements draw on the history of the region and/or 'talking claims' of the local people in their assertion of environmental impacts. These accounts are claimed to be true, can be verified as such, and originate in the same reality that the development project seeks to impact but are often divergent. At policy levels, these claims did not find any place in the social impact assessment studies till recently. As a result, theorizing within the emerging discipline of environmental sociology is in a state of crisis. The knowledge generated by social impact assessment studies and that generated by historical and interpretative understanding are often contradictory to one another. In order to continue to be meaningful and relevant to policy planners and decision makers, the emerging discipline will have to be able to explain this discrepancy. A comprehensive critical theory of environment is proposed here to better explain the environmental impacts of development projects. I suggest a research programme for developing a critical theory of environment, consisting of a complex of theories and multiplicity of methodologies that would be required to adequately capture this reality.

Such a critical theory of environment is a humanist variant of the self-estrangement theory that seeks to simultaneously explain the world and criticize it, and to do it in such a way that it would empower its audience to change it. This book is an endeavour in that direction. What I observed in the unfolding of events related to development project sites is that the project undergoes changes through distinct phases. There is an initial enthusiastic optimism regarding the project in the region before its initiation. During the construction phase, stories of 'injustice' start circulating in the local media and through 'talks' among people. Very soon, project-affected people, if they are not completely marginalized, are able to mobilize resources and begin resistance movements against the project. This usually coincides with the time the project is commissioned. Project commissioning is also the time that the movement peaks; over time the protests die out but the movement continues to simmer and uneasy peace prevails between the project-affected persons (PAPs) and project promoters. But the 'talks' about injustice and the resistance by the project-affected persons exist. Even though these 'talks' are not overt or easily visible, a closer examination of the PAPs in the context of such development project will always reveal them.

The pattern reflected in the case studies I have cited here is often paralleled in our everyday reality, whenever events put us in a catch-22 situation. Such a situation forces us to critically rethink our priorities and balance pros and cons in order to reach a decision. Therefore, decisions reached on ways to resolve crises to the best advantage, or often, with the least harm to ourselves, are a result of self-reflection. Self-reflection as process derives both from current contingencies and past experience; therefore, as Habermas suggests, transformative strategies are products of personal social histories. This, then, is the crux of my hypothesis, which has been validated in the context of groups of people faced with the socio-cultural and environmental impacts of development projects.

This dilemma is at the crux of the crisis faced by PAPs in any development project. Its resolution in different contexts by different project-affected persons is the subject matter of the book. The subject of the environmental impacts of development projects in developing countries is vast. So I cannot offer a comprehensive super-highway but only a series of footprints that I was involved in generating, and of which therefore, I possess a more intimate knowledge. I have studied each of the projects presented here, first hand. These are medium-sized projects involving a few thousand project-affected persons and the project impact areas are fairly localized within a 5 to 25 sq km radius. Each of these examples, though based in India, may be regarded as typical of many others in other developing countries in the world. I do not make claims about providing all the answers. All I have are my personal experiences from specific projects, with the environmental impacts and articulation of these impacts by various stakeholders and a sociological imagination. The last decade coincides with my entry into the discipline in a very narrow sphere of tourism, infrastructure and industrialization projects. My focus has always been that of a specialist trying to understand and capture social impacts within an environmental impact assessment statement needed for policy decisions. I claim to know enough about these because I have maintained a continued interest in these projects and often revisited them over time. On the basis of these experiences, I propose a critical theory of environment with a practical intent. I hope that this journey can take us beyond the theoretical divisions between sustainable development, dependency theory and a humanist variant thereof, that exist in the newly developing field of environmental sociology, to a broader view that recognizes a convergence in theory and methodology so essential to the growth of the discipline.

Last of all, the present volume is an outcome of an academic year spent at the Department of Sociology of Macalester College in St Paul, Minnesota. The work could not have been completed without the invaluable suggestions and help provided by Professor James W. Laine, Arnold H. Lowe Professor and Chair of Religious Studies at Macalester College, and the Scholar in Residence Program Fellowship sponsored by the Fulbright Foundation, New Delhi. I express my heartfelt gratitude to both Professor Laine and to the Foundation for giving me the opportunity to develop new insights into my field of work.

One

Introduction

Human activities resulting from modern industrial and infrastructure growth are seen as being essential for bringing about rapid economic growth and social justice. They are also the main trigger for a call for ecological justice and respect for nature.

In developed countries, justice for all living beings beyond the human species, involving both plant and animal life (described loosely as flora and fauna, respectively), is the driver for environmental studies generated by Western scholars. The basic premise is that environmental impacts of industrial development activities lead to destruction of physical environment, mainly due to pollution. Therefore, conservation and preservation form the focus of activities aimed at bringing about environmental justice, and aim to challenge the practices that involve particular technological processes resulting in the destruction of fauna and flora. Technological change has been seen as a solution and new eco-friendly technologies have evolved to take care of this issue.

Scholars from the Western world, mainly Americans (Dunlap and Catton, 2002; Rudel, 2002) have divided the subject matter of environmental sociology into two categories: natural resource sociology and environmental sociology. The former refers to environmental projects related to natural resource extraction, such as forestry, wildlife conservation projects, mining projects, etc., and is a matter of interest to environmentalists in developing countries. The latter refers to the issue of environmental pollution, and disposal of toxic and hazardous wastes, which are matters of interest for environmentalists in developed countries.

But the Third World perspective on industrial and infrastructure growth taking place in these countries is different from the call for environmental justice given by Western scholars and the compartmentalization of environmental projects proposed by American scholars. It is rooted in a different set of realities and challenges, faced by Third World industrial and infrastructure development. These projects in developing countries have to be located on lands that have pre-existing residents making claims to these lands and their produce. Their livelihoods and the emergent cultures depend on land and the resultant industrial and infrastructure growth threatens its destruction. This was rarely faced as a substantive issue in the Western industrial world, partially because land-ownership was clearly established through a series of legislations that preceded industrial development and that drove many people from rural areas into urban centres, and partially because plenty of barren land was available or made available through brute force against the native population, for industrialization in the 'New World'.

In order to bring about rapid economic growth and social justice, developing countries like India implement large infrastructure development projects. The project development usually goes through four distinct stages (Chakraverty, 1996), which are the planning and conceptualization stage, initiation stage, construction stage and operational stage (planning, implementation, construction and operation—PICO). The planning and conceptualization stage of the development project usually takes place away from the actual site of the project. The decision to situate a project in a particular region involves complex processes of advocacy and political bargaining among various social actors at various national, and often, international levels. Once the decision to locate a project at a particular site is made, the initiation, construction and operation stages of the project expose the people living in the surrounding areas, referred to as the project-affected persons (PAPs) of the project site, to different kinds of risks. But the realization of these risks by the PAPs usually comes 'after the fact' of the project. This results in the policy makers and the project promoters undermining the legitimacy of various claims made, and resistance put up, by the PAPs against the project. More recently, this has resulted in an environmental backlash against development projects in general, causing delays and cancellation of projects. It is not the most desirable outcome for a developing country like India. Therefore, there is a need for a comprehensive theory of environmental sociology, with empirical applicability. Such a theory would simultaneously understand and explain the interaction between PAPs and the project, and do it in such a way that the explanation provides the solution to issues in environmental sociology. This is the primary objective of this exercise.

The book focuses on the environmental impacts of development projects in India. The impact of a development project is dynamic, spanning over years, with the initial impacts being more favourable to the PAPs and the subsequent impacts being increasingly adverse. This is mainly because the status quo is disrupted and power relationships within the society that the PAPs belong to change for the worse, particularly for the elites, over time, due to the project. These projects straddle the line between the two categories of interests of environmentalists, namely, natural resource sociology and environmental sociology. The combination of multiple theoretical frameworks is increasingly becoming relevant as more and more modern capital-intensive development projects are being located in a developing country like India.

Development and Environment Theories

Theorizing about the environmental impacts of development projects roughly falls into two dominant categories, namely, the modernization perspective and its environmental variant, sustainable development, and the dependency perspective and its variant, the political ecology perspective. The least explored—the Weberian perspective in the theorizing of environmental sociology—draws mainly on Max Weber's works on agrarian sociology, comparative sociology and the rise of capitalism in modern Europe (cf. Kalberg, 1994; Weber, 1958, 1998 [1908]). These are relevant in understanding the impacts of the development projects in a developing country like India, mainly because agrarian societies are affected by the effort to promote capitalist industrial growth, and a comparative perspective of the resultant changes over time (historical, diachronic) and across projects (synchronic) facilitates a better understanding of the common thread running through the diverse projects. Weber treated environmental factors as interactive components of complex causal models, by favouring the selective survival of certain social strata over others (Buttel, 1986). The development of this perspective in the form presented here spans my entire career. I shall describe this personal and professional journey shortly.

The essence of environmentalism is the critique of the dominant economic development paradigm, independent of whether the belief is in sustainable development or dependency theory. The critique is indicative of a crisis within the discipline of environmental sociology. This is not to suggest that the discipline will die out, but to propose that a critical rethinking in the theorizing within the discipline is essential to ensure its survival. Therefore, the environmental impacts of development projects are to be understood within the context of development theories. At the same time, it is equally important to conceptualize the environmental impacts of development projects on human groups and communities within the context of interaction between human beings and their physical environment, as conceptualized by different ecological theories, mainly within cultural anthropology (Bennett, 1976).

The dominant theory in development literature is the modernization theory and its environmental variant, sustainable development, and the dependency theory and its variant, political ecology as the radical, often explicitly Marxist, critique of development (Scott, 1995). The growth of the sustainable development paradigm was marked by debates on the future of the environment in the early 1970s. Rachel Carson's *Silent Spring* (1962), which focused on the enormity of ecological damage brought about by industrial effluents being dumped in the rivers, started the ball rolling. In the early 1970s was published the epoch-making article, 'Only One Earth' by Barbara Ward and Rene Dubois (1972), funded by the United Nations Development Program (UNDP). The article suggested that the biosphere of man's inheritance and the technosphere of his creation are in deep conflict. The modification of the environment due to industrialization has a positive aspect. It reduces the apparent long-term insolubility of many historical and current problems of food, energy, clothing and other material comforts. But if the present trend continues, then the negative aspects of pollution and resource depletion will far outweigh the positive aspects. A balance needs to be maintained to sustain life on earth. Similar predictions were made by a group of studies funded by independent scientists called the 'Club of Rome'. The 'Limits to Growth' (Meadows et al., 1972) report published by them was based on data collected at global scales and the mathematical model of the world system was used to predict the future. The model predicted doom and stated that continued resource shortage, crowding, pollution, food failures or some equally powerful force will soon control current trends in population growth, natural resource exploitation and capital investment in agriculture, if persuasion and psychological factors fail to do so. This model was heavily criticized (King, 1975) and similar studies with different assumptions were cited to show other results (Barney, 1981; Forrester, 1972; Mesorovic and Pestel, 1975).

The assumptions of the 1970s' environmentalists were based on the perception that human beings and their environment can be treated as independent entities interacting with one another. Theorizing within these genera of studies is in the form of the systems approach, and positivist quantitative methodology is used to substantiate it. These findings had international political implications. The popular analogy for industrialization was that of a 'runaway train' and the question was one of approaching the problems generated by it. Logically, one could try to instal brakes on the train to slow it down. The more liberal interpretation was that the slowing down had to be done by the industrially developed countries, as they had the technologies and resources, could see the pitfalls, take precautionary measures to avoid them and share their experiences with the less developed world. The less generous interpretations by the conservatives in the developed world also had an associated action plan. If there were finite limits to growth, then the 'tragedy of commons' and the 'lifeboat metaphor' (Hardin, 1968, 1974) were often cited by 'doomsday' professors to be the natural outcomes of resource exploitation. The 'tragedy' doctrine cites an example pertaining to common grazing lands in European countries. Simply put, individuals wanting to maximize their profits would own more and more cattle, resulting in the over-exploitation of common grasslands leading to the 'tragedy' of resource depletion beyond rejuvenation. In pursuit of individual greed, the commons would be depleted. Similarly, in the case of a sinking ship, only a limited number of people can be allowed aboard a lifeboat, or else everyone would sink. Both these conservative perspectives emphasized that since the earth's resources are limited and the developed world has to survive, they should limit developing countries from accessing the 'global common resources' or the natural resources would be depleted and the 'lifeboat' for the developed world would sink. Therefore, putting appropriate brakes in place meant limiting the access to the commons, essentially implying that the less developed world should not be allowed to develop quickly.

The scientists had their own interpretations and solutions. Technologically optimistic models proposed that pollution abatement strategies would ensure that we stay within limits of resources. The technologically conservative models emphasized the 'three Rs', namely, 'reduce, re-use and recycle' resources to ensure sustainable development. The technologically pessimistic models called for a 'return to nature' and 'back to basics', whereby small, simpler technologies should be explored and adopted (Schumacher, 1984).

Thus, the sustainable development theory believes that the root cause of environmental crisis is that human beings control nature in the process of techno-economic development, leading to the destruction of various species and habitats. Therefore, solutions to environmental issues lie in better pollution abatement policies or better wildlife conservation policies. Over time, this theory has resulted in practical policies, in the development of Environmental Impact Assessment (EIA), including Social Impact Assessment (SIA), methodologies. These methodologies have become fairly standardized and handbooks are available to routinely record environmental impacts in the form of checklists. There are many such published handbooks that provide guidelines to applying the systems approach. The more recent ones typically include a checklist on population profiles and socio-economic and cultural impacts (Barrow, 1997; Morris and Therivel, 1995). These checklists establish a baseline of population and socio-economic activities before the project is initiated in the region, and measure changes in the baseline after the project is completed. In anticipation of the adverse impacts of the project, certain mitigative measures are also incorporated in EIA studies. These impacts are considered for decision on the project 'costs and benefits', and if the benefits exceed the costs, the project is sanctioned. But these suffer from a quantification bias. The impacts that cannot be measured quantitatively tend to get ignored. However, these methodologies are applied in a narrow sense to projects in developing countries, and to impacts within the boundaries of a stated project. This narrow approach is mainly responsible for the adverse reaction to these projects by the local population. The secondary impacts resulting from the project, and often extending beyond the specific project site, are considered to be outside the scope of these studies as far as the project authorities are considered. This is true in India and rightly so, as the responsibility for mitigation of the impact of regional economic growth should rest with the state or regional planning authority. It is the gap between the impacts and the mitigative measures that is mainly responsible for the protest against the project.

The other dominant perspective in the development literature is the dependency theory and its environmental variant, political ecology. Dependency theorists believe that the root cause of the environmental crisis is that human beings, in their pursuit of control over nature, easily transform this pursuit in terms of control of some human beings over others through their desire for individual wealth and property. Therefore, solutions to environmental issues lie in policies aimed at ensuring distributive justice and social equity. Theorizing takes on the form of variants of the Marxian and dependency theories, and methodologies are dictated by a historical and qualitative analysis to substantiate it. Another variant of the Marxian theories is the political ecology (Guha and Martinez-Alier, 1997) perspective as a critique of existing positivist empirical theory.

James O'Connor (1998) suggests the most comprehensive political ecology perspective with an emphasis on new social movements. A decline in the three political economic models—Keynesian welfare economics, socialist planning, and the nationalist development models of the South—have led to a theoretical crisis. Each of them is proving to be, in its own way, bureaucratic, inflexible and nationalistic—failing to incorporate the impacts of global transnational businesses and urban-centric growth. There have been broadly two popular responses to stagnant wages, growing economic insecurity and marginalization, degradation of the environment and of community life, and the conditions of production. The first has been a call for reduction in the hours of work, particularly in Europe. The second popular response to unemployment marginalization and the socioeconomic malaise of our times is the advent of new social movements. O'Connor theorizes new social movements, in general, and ecological movements, in particular, in terms of political economy, specifically Marxism. Environmental social movements have objective referents in production conditions, and ecology and environmentalism in natural conditions. In Polanyi's (1944) terms, these new movements are societies fighting against the commodification of production conditions. The neglect and subversion of conditions of production as a consequence of capital accumulation are many and varied. On the basis of the preservation first! (PF!) principle in their respective production conditions, people have evolved strategies of non-capitalist forms of production. These take the form of community businesses, co-operatives and mixed enterprises, and are viewed as forms of socioeconomic organization and monetary expenditure, required to preserve, define and enhance the conditions of life and life itself. These movements claim to preserve a healthy, cultured, civic-minded and reasonably happy population, liveable communities and the integrity of the 'environment'. In sum, the preservation first! principle is labour intensive, and governed by egalitarian principles and sociopolitical logic, rather than by purely economic logic. Preservation first! may contain affective and aesthetic meanings as well as instrumental ones. Thus, environmental protest movements are subsumed under the political economy perspective as a protest against the predominantly capitalist form of production. The dependency perspective and its associated methodologies, rooted in historical and qualitative analyses, are popular among social activists and Marxian scholars. The focus is on social change. These scholars are interested in organized social protest movements resulting from mobilization of the PAPs of a development project. The emphasis is on ways in which people organize themselves, the form of protest and the use of mass media to gain political mileage and thus the attention of policy makers, to bring about changes in existing policies to favour the PAPs. Thus, these studies are reactive rather than proactive and typically occur after the project is initiated and sometimes even after it is implemented.

In essence, both the modernization and development theses and their variants propose that, to the extent they can understand the relationship between environment and human beings, they can change the future through human interventions. The Weberian perspective, on the other hand, believes that reality is so complex that one can only try to understand the functioning of reality. Therefore, 'understanding' and not manipulation and control, should be the objective of social research. I agree with this, but I believe at the same time, that it is possible to take a normative stand based on the right, truthful and just outcomes of the processes. The groups that believe in sustainable development look upon environmental domination by humans as the crucial issue and are likely to focus on species destruction and environmental abuse through industrial and other effluents, and criticize dependency theorists for their insufficient focus on larger environmental issues. Dependency theorists believe that it is counter-productive to talk of environmental pollution and species destruction without addressing the issues of equity and social justice. Therefore, it would be more productive to talk about alternate technologies, rights over common property resources and sustainable livelihoods, which would have resonance in the minds of people living in the rural areas of developing countries. Proponents of sustainable development make little sense to people in rural areas, but appeal to the urban middle classes of developing countries. India is no exception to both these observations. While Weberian theorizing would incorporate both of these interpretations in understanding outcomes, such a theorizing may not have a populist appeal.

The dominant debates in environmentalism provide the context within which the environmental movements across the world can be classified. In the developed world, in recent years, most development projects have not resulted in the displacement of the human groups during the construction of a new project. The sustainable development paradigm and its associated theories in the developed world therefore predominantly focus on habitat preservation for species other than human brings. This shapes environmental movements in the developed countries. In developing countries, the story is more complex. There are socio-political consequences of development projects, in terms of the locality of the project site, in addition to the environmental consequences. Thus, both the issues, that is, the preservation of the environment and survival of the PAPs are equally crucial issues from the perspective of developing countries. To the extent that group identities are closely linked in techno-economic systems that do not use complex forms of energy and depend on the preservation of natural environment, the PF! principle applies to these groups, and therefore, the Marxist interpretation of environment movements in the developing countries is valid. It ensures a chance of 'development at their own pace' for the PAPs. This argument runs into problems when the PAPs are not dependent on subsistence economies, and the project involves complex techno-economic systems, as most development projects—such as those pertaining to power or industry—do.

The dominant form of theorizing the Third World environmental protest movements is rooted in the preservation first! principle which essentializes such movements as being representative of pristine and sustainable development initiated by the people, and economic growth and industrialization as the root cause of all evil, including human rights violations (Barik, 2000). This has led to a backlash against development projects in the Third World and the dissociation of the urban middle classes from the Third World and the First World alike, from the global environmental movement. It is therefore essential to restore a link between various paradigms to bring together alienated people in the interest of a global environmental movement, which is even more relevant now than before. A humanist combination of the growth and sustainable development paradigms is required to restore this link.

On the basis of fieldwork related to my case studies, I propose that the new movements and their dominant rhetoric for reclaiming their rights to commons in their environment are not indications of some primordial call for 'return to nature', but a strategic action on part of the participants to negotiate with the agencies of state with which the new movements have to deal. The possibility of using the environmental protest movement to ensure economic growth and social justice within the sustainable development paradigm is a new way of understanding these movements. This possibility is explored here.

At any particular point in the lifecycle of the movement, those engaged are heard to say more or less the same things, such as 'the state is unresponsive, oppressive, and too bureaucratic, relies on expert conclusions, vital statistics and lies, and cannot get anything done'. In the face of this typical response to the state, three alternative political strategies are possible for the movements, according to O'Connor (1998), which are: the anarchist strategy, efforts to mainstream environmentalism through reform in liberal democracy, and democratization of the state. The last option is particularly favoured by O'Connor. It involves decentralizing the power of decision making and actions of the state, in order to make state agencies more responsive and accountable to the local struggles. I propose that the process of 'mainstreaming environmentalism' and 'democratization of the state' are two sides of the same coin and have to happen simultaneously. I would argue that mainstreaming environmentalism through a relatively open-ended environmental policy, as in the case of an urban transportation project discussed in the last chapter here, is a distinct possibility, but that the efforts to mainstream environmentalism through reform should still be the long-term objective, which should evolve through decentralization and making state agencies more responsive and accountable to local struggles.

Human Ecology

Human control over nature is a basic premise of development theories. It is the problematic of ecological theories of the human–environment relationship, and is as old as the discipline of anthropology (Bennett, 1976). Conceptualizing the 'man–environment' relationship in the discipline begins with simple linear and deterministic models of anthropo-geography. In the paradigms of environmental possibalism, the linear nature of the interactions maintained by these models is discussed. They propose that the environment provides possibilities by way of several ecological niches from which different groups of people choose one or the other, thus reducing co-operation and competition. The more complex paradigm of Stewardian cultural ecology takes into account the impact of culture. This model considers a feedback loop, which suggests that just as human culture is shaped and modified by the environment that these social groups live in, culture is equally responsible for altering the physical environment. Thus, a complex feedback loop exists between culture and ecology, which simultaneously shape and change each other.

The more complex eco–systemic models are an offshoot of this. The adaptive systems are made up of multiple elements that are in dynamic equilibrium with each other (Bennett, 1976) so that changes in any one of these elements affect the system as a whole, but in different ways. Thus, these eco-systemic models are based on the assumption that if the relationship between the various parts of the system is known, one can predict the systemic changes brought about by changes in any one element.

Each of these eco-systemic and socio-cultural models of human interaction, with their physical environment, have developed in isolation. So far, there is no unifying theory that would bring these two spheres—the eco-systemic sphere and the socio-cultural sphere—together in understanding human interaction with the physical environment. The fact is that over time, ecological transition in human societies has been towards larger resource-consuming instrumentalities as a result of certain techno-economic superstructures. To take the argument one step further, not having a comprehensive theory that can incorporate all these realities without any of them losing the legitimacy of their claims, has gone against the interests of the PAPs, and subsequently, against social justice. This would indicate that in the interest of a more holistic understanding of human environmental interaction, there is a need to unify these independent developments in the spheres of ecology and culture under a comprehensive theory of environmental sociology and anthropology.

While the two theoretical paradigms are consistent in themselves, knowledge about the social and environmental reality generated by these two paradigms is very diverse and often conflicting. But the fact that these paradigms reflect two sides of the same coin is often ignored. There is a need to creatively combine these two apparently disparate approaches. The inability to agree on the root cause of the environmental crisis emerging from the process of development has plunged theorizing in the newly emerging field of environmental sociology into a deep state of crisis. The prognosis is not that the 'patient will die', but that there is a need to give the discipline a new lease of life by creating an alternate 'critical theory of environment' as a humanist variant of the self-estrangement theory. Such a theory, which draws upon an existing environmental theory and a social theory, and creatively combines them into a critical theory of environment, is proposed here. Thus, it is imperative to develop the third and equally important approach proposed by Weber in sociology. Weber treated environmental factors as interactive components of complex causal models, favouring the selective survival of certain social strata and social actors over others. Here, primacy is given to the actors, the meanings they generate and their transformative actions that bring about social change. Human beings cannot avoid action; it is not in their nature. They act rationally, given their limited knowledge of a situation, even if the outcomes are beyond their control. At a methodological level, critical realism is suggested as appropriate to incorporate these elements. A four-point research programme is proposed in the following chapter to develop such a critical theory of environment.

Reflections on the relationship between the development of theory and its practice in the environmental context, have been going on simultaneously throughout my academic career. I was able to develop the appropriate environmental theory, but not go beyond it. Subsequent project-related experience as an environmental sociologist/anthropologist, helped me acquire new insights into the ways in which different groups of people make various claims on the basis of their interests. These claims change over time, and therefore the legitimacy of the claims they make becomes questionable. If this is the typical behaviour of people, are they being untruthful or are they changing rapidly to adapt to the changing physical environment that works as a catalyst for changes in their social environment? What kind of theorizing will be needed to understand these sifting claims of PAPs, governments and project promoters? These were some of the questions with which I started.

What emerged was a systemic pattern of PAP behaviour over time. This is the common thread running through the case studies presented here. There was the rhetoric of a promise of the 'brave new world' as a result of the project, in the form of jobs and economic prosperity at the initiation stage, dissent and then protest or resistance to the project over time, and repetition of the pattern project after project. I had a wide variety of experience of EIA and SIA to choose from. The nature of the projects varied from recreational tourism to technology transfer to infrastructure projects like power, irrigation, water augmentation, industrial pollution treatment projects to environmental management plans for an urban metropolis to transportation projects. The six case studies presented here are chosen from about 15-odd projects that I had the privilege to be exposed to so far. Although the pattern of initial acceptance of the project to the ultimate rejection of these projects by the PAPs was universal, the specifics of the protest varied and there were limits to which the PAPs could take their protests. Ways of resisting the projects were unique to each group of PAPs. The project promoters were always 'outsiders', the PAPs were the natives, and the state or Central Government officials were responsible for promoting or not promoting the project. More recently, a new breed of PAPs has emerged, that of the public sector technocrats who are adopting the strategies used by PAPs to resist privatization of utilities. The six case studies presented here are typical. Each of the three main categories of actors, that is the project promoters, the PAPs and the government agencies, play a unique role in the project outcomes presented here. The PAPs form three categories: those who can afford to resist and in the process, have tested and reached the limits of action for the present; those who cannot afford to resist; and the public sector employees acing as PAPs. The project promoters belong to both the public sector and private sector, while the government agencies range from local, to state, to the Central Government.

Capturing this diversity of the case studies required an appropriate methodology. I was disillusioned by positivism, and being an anthropologist by training, the doctrine of cultural relativism was ingrained in me. Having explored the limits of the relativist approach and at the same time, while learning to differentiate between tools or 'methods of data collection' and 'research methodology', I realized that I needed a methodology rooted in 'critical realism' to tie up the theoretical insights and the case studies. This methodology captures the dynamism inherent in the environmental impacts of a project coming to a region. It allows me to use different methods of data collection and weave a comprehensive story of the real-life environmental impacts of a project on different sets of affected people, and the way they deal with these impacts over time. I shall elaborate upon this methodology in a separate chapter subsequently.

The Indian Context

Theorizing about the environmental impacts of development projects in India so far falls into two main categories: the modernization perspective and the dependency perspective, with an explicit Marxian framework (Savur, 1999), and its variant, the more recent political ecology perspective with its emphasis on ecological distribution conflict (Guha and Martinez-Alier, 1997). The varying perspectives depict different realities of the social environmental impacts of a development project, often contradicting each other. Development projects, as they have come to be identified over the last few decades, refer to large engineering infrastructure development projects aimed at the rapid economic growth of that region, in particular, and the country, as a whole. Such infrastructure development projects include irrigation and water supply projects involving dams, transport projects like highways, airports, railways and ports; energy projects, including mining and power projects, industrial development parks; and more recently, tourism development projects, including eco-tourism, following the creation of national parks and wildlife sanctuaries.

Economic liberalization adopted and implemented in India since the late 1980s and the early 1990s has led to the opening up of the Indian economy to multinational corporations and a push for an economic reform agenda that facilitated the flow of foreign capital into the country. Infrastructure investment in the agricultural sector through large irrigation projects with dams and the use of high-yielding varieties of crops and fertilizers to usher in the Green Revolution, is an old story. The opening up of the infrastructure sector in the areas of telecom, roads and highways, power, mining and drinking water supply, sewage and storm-water drainage and even tourism development projects, is a more recent phenomenon. Beginning with the early 1990s, infrastructure funding for large urban and industrial infrastructure projects in major cities and towns in India became available through multilateral donors in the form of economic aid and technology transfer. This is the dominant theme for four out of six development projects considered here. The two others raised capital through domestic and foreign markets.

Once a decision to locate a development project is taken at the political level, a development project broadly goes through four stages, the PICO, mentioned earlier. These projects typically do not cause large-scale displacement, resettlement or ecological changes that irrigation projects do. Nor can all the negative social, economic and environmental consequences be directly and causally attributed to these projects. They do result in stipulated benefits in the social, environmental and economic spheres. In spite of this, in India these projects are sites of active resistance by local communities with the help of environmental NGOs. Conflicts between project promoters and local communities exist virtually at all sites, irrespective of the type of project or the state within which the project is located. Some of these conflicts result in environmental protest movements that are fairly vocal, and sometimes violent.

The timing of the struggle is important, as these conflicts begin at the construction stage and peak at the time of the operational stage of the project. One often wonders why there is no obvious resistance to the project during the planning stage, when the decision to locate the project in a specific region is taken, or at the initiation stage, when the project site is measured and marked. When the protest movement emerges, there is discrepancy between the environmental impacts resulting from the project, as stated in the official documents of the Environmental Impact Assessment studies, commissioned at the beginning of the project, and the claims made by the proponents of the movement. More importantly, certain projects of a similar nature, implemented 20 years ago did not evoke similar adverse community reactions.

The outcomes of these struggles vary, but what is common across these struggles, regardless of whether they are spearheaded by active environmental NGOs or by local leadership, is the 'moral economy argument', which allows them to effectively catapult what is essentially a local struggle into a national or global environmental resistance movement. There is a much higher sensitivity among multinational organizations and international aid agencies to environmental issues than to poverty or social inequality, when they are dealing with projects in developing countries. Discourses on transnational environmental issues and claims of moral economy and subsistence ethics are better articulated in Western cultures. It is easier to conjure up images of a pristine nature and of local cultures being destroyed by transnational power than images of pot-bellied children with different skin colour and racial features, being adversely affected by these projects as these images of environmental disasters have a better transnational appeal. The forms of articulation, their language and their use of media, are common across the NGOs involved.

Finally, over the last few years, new alliances are being formed between stakeholders that historically stood on opposite sides for project-related negotiations. More recently, the large public sector bureaucracies, in their fight against the economic liberalization agenda that would allow privatization and competition, are using the same rhetoric. It is used to delay the process of decentralization of governance, and the regulation and entry of multiple new players in the form of competition. Even the 'full' implementation of an already approved infrastructure project can be re-negotiated using this rhetoric, as in case of the Dabhol power plant case study presented here.

State of Theoretical Knowledge

Literature on social protest movements is as old as colonial history in India. Not surprisingly, environmental history in India is dominated by protest movements of natives against the colonizers, in the context of forestry. In the late 1970s and the early part of the 1980s, studies on environmental sociology focused mainly on issues related to forestry and dams. Timber-logging related to the commercial exploitation of forests and the subsequent demarcation of national parks and wildlife sanctuaries, and the impact of these old and new developments on the local communities, mainly tribal groups, were the focus of studies related to forestry. While dams and irrigation projects resulting in the displacement and resettlement of people in the submergence areas were subjects of studies related to agricultural projects, the social-environmental impacts of industrial and infrastructure projects are of relatively recent origin.

The pre-project socio-economic impact assessment of the projects before the 1970s was through the cost-benefit analysis and quantification that it offered within the systems approach of development studies. These studies had to indicate the economic justification of the project in terms of the cost-benefit analysis. If the benefits outweighed the costs of implementation of the project, the implementation was justified. These studies usually preceded all the dam and irrigation projects. A similar quantitative framework was extended to the environmental impacts of these projects after the mid-1970s and was identified with the sustainable development methodology. This provided the necessary impact assessment framework for mainly the empirical quantification of the socio-environmental impacts of the project.[1]

The documentation of revolt or resistance by local communities, mainly tribal groups in forestry (Guha, 1989), and irrigation projects is dominated by highlighting the conflict with the state agencies (Drèze et al., 1996). The theoretical orientation of Marxian sociology, with its emphasis on historical factors fitted in with the colonial policies related to the forest sector in India in the past. The continuation of the policies in independent India leading to a further marginalization of the marginal groups like migrant plantation labour or tribal groups, and the degradation of forest lands was the focus of studies in environmental sociology (Grove and Sagwan, 1997). The crisis of forest degradation is being handled through corrective action in the form of social forestry projects and newer experiments therein such as the 'Anna Bari' system in West Bengal, wherein the community got the rights to non-wood forest produce in exchange for protecting the trees planted by the forest department. Dams and irrigation projects resulting in the displacement of people and the destruction of ecology upstream, constituted the other focus of environmental sociology (Baviskar, 1998). Since major dam projects were undertaken after Independence, this context and the resettlement and rehabilitation strategies lent themselves to the dependency theory and the political ecology paradigm.

The more vocal environmental struggles like the fish workers' agitation or the *Narmada Andolan* or the *Chipko Andolan* against commercial forestry have been conceptualized as 'new protest movements', on the lines of Habermas by Gail Omvedt (1993). The 'new social movements' which emerged between the 1970s and the 1990s can be loosely identified as: *(i)* the women's movement; *(ii)* the anti-caste movement; *(iii)* environmental movements; and *(iv)* farmers' movements or peasant struggles over issues of market production (Omvedt, 1993). The emergence of these movements is a result of people beginning to struggle in new ways and formulate new theories

---

[1]For a few studies using the systems approach and EIA methodologies, see Agarwal and Narain, 1998; Bapat, 1995a; Development Alternatives, 1989, 1989–91; various EIA Reports (1992a, 1992b, 1995); and Pareikh et al., 1985.

and ideologies in confronting realities that do not fit rigid analytical categories.

The 'new social movements' are social movements in the sense of having a broad organizational structure and an ideology aimed at social change. They define their exploitation and oppression in new terms—related to the conflict school, but having clear differences with it. These groups are exploited in ways which are related to the new processes of contemporary capitalism, but which are left unconceptualized by 'traditional' conflict theorists. The environmental movements within the new social movements express the concerns of groups of people regarding the depletion of water, degradation of land and other changes in ecosystems affecting the traditional patterns of natural resource exploitation. These movements generally take place in rural areas, and the leadership for the movement generally comes from outside the community that is adversely affected. The secret to the more successful environmental protest movement is its ability to retain its legitimacy. The most effective strategies of 'non-violent protest' through *satyagraha* perfected by Gandhi, are still at the core of the more successful environmental protest movements like the *Narmada Bachao* and the *Chipko Andolan*s.

The ecosystems perspective and the carrying capacity models, however, have very limited impacts because of the difficulties of modelling such complex systems. Attempts at energy modelling in the Indian context indicate that these models have very limited applicability. These are optimization models based on theoretical assumptions of state equilibrium. In short, various elements of the complex system are incorporated into a simultaneous equation. A single number, the parameter, represents the relationship between one element and others. This kind of modelling exercises dominated energy studies. The accuracy of the model and its predictability thus depend on the accuracy of the estimate of the parameter, the possible quantification of the elements that constitute the model, and minimal disruption within the system. All these prove to be impossible conditions in a complex real world situation.

Even if an optimal solution to a particular issue is arrived at, bringing about the necessary changes in the behaviour of people is always a problem. For example, if one did predict, say an optimal solution to the issue of loss of forest cover due to increased fuel wood consumption, by increasing the consumption of kerosene in the system, bringing about changes in people's behaviour so that only a limited number of people will change their behaviour in the desired direction, always remains a problem. The relationship between policy changes and human behaviour is still a grey area, particularly in these modelling exercises.

Pragmatic Interest

This brings us to the pragmatic interest in environmental policy. As indicated earlier, there are a multiplicity of theoretical approaches for understanding the environmental and social impacts of development projects that are often in conflict with each other (Bapat, 1998). While choosing approaches that support certain interests over others, in donor-funded development projects, policy makers conveniently use this multiplicity of theories. The Department of Environment and Forests usually supports the approach that results in 'least cost' to the project promoters by claiming it to be more rational. Very often, the various state departments or the public sector are partners with the promoters of the project. The dominant approach of the cost-benefit analysis that quantified and converted all cost and benefits into monetary terms, held sway over other approaches till the early 1980s mainly because it resulted in the least cost to the project promoters, as most of the environmental impacts, especially on rural partially-monetized economies could not be fully quantified and monetized.

To the extent, that the unintended and unforeseen negative impacts of a project were faced by dispossessed communities, project promoters were able to implement the project with the least social resistance. This is not to suggest that no community suffers negative consequences, but to point out that the social skills and resource access needed to mobilize the social protest movement highlighting their suffering through the media and to influence policy, may be lacking among certain groups of affected people. Subsequently, increasing criticism of the analytical framework emphasizing the quantitative and monetary impacts, and the mounting major environmental protest movements forced policy makers to realize the qualitative and non-quantifiable costs. But this criticism was given only a token recognition because of the difficulty of the task. Implementing the methodologies to incorporate the qualitative livelihood-affecting changes in the discipline of environmental sociology still remain a challenge.

Not having a comprehensive theory and methodology within environmental sociology has gone against the PAPs and especially those who depended on common property resources for their livelihoods. The cost-benefit analytical framework to measure and convert everything into monetary value is problematic because complex bio-social systems that the tribal and rural communities live in, do not easily lend themselves to quantification. The human groups that form a part of the complex have cultivated complex skills that are adaptive to the particular ecosystem that they are a part of. These skills do not translate easily into other complex socio-ecological systems like agrarian ecosystems or urban ecosystems. So assuming that they can be trained, when human beings well-adapted to one type of ecosystem are relocated to a new system, usually need time and training to adapt to the new situations. But the tools and the methodologies needed to understand how much time or what kind of training these displaced people will need to be rehabilitated, are not fully understood and hence cannot be effectively quantified and therefore monetized. Therefore, compensation packages cannot be adequately calculated. There is recognition of this issue among policy planners, but never beyond a token one.

The alternate understanding of these impacts is documented in micro-level anthropological studies. But they use different methodologies including historical and interpretative analysis. Destruction of the habitat resulting from major irrigation and forestry projects leading to displacement and resettlement of tribal communities forms the core of this literature (Dreze et al., 1996). The livelihoods of tribal inhabitants and their subsistence economies are intricately linked with their habitats. Relocation forces them into situations that are market-oriented and are linked with monetary economies. Lack of formal education and technical skills in these economies can be a major handicap. Displacement and resettlement spell disasters. Relocation without any sensitivity to the kinship networks and living arrangements often leads to separation of the kin group and the social support that they provide to each other, which adversely affects their health and nutritional standards.

But not having a comprehensive theoretical and methodological framework to reconcile these two, often posed as opposing understanding of the impacts, is an important issue. It goes against the grain of social justice to which all development projects are committed. It is this major lacuna that is filled by the critical theory of environment proposed here.

Overview

Chapter 2 elaborates the critical theory of environment that is a variant of the self-estrangement theory and draws extensively on Habermas' critical theory, and anthropology. Theorizing the 'ideal-typical' sequence of events resulting from environmental impacts of development projects in India is the objective here. Development projects are defined as projects that promise to bring about rapid economic growth within a region, leading to modernization. They have a promise of jobs for people and technologies that would cause minimal damage to the environment. The impetus to locate the project in a particular region is external to the actual local site and its context. The development project once selected for a specific location, goes through four distinctly identifiable stages, the initiation stage, the planning and implementation stage, construction stage and operation stage. These stages are roughly chronological in nature but the boundaries between these stages or the time duration are often indeterminate.

Associated with each stage in the development of the project is the 'ideal type' of reaction of the local communities to the project. A process of political consensus-building to support the project usually takes place as a result of the various behind-the-scene negotiations that are instrumental in locating the project at the specific site. Associated with the project planning and initiation stage is euphoria about the project coming to the region and a belief in the promise of development and economic prosperity of that region. Once the implementation stage begins and actual transfer of land through a process of land acquisition takes place, it marks the beginning of the 'voices of dissent' that start being heard, usually in the local media. The construction stage also marks the entry of construction labour and related migrants into the region. This coincides with an increasing crescendo of dissent among the local communities and is usually articulated as loss of access to common property natural resources by the local media and is often picked up by the national print and audio-visual media. This rhetoric of injustice peaks by the time the operations stage is reached. Some negotiations, usually informal in nature and mediated through a political leader, between the project promoters and the local communities, take place. This results in a temporary 'truce' but the resistance to the project by local communities continues, and often erupts into a crisis from time to time.

It is this reality of the environmental impacts of development projects that is explained theoretically through a research programme consisting of a complex of theories logically interconnected to one another. A variant of the self-estrangement theory proposed by Habermas and creatively combined with an ecological paradigm proposed by Bennett (Bennett, 1976) provides the theoretical framework and the methodological grounding. A four-point research programme (Fay, 1987) is used to further develop the paradigm into a critical theory of environment in the following chapter. This provides the necessary theoretical framework to understand the chronology of events leading to the resistance of the local PAPs against the project in their neighbourhood.

Chapter 3 elaborates an appropriate methodological approach from among the available methodologies, to connect the theoretical conceptualization and the case studies to which this theory is applied. It is able to act as a bridge between the theoretical paradigm and the real-life experience of the project implementation.

The subsequent chapters draw on six case studies in India in different techno-economic contexts and different regions, based on research carried out by me in the field. These are documented as case studies to indicate the multiplicity of projects, multiplicity of social actors, and related changes that can be understood by using this unifying framework of the critical theory of environment. The first two case studies in Chapters 4 and 5 document the two separate ways in which the project-affected persons react to a similar stimulus of an amusement park-related tourism project. The project location is in the 'green' or the no-development zone of the urban metropolis of Mumbai. The first project is funded and implemented by a private corporation in Gorai. Commissioning of the project drew a very vocal social protest movement against the amusement park. The amusement park carved within a national park and a leopard sanctuary in Borivali, promoted by the state government forest department, did not face any obvious voices of dissent. Subsequent interviews with the project-affected persons did provide clues to their forms of resistance and their double marginalization, which is elaborated in Chapter 5.

The following two case studies, in Chapters 6 and 7, respectively, necessitate a more expanded definition of the PAPs, who 'were there first' and hence the legitimacy of the moral claims of their 'survival first' principle. These two refer to the resistance offered by the public sector technocrats in two infrastructure projects. One is a mining project located in Dhanbad, Jharkhand, and the other is a power production project located in Dabhol, Maharashtra. The emphasis on liberalization, and promoting competition or technological efficiency, are claims towards a more rational order based on economic efficiency. While the establishment of the public sector enterprise was based on the principle of equity and social justice, the subtle but effective resistance of the public sector employees to the liberalization agenda of the nation state is documented here. The ingenuity and creative manner in which they are able to co-opt the subaltern rhetoric to ensure their survival as an organization, is interesting.

The case studies in Chapters 8 and 9 are very different. Chapter 8 refers to the limits of an environmental protest movement to push for industrial pollution control legislation. Chapter 9 discusses an urban transportation project and provides the new potential of environmental NGOs to bring social justice and equity on the negotiating table, and to effectively shape the future environmental legislation, in urban infrastructure projects, in particular, and other infrastructure development projects, in general, in India.

The final chapter re-visits the critical theory framework. It explains how the critical theory framework of environment provides a unifying and comprehensive explanation to all these case studies. The theory linked with the appropriate methodology, provides an understanding of various stages in the development of the projects and the underlying principle that explains the resistance to the project. The multiplicity of the case studies suggest the creativity of the affected groups in using the basic principle in different contexts, effectively. Finally, it summarizes the outcomes of various projects to point to the crucial role played by state agencies in the project outcomes. Thus, ironically, in spite of liberalization and the advent of multilateral donors and the alleged erosion of state power, in the triad between the PAPs, the project promoters and the government agencies, the agency which wins is that with which the state chooses to 'thrown in' its lot.

Two

Critical Theory of Environment*

Theorizing the 'ideal' sequence of events resulting from the environmental impacts of development projects in India is the objective here. Development projects are defined as projects that promise to promote rapid economic growth, environmental sustainability and social equity in a region, leading to modernization.

Research Programme

The Weberian perspective in the theorizing of environmental sociology has been explored here through a critical theory of environment. Weber treated environmental factors as interactive components of complex causal models, by favouring the selective survival of certain social strata over others. The question is, if the theory supports the selective survival of certain social strata, could such a theory be normative? My answer to this question is in the affirmative. Without the implicit normative support, the survival of certain social strata is not sustainable in the long run.

A comprehensive theory of environmental sociology should begin with a theory of the environment. It should be able to explain human interaction with the environment, and should be a sociological theory only subsequently. Proposed here is a four-step research programme (Fay, 1987) to develop a critical theory (Connerton, 1976; Dreyfus and Rabinow, 1987), of the environment, which is environmental

---

*I wish to thank the late Professor R. Sundara Rajan of the Department of Philosophy at Poona University, who helped me greatly in the preparation of the paper on which this chapter is based. His insightful comments enabled me to separate the grain from the chaff.

and sociological at the same time. The first step is to identify an appropriate environmental theory that can be combined with a critical sociological theory to develop the basic theory of human adaptation to the environment. The second step of the research programme addresses the question as to who is an environmental critic. The third step is to understand how the critic understands the environmental crisis that helps in the long-term physical and cultural survival of the group. The fourth step of the research programme involves exploration of the actions that the critic adopts in order to transform the situation in their favour, successfully. The programme combines the environmental theory with a humanist variant of the self-estrangement theory in order to develop a critical theory of the environment. The critical theory of the environment proposed here reveals how a particular social environmental order functions, how it shows the ways in which it is fundamentally unsatisfactory to those who live in it, and how it does this in a manner that it itself becomes the moving force, helping to transform this order into something radically different.

Adaptive Dynamics

As a first step, we identify from among the existing theories of the human environment relationship, an appropriate theory, point out the ways in which it is inadequate to fully understand the critical issues arising out of the environment-development nexus; propose an appropriate critical theory that is most suited to combine it with the environmental theory; and suggest modes of combination of the two theories to form the critical theory of environment. The objective of this exercise is to develop a theory of the human–environment relationship based on omissions and underdeveloped implications of the two frameworks of environmental theory and critical theory. Such a theory will need to be further developed to create a 'critical theory of the environment' with a practical intent. Since the theory recognizes emancipatory interest to be fundamental to the theory, it is a variant of the self-estrangement theories.

The 'adaptive dynamics' paradigm (Bennett, 1976) is identified as a viable environmental theory, albeit with modifications, while Habermas' critical theory is identified as a viable social theory. This is an attempt to develop a new paradigm for human and environmental relationships by means of a synthesis of these two frameworks. Such a task would demand theoretical analysis and a critique at three levels. As a first step, a clear theoretically sensitive discussion of the basic concepts and propositions of the two theoretical frameworks is required. Next, it will have to be shown that the incompatibility *between* these two frameworks is only apparent. This will be supplanted with the reasons for a theoretical synthesis. This final level of analysis relates to the modes of combination and the appropriate methodology required for such a combination.

Basic concepts and propositions

The adaptive dynamics paradigm originates in the general system theory. The fundamental propositions of the theory are:

1. The theory begins with the assumption that socio-cultural systems are examples of organized complexity.
2. These complexities are to be studied as processes in time rather than entities.
3. These processes are determined by various parts in the system.
4. These processes follow their logic. This logic is mathematical and formal. It can be explicated through mathematical modelling. Such an exercise would help human beings understand these processes in a better manner so that they can be subject to manipulation and control.

The socio-cultural systems fall under adaptive systems. The complex adaptive models are characterized by the elaboration and evolution of the system. They thrive on disturbances and varieties in their environment. A typical response of an open adaptive system to its changed environment is that the system changes. These changes can be either ontogenic, that is, 'within system changes', or phylogenic, that is, 'of the system changes'. The ecological models that arose from these processual adaptive dynamic models have guided major studies in the man-environment relationship. To name a few, these include models used by the 'Club of Rome' studies (Gabor et al., 1976; Meadows et al., 1972; Mesarovic and Pestel, 1975; Tinbergen, 1976), the system dynamics (Forester, 1974), and the ecological carrying capacity models of Edinburgh University.

The paradigm

The 'adaptive dynamics paradigm' suggested by Bennett (1976) is a highly structured model of interlocking loops. The first linkage that is identified by the paradigm is the production process, wherein the first step in human and environmental relationship involves a cognitive step of identifying certain elements of nature as raw materials that feed into the techno-economic structures to create goods and services. The second loop is a feedback loop that consists of informal subliminal controls that control the production and consumption of human societies. The third loop consists of socio-cultural and political systems determined by values and processes that, in turn, feed into the production process. The fourth and final loop is a loosely defined feedback into human biology wherein the impacts of production of goods and services, and pollutants may have long-term impacts on human biology, directly or indirectly. There are interrelated loops, with each of the sub-systems in these processes being fairly autonomous in their functioning.

The model is thus based on the systems approach (Forester 1974; Gabor et al., 1976), but Bennett asserts the primacy of techno-economic factors over the environmental ones. He has defined human ecology as a historical ecological transition in human beings. It follows the dynamics of adaptation of humans to their environment in three spheres: population, technology and energy consumption. He goes on to identify the uniqueness of human ecology. He identifies two steps that are unique in human ecology, first, the symbolic step of naming certain substances of physical environment as 'natural resources', and second, allotting economic value to them. This is a cognitive step in human interaction with the environment. This step enables humans to act upon the physical environment and extract substances from it to produce and transform energy. Assigning economic value to goods is a cognitive step that arises through and within social organizations. These values are not determined by biological needs alone but by culturally determined wants for goods and energy. Since there are no absolute standards for these cultural wants, there is no automatic biologically determined control over them; it is, however, substituted by the cultural feedback loops of information flow and communication, which are cognitive in nature. Since the control is cognitive in nature, at best, it is imperfect. It serves both the interests, namely the purpose of action and means for control of these actions, when they become dangerous. It is possible to develop the means of control over actions, by reflecting on the meaning and consequences of the act and after reflection, subject it to control.

It is these cognitive steps in the ecological paradigm that are parallel to the Marxian theory. The ability of man to extract natural resources and subject them to forces of production, and the ability of self-reflection in human beings are finding added emphasis in the interpretative theories of today. These cognitive steps that make human ecology unique are correctly identified and given their central position in the paradigm proposed by Bennett. Thus, he is able to rise above the deterministic processual model of the systems approach, partially.

But Bennett (1976) still adheres to the systems approach when he posits an external origin to 'change', and when he traces the causes of ecological transition in man. Bennett goes on to trace the peculiar problems faced by human societies, when he seeks to answer the following questions:

1. How do human societies maintain short-term equilibrium?
2. What causes disequilibria in such societies?
3. What kind of adaptive strategies are used to restore equilibrium?

The maintenance of short-term equilibrium is attributed to what Bennett calls subliminal controls that exist in low energy consuming societies. These controls are exercised traditionally through rituals and work practices in these societies. When such societies come into contact with other societies, which have larger resource-consuming instrumentalities, and which initiate a higher techno-economic development as modernization, the subliminal controls embedded in the cultural values and norms related to environmental resource extraction, tend to break down. This transition from equilibrium to disequilibrium is demonstrated in the highly generalized adaptive dynamics paradigm of human ecology as mentioned above. When disequilibrium is caused due to the breakdown of subliminal controls as a result of the modernization of societies, formal controls in the form of laws and legislations in the pollution control of air, water and soil need to replace them, to restore the balance. The formal controls indicate that subliminal regulations have not been historically sufficient to preserve the system from the over-use and abuse of resources. Therefore, formal controls such as environmental legislation, based on information and feedback, become necessary.

Points of disagreement

Thus the paradigm is based on the premise that the social processes have a primacy over the individual 'self'. In fact, the systems follow a logic of their own, over which nature has no control. This is in line with one possible interpretation of Kant (2003[1929]). He argues that the basic mode of human action is 'freedom'. But because humans are posited within the causal laws of nature, this struggle for freedom remains unexercised. This forces human beings to return to the 'inner self', that is, subjectivity in order to attain transcendence. But in opposition to Kant, Hegel was able to demonstrate phenomenological self-reflection of knowledge as the necessary radicalization of the critique of reason. It is this phenomenon of self-knowledge that provides the critical human being with moral and ethical justification for undertaking transformative actions, and the moral and ethical nature of these transformative actions. Habermas (1971) extends this Hegelian argument to link the return to inner self as a path to action and not an escape from a reality wherein freedom remains unexercised. Thus, though the ecological paradigm proposes the primacy of society over the individual human beings in restoring ecological balance, this is only one possible interpretation of the paradigm. There is room to believe that through self-reflection and enlightenment, human beings can undertake actions to transform the situation in their favour.

Habermas agrees with this enlightenment doctrine, which assumed human estrangement. He proposes (Giddens, 1977) that understanding human conduct is not only a causal endeavour, but it also consists of uncovering its intelligibility by relating it to the rules that constitute forms of life. Habermas stresses the point that the generalizing sciences which dictate the systems approaches in positivistic sociology and hermeneutics have, for a long while, gone their separate ways. The problem is to show that logical relations connect them on the level of epistemology. Science can only be comprehended epistemologically, which means that one category of possible knowledge and the evolution of scientific disciplines have led to scepticism about other forms of knowledge, including self-reflection. This has resulted in the conviction that we can no longer understand science as one form of possible knowledge, but rather identify knowledge with science. Thus, it conforms to only one type of knowledge-constitutive interest, that of prediction and control of occurrences, or technologically exploitable knowledge. This kind of knowledge denies the diachronic process of social systems. The systems theorists advocate a synchronic dimension. Chess is usually cited as an example. Just as a game of chess has various elements, so do social systems. If the relationship between these elements and the rules of the game are known, then anyone can play the game, from any point, within the game. The systems theorists argue that social systems follow a similar logic. These rules and relationships between social elements can be extricated. Just as in a chess game, the present situation may be arrived at by any possible earlier moves and thus they have no bearing on how the game can proceed. Similarly, the present social situation cannot be used to predict future evolution.

But this approach is unable to adequately explain the emergence of new social elements beyond those assumed earlier. It portrays a static image of society. It is a fact that social systems undergo change and evolve over time. This, the synchronous approach is unable to account for (Gouldner, 1970). It is this crisis that has led to the emergence of hermeneutics and critical theories. Habermas (1988) has stated that such a synchronic approach is only one possible logical form in which discourse can take place and is directly connected to instrumental or purposive rational action. The second type of knowledge-constitutive interest is emancipatory. This communicative interest assumes interaction. Interaction is dialogical rather than monological. A dialogue assumes a degree of normative consensus between communicating individuals. One cannot, therefore, be concerned with interaction without being able, in principle, to enter into a dialogue. This is the locus of hermeneutics, which conforms to knowledge-constitutive interest in understanding. Hermeneutic problems relate to the intertwining of language and experience in different forms of life, which ordinary language both expresses and mediates.

Habermas takes reflexivity to be fundamental to the interest in emancipation, just because it is in the course of self-reflection that the subject is able to grasp and transform the conditions under which he acts, by embodying his knowledge of these conditions within the rationalization of his actions. Thus, for a critical theory, the shift to historicity is a necessary condition for self-reflection and emancipation.

While the adaptive dynamics paradigm takes into account the historicity of human adaptation, it is this equally important emancipatory interest in dialogue and reflexivity that is ignored by the adaptive dynamics paradigm while laying emphasis on the prediction of the future evolution.

There are thus two main reasons to retain this paradigm, albeit with modifications. First, the adaptive dynamics paradigm, though rooted in the systems approach, does recognize the importance of historicity and therefore transcends the purely instrumental interest. It attempts a theoretically generalized history of human ecology, even as it maintains its systems approach. The second reason to retain the paradigm is that this is the only paradigm that recognizes 'social production' as well as environmental dimension. The alternative Marxian theories are not adequate in explaining environmental domination by man. This has been elaborated by Isaac Bulbus (1982), when he considers the Marxian structuralist theory of production. Bulbus points out that both the optimistic and pessimistic theories of technology are unable to serve the emancipatory interest of man. Thus, contrary to Marx, the social relations of production possess a partially autonomous logic of development. This takes us back to Marx's instrumental theory, coupled with the insistence that the logic of technological development is repressive, which is what Weber argues—that there is an inherent identical logic underlying industrial production as such, and this logic is repressive. Bulbus answers this problem by identifying and promoting technologies that are not destructive to the environment. But this only partially solves the problem. The domination of nature and the problem of domination by humans remain.

A way out is to develop a critical theory of the environment that is rooted in the emancipatory intent and is able to adopt an environmental dimension to the social production. The adaptive dynamics paradigm (Bennett, 1976) is identified as an environmental theory, to be suitably amended to incorporate the emancipatory interests of human beings. The paradigm in its present form gives primacy to the techno-economic production sphere.

Following the lead by Habermas in his re-interpretation of the base-superstructure theorem, there is sufficient empirical evidence in the cases presented here to indicate that the socio-political and cultural superstructures (communicative actions) play a decisive role in the selection of the techno-economic base as well as decision of the siting of these projects. There is evidence to suggest that behind-the-scenes negotiations between national level technocrats/bureaucrats and international aid agencies and/or multinational corporations do take place for the selection of a particular techno-economic project. At the national and state levels, similar battles are fought for locating a particular development project within a particular state and in a particular region within the state. I would argue for primacy of the socio-cultural and political superstructures that determine the emergent techno-economic base, in general, and for the projects I have reviewed here, in particular. Thus the adaptive dynamics paradigm should grant the primacy that it deserves to the socio-political spheres.

Second, the paradigm needs modification as it posits an external point of origin to changes that take place within society. This is because it lacks a grounded 'theory of learning' to locate the origin of change within human society. The changes in the techno-economic systems taking place in their neighbourhood, force a crisis within the individuals at different levels, as discussed later. This crisis forces human beings to return to the 'inner self' and reflexivity that dictates the future course of action, thereby locating the origin of change and emancipation within the society. This emancipatory interest provides the guiding inspiration for the critical theory (Held, 1980). Thus theorizing human interaction with the environment needs to ride the two horses of hermeneutics and social production, simultaneously.

Crisis, Critique and Enlightenment

The adaptive dynamics paradigm needs to be retained but requires modifications. First, the paradigm should grant primacy to socio-political cultural systems over techno-economic ones. Second, it should locate the origin of change within the society. Introduction of a new techno-economic system in an existing socio-cultural context precipitates an environmental crisis. This raises three basic and inter-related questions, the answers to which would determine the future course of environmental policies. The basic questions are: what is the crisis?, who is the critic?, and, what is the enlightenment/learning that leads to action? So far the answers to these questions in the context of development projects are assumed to be self-evident. The crisis in environment is viewed as an imbalance in the proportions of certain chemicals in the physical environment that cause pollution. The job of the critic is to correct these imbalances to restore environmental equilibrium through technologies and policies, broadly classified under the rubric of environmental pollution abatement actions. As argued earlier, the adaptive dynamics paradigm, lends itself to alternate and equally valid answers to these questions that are very different from these. The rest of the section elaborates the philosophical arguments that support such an interpretation, drawing mainly on Habermas' development of the critical theory of society.

The more crucial questions in the context of the critical theory are: who is an environmental critic?, and, what is the environmental crisis? Habermas provides such a critical theory that would help us find different answers to these questions. He has developed a research programme, which is at once philosophical, critical and pragmatic (Held, 1980). Habermas' critical theory has the following three major propositions that have relevance to ecological attitudes and ethics:

1. As a philosophical theory, that is, an epistemic problem,
2. As a meta-scientific mode, that is, critical theory as a philosophy of social sciences, and
3. As a substantive social theory, that is, the hermeneutic dimension.

These are rooted in various ways in which the term critic can be interpreted. The first clue to the notion of the critic is as its association with a 'crisis' situation. The relationship of association was described by Hippocrates in a medical context. He regards a 'crisis situation' in an individual organism as determined by ups and downs in the health of an organism. Thus, a disorder or a structural imbalance in an organism is identified as the root of the 'crisis.' But merely a disorder is not a sufficient condition for the need of a 'critic'. This systemic disorder has to be identified as such by the organism itself through its perception of the malaise. Thus, Habermas suggests that such a situation has an objective structure and a subjective hermeneutic dimension. The significance of the crisis is not that it represents a structural disorder but that this disorder is perceived to be such by the organism. In this case, the person who is capable of recognizing a system of crisis and of prescribing remedial steps becomes a 'critic'. In the case of an organism, the critic is a healer. Here, apart from other notions, the central idea is that a physician, while diagnosing the disease, is guided by the conception of 'well-being'. This normative idea is a guiding principle and a goal for medical practice. Thus, the activity of the critic is to talk to the patient for understanding what 'an illness means to the patient'. Therefore, the investigations, besides being subjective and objective, will have to be normative in nature.

Michel Foucault (see Dreyfus and Rabinow,1987) suggests a methodology for identifying the concept of 'well-being'. His methodology states that in order to find out what our society means by environmental 'well-being', we must investigate what is happening in the field of environmental 'crisis'. Thus, a critical theory as a philosophical theory ought to enumerate the conception of what is 'normal' in a society, if a 'crisis' is to be identified. The normative principle of sustainable resource exploitation can become the guiding principle in the case of environmental well-being. The critic is a person who possesses such a conception of 'well-being' in an environmental context.

The second meaning of critic, as understood by Habermas, pertains to Aristotle. In a socio-political context, Aristotle observed that a state had certain multiplicities leading to a system. Thus, these various structures would, at some time, indicate certain structural imbalances over what is 'just and right'. A social system can encounter a period of crisis, which is expressed as 'conflict'. The critic is a person who is able to identify disorder and take corrective measures.

In an environmental context, this crisis is manifested in the nature in which important problems exist in human ecology today. The present way of techno-ecological exploitation rakes up certain problems, in the context of increasing knowledge about environment, which are listed here:

1. The mastery of some men over others as a consequence of technical interest in resource exploitation conflicts with the egalitarian principles accepted as a 'world view' (Bennett, 1976).
2. 'Economic growth' as a criterion for development is increasingly questioned as against 'quality of life'. This is because there are limits to growth in material spheres due to environmental constraints. At the same time, increasing material standards does not guarantee distributive justice (Jenning and Hobel, 1958).
3. The technical interest dictates that nature be treated as an instrumentality, but increasing knowledge about nature dictates that nature be treated as a system of great complexity that is not fully understood (Schroyer, 1983).

The third meaning of critic originates in the Roman medieval periods. During the Renaissance, the Romans depended on Greek scriptures for the borrowed civilization that they reconstructed. This was a literary critic, whereby alien meanings had to be a 'hermeneutic activity'. This notion of critic as a hermeneutic activity is important. For a proper understanding and re-interpretation of scriptures, the appeal has to be to human reason. When this happens, the appeal is only to faith and reason. Thus, reason is not just a tool but also the final arbitrator. At this final stage, reason is public. But for Kant, a critical reason had to be a critique of pure reason. Thus, for him, a critic becomes self-critical and reason becomes 'a-public'.

Who is a critic?

According to the first interpretation, a person who has a concept of environmental well-being, against which an environmental crisis can be compared, would be a critic. Thus, any human being, including any of the project-affected people, who has a concept of what environmental well-being should be, and can measure and identify the environmental crisis against this, then becomes a critic.

According to the second interpretation, various socio-political structures may sometimes indicate certain structural imbalances over what is just and right, leading to a period of crisis, which is expressed as 'conflict'. Thus, all project-affected people involved in the conflict become critics because they try to resolve what is the right and just impact of the development project to everyone in general and to themselves in particular.

The final interpretation of a critic is one who adjudicates alien meanings and arbitrates according to pure reason. Any human being capable of pure reason is therefore a critic, which includes project-affected people.

These interpretations remove the onus of the critic from being a 'specialist' to a person who is able to identify a crisis and suggest remedial action. People who are affected by the environmental impacts of a development project, who can identify an environmental crisis in the light of a concept of 'environmental well-being', who identify the 'structural imbalance' over the definition of what is 'right and just' and take corrective action to restore it, and those who are able to 're-interpret' 'official' statements of environmental impacts based on pure reason, would qualify to be environmental critics.

Here we return to Habermas and his contribution to the critical theory of society to take clues for the further development of a critical theory of environment. Habermas suggests a research programme to develop a critical theory of society. The ground level consists of a general theory of communication. At the next level, it serves as a foundation for a general theory of socialization in the form of a theory of acquisition of communicative competence; and finally Habermas sketches a theory of social evolution based on the previous two levels which he views as a reconstruction of historical materialism.

Following the lead, we shall first develop a general theory of ecological competence; at the next level, we shall develop the concept of reconstructive adaptive strategy based on the acquisition of ecological competence. Implicit in the concept of reconstructive adaptive strategy is the idea of a 'normal' human-environment relationship. This idea can be validated methodologically by studying the different circumstances in different development projects that give rise to distortions resulting in resistance by PAPs. The terms of articulation of the various types of resistances will provide us with clues as to what is expected of a 'normal' interaction between human beings and the environment.

Lacuna

The contribution of Habermas to the theory of social evolution is twofold. He has developed a new theory of learning, which incorporates both communicative actions and instrumental actions under human action. While re-interpreting the base–superstructure theorem, he has stressed the primacy of communicative action. Thus, his reconstruction of historical materialism states that normative structures play an important role in resolving system problems in social evolution. He then sees systems as life-worlds that are symbolically structured. Social systems crises, according to him, arise in economic, political or socio-cultural sub-systems, leading to systemic changes. For example, due to internal contradictions, capitalist societies face danger from economic rationality and legitimation or motivational crises.

Like all Marxists, Habermas seems to have given almost no importance to ecological crisis. He states that the capitalist form of society has an established growth mechanism 'that compels population growth and an increase in production on a worldwide scale. This growth has two limitations—finite resources and population. These limits have not yet been reached, but one absolute limit to growth can be specified, namely the limit of thermal load imposed on the environment by the consumption of energy' (Connerton, 1976). Thus, Habermas considers ecological issues as technical issues (Bulbus, 1982). This seems to necessarily follow from his theory of constitutive interests, particularly the interest in control and domination. If this is so, new levels of social learning can only be social and inter-human. Such an anthropocentric view would limit the ecological attitudes and ethics. This Habermasian version of critical theory is possible. Insofar as new levels of normative learning would be anthropocentric, the prospect of new ecological attitudes and ethics would imply some modifications in the Marxian theory of technology. But Bulbus (1982) has argued that the modification of just relations of production would not produce technologies that are far less domineering, because domination is internalized in the very mode of production. Therefore, there is a need for identifying technologies that are non-domineering. Bulbus has proposed the doctrine of 'small is beautiful' as presented by Schumacher (1984).

This would be a narrow way of solving the ecological crisis because it proposes a partial solution. Therefore, the critical paradigm needs elaboration to encompass the environmental dimension including social histories just as the environmental dimension needs a critical dimension.

Mode of combining the paradigms

In the development of a general theory of communicative action, Habermas provides certain clues to the mode of combination. He states that in order to arrive at a general theory of communication, certain universal pragmatic rules of communication need to be reconstructed. In the light of these reconstructed rules/strategies, the 'communicative competence' of an individual can be established. These two would then form the foundation for a general theory of communication.

Similar steps can be followed to arrive at a general theory of environment. Drawing on the theory of adaptive dynamics and the critical theory, it will be possible to reconstruct certain universal pragmatic rules of human interaction with their environment by defining a reconstructive adaptive strategy and arguing in defence of universal ecological competence. This would provide the foundation for a general paradigm. These assumptions about the 'normal' interaction between human beings and the environment can be validated by understanding the 'abnormal'. The distortions within the human environmental interactions are what are seen in different forms of resistance, including social protest, among the PAPs. Clues about this normative ideal for any society can be derived on the basis of what is considered distortions and how these distortions violate what is considered 'normal' or the normative ideal about human-environment interactions.

How do we understand these distortions? The discrepancy between information produced through the official claims in the form of reports and documents and the 'talking claims' that are constantly made and reiterated through a discursive strategy by the PAPs will provide us with clues as to what is considered 'nomal' in the theory of the environment.

The terms of articulation of these types of resistances will provide us with clues as to what is expected of a 'normal' interaction between human beings and the environment. A theory of learning will provide us with moral and ethical claims made in the articulation by PAPs. The means of articulation adopted by each of the PAPs and the strategic thinking that is used to transform the social situation in their favour are some things that can be understood by a theory of transformative action. This will make a critical environmental theory empirical and scientific without being reducible to empirical analytic science.

Reconstructive strategies

Habermas uses the term 'reconstructive sciences' to designate explicit systemic reconstruction of implicit pre-theoretical knowledge. In the case of human ecology, such an exercise will have to define a guiding principle that is normatively ideal in the man–environment relationship. A clue to the normative ideal is provided in the adaptive dynamics paradigm in the context of subliminal control. These controls were socio-culturally embedded in the rules of everyday life and provided short-term equilibria in environmental systems. Such a normative ideal depicts how human interaction with the environment should be environmentally right, culturally sustainable, and socially just. Thus, reconstructive adaptive strategy should leave the physical environment better off, it should be sustained and strengthened by social organizations within which it is practised and it should be (socially) just to all the human beings involved. Thus, it should result in a 'win-win' situation for human beings and the environment, and the rules to arrive at it should be culturally incorporated.

The first step is to define reconstructive adaptive strategy. Here, adaptive strategy aimed at group survival is given prime importance and at times, it may not be adaptive to an individual in the short run. This is a very complex job, mainly because the problem with human-social systems is that they adapt to the environment by changing and not by resisting change. The feedback is positive and they do not work towards any one particular goal. When the criteria of what is adaptive shifts from an individual to a group, and to its welfare and survival, human ecology in the sense of having a 'practical intent' becomes an enquiry into the adaptive consequences of human activities. Several concepts of adaptive strategies are examined in order to justify and define a reconstructive concept.

Adaptive strategies adopted by individuals fall under two spheres: (*i*) biological adaptation (Huizenga, 1975; Jenning and Hobel, 1958), and (*ii*) socio-cultural adaptation between individuals as studied by social psychologists (Thomas and Zennenski, 1978) and between individuals and groups (Merton, 1968; Mills, 1960; Peel, 1972).

The systems theory as suggested by Talcott Parsons (1967) refers to the adaptation problem as the problem of providing facilities for the use of a system, that is, given certain goals to arrange resources to attain these goals. Thus, it is a means of solving the problem of self-maintenance. Parsons also studies adaptation as a value pattern in societies. In the systems theory, this definition of adaptation as a 'means' poses a question, namely which mechanism in the system can 'create adequate adaptation of the system to the environment'? Even if we find the mechanism, at what price would we be able to do so? For, only strategies that have already proved to be adaptive can belong to this object domain, and other adaptive strategies not thus proven will be ignored, thus excluding an independent evaluation of reasons. But can we ignore the fact that the normative validity claims of adaptive strategies meet this condition because they are well-grounded? It can be decisive for an analysis to know whether a population had acted on the basis of accurate or false information and opinion. In order to make a judgment, we have to be able to systematically evaluate adaptation claims in a rational, inter-subjectively testable way. We require a concept of adaptation with normative content.

But if philosophical ethics and socio-cultural theory can know nothing more than what is contained in the everyday norm consciousness of different populations, and if this cannot even be known in any different way, it then cannot rationally distinguish between adaptive and real-adaptive strategies.

Thus, the empirical concept of social science is not satisfactory because it abstracts from systemic weight on the grounds of validity. The philosophical is untenable because of the metaphysical context in which it is embedded. A third concept of adaptive strategies is the 'reconstructive concept'. This should satisfy the following. A recommended adaptive strategy should be:

1. in the general interest, and
2. satisfy normative validity claims.

Assuming that idea and reality do not split, the reconstructive adaptive strategy must fulfil the following three criteria:

1. It should leave the physical environment ecologically beneficial.
2. The adaptive strategy should be sustained and strengthened by the social organization, so that it becomes culturally acceptable.
3. Finally the satisfaction of both these criteria, one at the environmental level and the other at both the individual and group level, would lead to the satisfaction of normative validity claims, given a particular adaptive strategy.

In defence of universal value

Who would then possess the necessary competence to decide on an appropriate adaptive strategy? I have defined this as an 'ecological competence'. Ecological competence consists in identifying certain pragmatic features of ecological activities, which can be logically reconstructed. These feature are delineated here:

1. It is the ability of an individual to incorporate an environmental dimension into his/her everyday life. What is suggested here is that humans look upon their environment as something that is a part of them, and any action on their part would have consequences for themselves in the end, that is, to see their actions as having ecological consequences.

2. This would imply the normative basis, which accepts equality, non-domination and a dialogical approach to differences. Incorporated in the concept of ecological competence here are both the physical and social environmental aspects.
3. The human decision to be 'one' with nature does not depend upon any epistemic presuppositions or changing contexts. Humans in any ecological context are capable of engaging in this kind of action. Therefore, a universal and pragmatic investigation can be proposed.

The conceptualization of experiences and the physical environment simultaneously, at a normative level, accepting equality and non-domination between human beings and the environment, and taking corrective actions to resolve conflicts that adversely affect the individual, the group, and the physical environment, are uniquely human capabilities. The ability to see the impact on the self and the environment simultaneously is independent of any ecological context. Thus, I argue in defence of the universal value of ecological competence. Every individual possesses 'ecological competence' as part of his or her basic human nature.

Thus defined, a reconstructive adaptive strategy gives primacy to 'life-world' or everyday life and grants ecological competence to any human being who finds himself facing the environmental consequences of a development project. Techno-economic systems are sub-sets of 'life-world'. They therefore constitute one possible interpretation of the human–environment relationship. If these techno-economic systems are found to be disruptive to the larger life-world and the inter-subjectively shared common sense understanding of it, they are subject to challenge by the very individuals, who may have accepted them in the initial stages.

We have so far defined the pragmatic rules of human environmental interaction as reconstructive adaptive strategy and argued in defence of the universal value of ecological competence. Thus, the reconstructive adaptive strategy allows humans to be one with nature—this is the 'normal' interaction between human beings and the environment. How does one know what this normal state of interaction is? The answer to this is through the adoption of the methodology proposed by Habermas. He proposes that clues to the normal are to be gathered from what is considered as abnormal by people who, faced with a situation of environmental crisis, have become critics. They make 'talking claims' about their own situation and the environmental situation around them.

Why does an environmental crisis occur? It is Habermas' contention that the human species organizes its experience in terms of prior interests. The fact that there is a basis for interest follows from an understanding of humans as tool-making and language-making animals. Their interest in the creation of knowledge, which helps humans control objectified processes and maintain communication, is of two types:

1. A technocratic interest in the control of nature, and
2. An interest in the reflexive appropriation of human life—this is the interest in the reason, in the human capacity to be self-reflexive and self-determining; to act rationally is an emancipatory interest.

Habermas claims a universality of hermeneutics, whereby he argues that interaction is founded in ordinary language communication, which is the organizing mode of inter-subjectivity. The norms governing everyday communication are rooted in the practical demands of sustaining community existence. Language is a medium whereby an inter-subjectively formed social life is carried out. Language is a medium of doing things through communication with others. Interaction is, thus, dialogical rather than monological as is the case in instrumental actions guided by technocratic interest. One cannot be concerned with interaction without being able, in principle, to enter into the dialogue. This is the locus of hermeneutics, which conforms to the knowledge-constitutive interest in understanding.

Habermas acknowledges that science, as understood epistemologically, is one category of possible knowledge, which is guided by the interest in controlling objectified processes and technological interest dictated by instrumental rationality, resulting in strategic action. The domination of this interest in today's world has led to 'scientism'. This has resulted in the conviction that we must identify knowledge with science. As a result, the knowledge-constitutive interest in understanding and emancipation has suffered and human ecology is facing a crisis at both normative levels as well as material levels.

The challenging of the false consciousness created by one type of claims based on one type of knowledge-constitutive interest in domination and control of the environment is the beginning of crisis. In the face of the consequences of the instrumentally rational actions dictated by these knowledge-constitutive interests in prediction and control, the PAPs are faced with a dilemma. The central dilemma before the PAPs is that if they believe in the dominant discourse of the development and follow the path of profit maximization through the sale of their assets or claims to new sources of employment opportunities, they meet limited success. But the subsequent changes in the socio-cultural and political sphere, make them run the risk of losing what they already possess and what had historically ensured their survival, albeit at subsistence levels. If they continue at the subsistence level, they miss the chance of ensuring their own economic development which may be possible due to the project. Since they cannot afford to pass up the chance, the crisis pushes them into self-reflexivity and enlightenment. The crisis is a realization that if they accept the dominant rhetoric associated with the development project and engage with it, they lose. The dominant rhetoric asserts that the project is right, rightful, and just to all the people involved, including the PAPs. The PAPs may not lose in absolute terms but they 'lose out' relative to other social groups who come 'after the project'. The migrants rarely constitute a homogeneous group and usually move into the region as a consequence of the development project. The 'original settlers' or the PAPs get marginalized due to the new economic growth and associated changes, over which they have very little control. But if they choose not to engage in the dominant rhetoric of development, and allow all the various new claimants to take what they claim, the natural and social resources left for them would not ensure their subsistence or survival as a distinct ethnic group. The crisis is in the realization that despite negative consequences of projects, they must engage the project authorities for their own welfare. The reality, as defined by the dominant rhetoric associated with the project, is heavily stacked against them. Therefore, they must assert and claim an alternate reality rooted in survival and subsistence claims or a 'fair share', to ensure their survival.

In the present context of development projects, the series of crises experienced by local communities in the form of alienation from land, labour and environment, and the realization of relative deprivation and inability to challenge the perceived injustice and alienation, lead to the Kantian crisis: the struggle for freedom remains unexercised. The dilemma faced by the PAPs is that their traditional lifestyle becomes untenable due to the changes brought about by the development project while the new lifestyle is beyond their reach. This forces the local communities to return to the inner self, reflexivity forces the critic to become a self-critic in order to seek emancipation from the present situation. This critique is itself a form of knowledge. Hegel points out that the critique of knowledge does not possess the spontaneity of origin. Reflection is instead dependent on something prior and given, which it takes as its object while simultaneously originating in it. Thus, the choice of the first frame of reference and the sequence of the additional stages of investigation remain arbitrary. The former can no longer claim to fulfil the intention of the first philosophy, but this need not entail abandoning the critique of knowledge itself. The circular character of argument (how do you know when to stop being a critic and move to the next stage of the investigation?) that is problematic to epistemology in this methodology proposed by Reinhold, is justified in phenomenological experience, as the form of reflection itself. It pertains to the structure of self-knowledge that one must have apprehended in order to know explicitly. Only something already known can be remembered and comprehended in its genesis. This movement is the experience of reflection, thus the critique of knowledge is destined to take place after the fact. It begins with the data of consciousness that it first confronts empirically (Habermas, 1971).

The only way they can claim a 'fair share', that is, a share biased in their favour, is, by creating and asserting a new alternate reality that is favourable to them. The only social reality that they know and claim to be fair, something that was always 'theirs', is historically located in their relationship with their environment. This was their usufructuary right over natural resources in their regions linked with the subsistence economy. That arrangement had ensured their survival for centuries and generations in the past, without actually having 'ownership rights' over these resources. Whenever these rights were disrupted due to regime changes, the PAPs had always resisted it and reclaimed their rights, usually to a substantial extent. These stories of past victories over regime changes are linked with identities and indigenous cultures, and form a part of the collective social histories of all social communities that are linked to a place over time.

This new learning, resulting from their ability to make these connections between their histories, re-interpreted, in the present context of a development project, is important. The consciousness (of the self-reflexive critic, in this case, the PAPs) in its genesis can make apparent only something that is already known, albeit from their past. This is the moment of genesis. The capability of self-reflection and the ability to infer new meanings from an objective social reality, when an existing meaning about reality becomes problematic to individuals, is not new to sociology. The objectification of physical environment as a source for drawing 'natural resources', both in Marxian theory and the adaptive dynamics paradigm, is directed by the technical interest in control and mastery over the environment. This has led to contradictions and new learning in human ecology.

1. The objectification of nature severely conflicts with the assumption of nature as a complex system. This assumption is increasingly supported by knowledge through technological evidence made available today (Schroyer, 1983).
2. The objectification of the subject, that is, the human being, which is necessary for the production process, is another contradiction. It conflicts with the emancipatory interest and belief in dialogue and interaction.

In his own work on historical materialism, Habermas has criticized Marx for ignoring communicative action, which is equally important in production processes. He has demonstrated this through historical studies. In fact, it is Habermas' contention that it is normative structures which determine the rules of communicative action. These play an equally important role in resolving system problems in social evolution. Habermas fundamentally suggests a reframing of the base-superstructure theorem. He states that it is the endogenous learning process (the superstructures) that provides the growth of technically useful knowledge (the base). The equilibrium, according to this, between forces and relations of production, is rare. Hence, endogenously caused development of productive forces makes structural incompatibilities obvious and this causes disequilibrium. It is the development of new norms and intuitive learning that may restore equilibrium.

The symbolic interactionist approach that has emerged in sociology and social anthropology emphasizes this perspective. Starting with George Herbert Mead (1865–1931), the tradition of viewing human group life from the perspective of the individual in sociology has produced a rich literature using the symbolic interactions approach. Cooley, Thomas and Goffman reflect this approach. This approach sees individuals as creative thinking organisms, able to choose their behaviour instead of reacting more or less mechanically to the influences of social processes. It assumes that all behaviour is self-directed, shared, communicated and manipulated on the basis of symbolic meanings by interacting human beings in social situations (Cockerham, 1998: 63). This is consistent with the basic human nature that is assumed by Habermas.

This return to reflexivity seriously challenges the data of consciousness that the PAP first confronts empirically, and the well-documented assumptions about the environmental impacts of development projects prepared at the inception stage of the project. In the context of techno-economic development projects in India, the role of the state and its bureaucracy is clearly stated through environmental legislation. This legislation passed in 1972 was also responsible for the creation of the Ministry of Environment and Forests (MOEF). The role of MOEF is to ensure that the project promoters create a documentation of the Environmental Impact Assessment (EIA) of a development project including its adverse impacts, and take mitigative measures to reduce these adverse impacts, within the boundaries of the project, as a pre-condition for approval of the proposed development project. Thus, the process assumes predictability and mitigation of the adverse environmental impacts resulting from the project.

The situational logic of the development projects is such that the unintended and undesired consequences of the project appear 'after the fact'. These impacts threaten the identities of original inhabitants in the area surrounding the project site. The threat to their local cultures, livelihoods and quality of life, form the basis of environmental resistance and struggle that is organized against the project sometimes. These impacts, by their very nature, can be experienced only after the project is sited in a locality. They cannot be anticipated and therefore cannot be documented in the EIA statement nor can they be measured within the geographical boundaries of the project. But they are very real and threatening to the local communities.

The individual-turned-critic is able to identify an environmental crisis, in the light of a concept of 'environmental well-being' as defined by him. He is able to identify structural imbalance over the definition of what is right and just from his perspective. He is able to re-interpret the 'official' statements of environmental impacts based on pure reason. Since 'ecological competence' is universal, any human being will be able to do this. Thus, he is able to come up with new and equally valid (to himself) interpretations of a social reality. The return to inter-subjectivity is the 'new learning' that challenges the dominant assumptions about the environmental impacts of the specific development project.

This moment of self-reflexivity gives rise to a critique of knowledge. The only thing at the beginning of the critique is the radical project of unconditional doubt. This doubt requires no justification because it legitimizes itself as an aspect of reason. And correspondingly consciousness that criticizes itself does not need to be trained in methodological doubt, because the latter is the medium in which consciousness constitutes itself as consciousness that is certain of itself (Habermas, 1971:13). The critique of knowledge does not possess the spontaneity of origin. It depends on something prior and given, which it simultaneously questions and challenges. This form of reflection originates in the stratum of experience. It is this commonsense understanding that gives rise to the consciousness of a world of everyday life. The recollecting power of reflection itself originates in this consciousness of the everyday world.

In reflection, consciousness cannot make anything transparent except the context of its own genesis. Only something already known can be remembered as a result and comprehended in its genesis. This movement is the experience of reflection (Habermas, 1971).

New Learning

Methodological individualism proposes that all human beings act rationally within the constraints of the social situation they find themselves in (Jarvie,1976). But when their perception of the situation changes due to new learning emerging from crisis and reflexivity, they modify their behaviour toward what is rational and appropriate to these changed circumstances. They are able to thus come up with new but equally valid interpretations of a social reality, which they use in strategic action to change a reality. The new learning that emerges as a consequence of self-reflection has to be based on new meanings that are environmentally sustainable and culturally acceptable to all. This can be done only through interaction. While asserting the claim to the universality of hermeneutics, Habermas states that interaction is the locus to hermeneutics, which conforms to the knowledge-constitutive interest in understanding and is hence emancipatory in nature. Understanding human conduct is a causal endeavour and consists in uncovering its intelligibility by relating it to the rules that constitute a form of life.

The methodology that dictates this kind of analysis has to be an interpretative methodology. There are two sequential aspects of social science methods. Weber distinguishes them as the difference between the 'what' and the 'why' of a phenomenon. The 'what' questions explicate adequacy at the level of meaning, the 'why' questions provide causal adequacy. Weber goes on to add that causal explanations are possible in interpretative sociology. According to him, it is wrong to suppose that since human action is subjective and therefore unpredictable, human conduct tends to be predictable to a layman or to a scientist to the degree to which it is rational in terms of the selection of the means to attain specific ends. Predictability pertains more to actions and is free of emotions. Explanation of motives definitely involves causal explanation because it can be attained via *a priori* grasp of the subjective meanings that are attached to their actions. The task of the social scientist is to concern himself with the interpretative understanding of social action, and thereby to supply it with a causal explanation of its course and consequences. Social action is expressed in terms of the subjective orientation of the agent. Action is social if the actor takes account of the behaviour of others. Understanding the problem of the other is problematic. At the core of Weber's analysis is the distinction between behaviour, *verstehen* (understanding) and action (Habermas, 1988). Each of these can be explained by the observer, but the behaviour cannot be framed in the subjective intent of the actor because it is habitual. Action, on the other hand, has to be framed in terms of its meaningfulness to the actor. The possible criticism of an interpretative approach is as follows. Since interpreting meanings involves an empathetic experience, meaning has to be understood and described with a great degree of certainty in the 'correctness' of the interpretation. Since there can be no absolute standards for a correct 'description', one can argue that interpretation will always be subjective. The way out is that one can perceive multiple meanings in the understanding of an act. The convergence of particular meanings through a process of dialogue is possible. Alternatively, one can study the opposite, a crisis to get clues into the ideal phenomena, as suggested by Foucault.

Thus, it is not surprising that one often finds people who are affected by a development project using a discursive strategy of 'talking claims' to assert and re-assert their claims to reality about the impacts. The leap from individually experienced crisis in the form of alienation to an inter-subjectively shared reconstruction of an 'ideal' is an important step that takes place through this strategy of talking claims.

The work of William J. Thomas (1863–1947) (Volkart, 1951) is also relevant for understanding crisis as residing in the individual's definition of the situation. Thomas stated that as long as definitions of social situation remain relatively constant, behaviour will generally be orderly. However, when rival definitions appear and habitual behaviour becomes disputed, a sense of disorganization and uncertainty may be anticipated. The ability of an individual to cope with a crisis situation will be strongly related to socialization experiences. Specific social histories of the group are important here. These collective, intersubjectively shared experiences are compared with past experiences to cope with new situations. In the process of preservation of the self, it would become necessary for individuals to create, share and communicate new meanings among similar individuals within the social group, to manipulate the social situation in their favour.

The transition from individual interpretations of a social situation, to the emergence of group meaning is a problem that is not very well addressed in sociology. More recently, 'talking claims' as a discursive strategy, is used to explain the emergence of group meanings. Constant assertion and re-assertion of claims are used as a strategy by individuals, who assert their claims to a new reality and legitimize it (Cooley, 1964).

The initial 'risk-taking' behaviour of the local elites in land transactions, new jobs, or new local businesses, resulting from economic and social changes in their vicinity, is the rational response to the new project coming into the region. In the context of a particular ecological niche occupied by the local communities, the socioeconomic changes resulting from the project make the traditional livelihoods untenable and the new livelihoods beyond reach. This realization comes from experience that is intersubjectively shared through 'talking claims'.

A critique of knowledge, when it casts off its false consciousness (of the dominant claim of the development project), gives rise to unconditional doubt. Consciousness that criticizes itself does not need to be trained in methodological doubt, as unconditional doubt legitimates itself as an aspect of reason. The result is the re-establishment of 'risk-averse' behaviour and the associated worldview, which is the experience of reflection. The 'moral ecology' claims carry with them the notion of ecological justice based on the notion of limits to exploitation, which is inherent in the subliminal controls of most traditional societies. Their working definition of exploitation is a loss of access to what is claimed to be theirs as a first principle: the common property natural resources such as land, water and air, and game, fish, wood, etc., which are linked with these natural resources and which are lost to them due to resource over-use and abuse or changes in property rights. This is seen as a serious breach of trust. To reassert a reliable subsistence for themselves and for their future generation, becomes a primary goal. All new relations are examined in this light. Risk-averse behaviour is already known to people living in rural areas in agrarian economies (Scott, 1976). A return to risk-averse behaviour and associated moral ecology is the 'new learning' that guides actions. Resistance to change then becomes a negotiating strategy. If the local agrarian elites are mobilized, the emergent local environmental movements work their way up a political system to get better bargains. If not, they would adopt other forms of resistance to arrive at the same goal. The primary goal is to ensure at least the minimum security of survival under the changed circumstances of the new project. This minimum security of survival was ensured in the past through risk-averse behaviour rooted in subliminal controls that exist in the traditional patterns of resource exploitation. Thus, it is important to realize that the call for a 'return to basics' is to be understood only as a discursive strategy of the PAPs and not be confused with the actual desire to return to lower levels of resource-consuming instrumentalities.

At a strategic level, every PAP who faces the consequences of a development project, makes 'moral ecology' claims.

Most environmental struggles are located in subsistence economies, and so the struggles make similar claims. The impacts of development projects, when cast in terms of a threat to their subsistence economies, is the only way they can legitimize their claim for a renegotiation without appearing to be anti-development and therefore anti-national.

The core of the argument of moral economy put forward by James Scott (1976), in the context of a traditional agrarian system, can be applied here. In traditional agrarian systems, cultivators and landowners share certain common norms. Various risk-sharing arrangements may evolve over time in different agrarian regimes, between the tenant cultivators and the landowners, resulting in a stable pattern of reciprocal obligations between the two. For example, in a bad year when the crops fail, depending on the risk-sharing arrangement, the landowner has a social obligation towards his cultivators. He may choose to waive his share of the agricultural production, or may even provide food to the cultivators from his own surplus stocks, to ensure their survival. Scott (1976) then traces the changes in the distribution of risk that results from a change in regime from landowner to colonial capitalism. This often results in the breach of stable exchange that may threaten the survival of the peasant during a bad year and under the right conditions, it may lead to a peasant revolt. The moral issue here is not how much of the surplus is taken away by the various claimants, but what is left for the survival of the peasant. Thus, for the same volume of surplus extracted, there may be no dissent in a good year; but in a bad year, in the absence of reciprocal social obligation between the peasant and the landowner, this may result in a revolt by peasants. Thus, Scott argues for the 'survival first' principle in the subsistence ethics of the peasant culture to explain the emergence of peasant revolt. But revolt is exceptional. Non-harmonious relations and coercion may exist, without revolt, under similar circumstances (Scott, 1976), as seen in the local discourse among the affected people in the form of narratives, in pilferage when the occasion permits, and in increased police control.

Moral economy (as defined by Scott) includes the notion of economic justice. PAPs' working definition of moral ecology, in a similar vein, involves the notion of ecological justice—their view about which claims to their ecology are tolerable, and which intolerable. Broadly speaking, the transfer of individual land through sale is tolerable, but a loss of access to common property resources such as common lands, forests, grazing lands and water sources are intolerable. Insofar as their moral ecology is representative of other environmental struggles elsewhere, we are moving towards a fuller appreciation of the normative roots of environmental politics. Return to safety and reliability that ensures survival of the family/community, is the first principle.

The local economy may or may not be strictly a peasant economy, nor is the tenant–landlord relationship strictly relevant here. But the moral economy argument still holds. There is a breach of social obligation, in a different way. There is a breach of social obligations by various claimants depending on the situation. In most situations, there tend to be three main claimants who breach the social obligation towards PAPs: first, the earlier landowners, in this case, the state, as all barren common lands are owned by the state; second, the new landowners, in this case, the project promoters who lease or buy the land from the state; and third, the elected representatives of the constituency in the local, democratically elected government.

In the process of creating the documentation that is used to justify and rationalize the introduction of the development project, the state and the elected representatives make claims to bringing about rapid economic growth, reducing social inequality and regional disparity, and promising environmental sustainability. The promise made by the state agencies and the political leaders is that the local community will be better off with the project than without the project. The bottom line is that the local community will not be worse off as a result of the project.

The moral issue here is not how much of the surplus is taken away by the various claimants, but what is left for the survival of the local communities, after the various claimants have made their claims. The economic profits made by the project proponents are not grudged by the local communities: they claim a share in the profits as a survival right, based on subsistence ethics. Thus for the same volume of surplus extracted, during the initial period, there may be no dissent among the local communities. Over time, they expect that some of the profits will come to them by way of income or charity, as a reciprocal social obligation between local communities and the project promoters. In the absence of this, and especially as the development project unleashes socio-cultural and economic changes beyond their control, the potential for a protest movement by the local communities may emerge. It may even result in a revolt by the local communities.

Transformative Action

While considering transformative actions as strategies of resistance to the project, the PAPs have to keep in mind that they have to deal with particular agencies of state. There are four alternatives before the PAPs in this situation depending on the perception of the weak or strong state vis-à-vis the PAPs: avoidance of conflict, adoption of an anarchist strategy, efforts to mainstream environmentalism, and appeals to decentralize the power of decision-making within the state in order to make state agencies more responsive and accountable to the local struggles. When the PAPs perceive the state agencies as strong, they adopt 'every form of resistance' (Scott, 1985). When the state is strong and so are PAPs, this results in a legitimation crisis and armed conflict. The anarchist strategy results in state agencies coming heavily against the PAPs. When the state is perceived to be weak or open to moral persuasion, and the PAPs believe that they can persuade the state to listen to them, efforts are made to mainstream environmentalism through reform, an appeal to the moral economy. Finally, if the state and the PAPs are seen as being equally matched, they are able to negotiate across the table. This results in decentralization of the power of decision making and actions in order to make state agencies more responsive and accountable to the local struggles.

Consequently, Thomas (Volkart, 1951) makes two important contributions: he notes that the same crisis will not produce the same effect uniformly in all people. Second, he explains the ability within individuals to compare a present situation with similar ones in the past, and to revise judgments and actions upon the basis of past experience. Therefore, the outcome of a particular situation depends upon an individual's definition and upon how he comes to terms with the situation. Thus, the concept of crisis is important because it emphasizes that crisis not in a situation, but rather in the interaction between a situation and a person's capacity to meet it.

People typically cope with crisis by trying to change their situation (compete when new opportunities present themselves), manage the meaning of the situation (re-interpret meanings) and/or keep the symptoms of stress within manageable bounds (controlled social protest without making it lose its legitimacy such as Gandhian non-violence). Each region would imbibe the development project with its own distinctive meanings. The historicity of the place drives the manifest forms of resistance and hence the transformative action (Ludden,1990). The transformative action sometimes takes the form of a social protest movement. Environmental protest movements can also be located within what are now called 'new social movements'.

Environmental protest movement is an exception and has been conceptualized within the political economy framework, based on the (preservation first!) PF! principle as stated in Chapter 1. What is proposed here is that PF! is only a professed goal of the PAPs who organize themselves into a protest movement. Their ultimate goal is to regain a privileged position in the newly developing social, political and cultural hierarchy, consequent to the location of the development project in their neighbourhood. PAPs are not happy to continue at subsistence levels in the face of a development project, and the resultant social protest movement is not a desperate cry of desperate people but an action resulting from new learning and strategic action undertaken by PAPs to change the newly emerging social hierarchy in their favour. Thus, they take strategic action to re-assert their identities, and to avoid a situation wherein they get marginalized and are no longer counted in the new society.

Just recognizing environmental social movements within the PF! principle leaves out a range of other forms of resistance by the PAPs, which are equally important. Environmental protest is an exception mainly because the PAPs perceive the state agencies as being 'strong' and consequently adopt 'every form of resistance' (Scott, 1985). Non-harmonious relations may exist without the emergence of an environmental protest movement, and the denigration of the project by PAPs in private conversation and in folk songs is a typical indication of this. These may take on various forms ranging from short-term migration and pilferage of project property through social banditry.

The deterrence to environmental protest movements is often not the survival alternative open to the PAPs but rather the risk of protest. These risks are largely proportionate to the coercive power of the project promoters insofar as the state government is willing to provide 'protection' through the police, but in a democracy, the state is usually constrained and the ability to use mass media to their advantage helps the PAPs in organizing civilized forms of protest like *morchas*, *dharnas* and *gheraos*. When the state is perceived to be weak or open to moral persuasion, and the PAPs believe that they can persuade the state to listen to them, efforts are made to mainstream environmentalism through reform, and an appeal is made to the moral economy. These actions do not de-legitimize the protest and help the PAPs to achieve a 'political visibility' for their agitation so that some re-negotiation is forced on the project promoters. The actual actions will depend on the PAPs' perception of the advantages accruing to them from these actions in the long run and their ability to mobilize resources to achieve more visible protests depending on their social history (Scott, 1985).

Finally, in a new and emergent trend in the reaction of the PAPs to a project, sometimes the state and the PAPs are seen as being equally matched, and being able to negotiate across the table. Usually the balance between the state and the PAPs is due to an external pressure such as that caused by a development aid agency threatening to pull out of the project. It results in decentralizing the power of decision making and actions in order to make state agencies more responsive and accountable to the local struggles.

To summarize, the theory proposes that the environmental adaptation of human beings to their environment is an adaptive dynamic paradigm: unique, evolving and mediated through socio-political and cultural systems. Historically, socio-political systems in human society dictate the interaction between human beings and their physical environment, leading to certain types of technologies used for resource exploitation that meet the subsistence needs of these societies. The over-use and abuse of natural resources, in non-fossil fuel using technologies, were kept under control through certain subliminal controls that were part of the cultural system resulting in a dynamic environmental equilibrium. Over time, the exploitation of natural resources due to fossil fuel use has intensified. These subliminal controls tend to break down and need to be replaced by more rational environmental regulations. The limits of physical environmental exploitation related to air, water and land are easy to establish and the pollution abatement technologies do precisely that. But the consequences of the deterioration of the physical environment on the socio-cultural environment and human societies of the PAPs is far more complex and very difficult to predict. So how does a more rational environmental regulation evolve?

Today, socio-political systems still identify development projects with their associated technologies. These projects demarcate certain elements of the physical environment as natural resources and use them to produce economic goods and services. This is the first step in the interaction between the environment and human beings that brings about desirable outcomes such as economic growth and development in the socio-political sphere. But at the second level, the use of these natural resources results in resource depletion and pollution. At a third level, the economic growth and regional development initiated by the development project lead to certain long-term sociocultural consequences due to the changed cultural ethos resulting from changes in the economy and ecology, and in population distribution and density.

All these primary, secondary and tertiary consequences have an impact on the PAPs as the project proceeds through its various development stages. The consequences at the primary level due to changes in land use and the price of land, are more or less predictable and leave the relatively elite among the PAPs, who own lands, economically better off. This is mainly the focus of soical impact assessment (SIA) studies. Similarly the preservation of fauna and flora due to pollution and resource use can be promoted through appropriate pollution control technologies. But the secondary and tertiary level consequences on the PAPs start manifesting themselves only towards the completion of the project and by their very nature, are non-predictable. The rural subsistence livelihoods are adversely affected due to changes in the access to common property natural resources and the lands associated with them. But resource depletion is mainly caused by the influx of people in search of new opportunities resulting from the project, leading to increased population density, and therefore cannot be considered as a direct impact of the project, though it may be attributed to it. The increased density of population resulting from immigration to this region could also lead to changes in the demographic and ethnic composition of the population. Economic prosperity leads to changes in local culture and the changes in demographic characteristics lead to an additional strain on natural resources like water and fuel wood, and on infrastructure resources like roads, power, and sewage and sanitation of the entire settlement.

SIA studies are responsible for only direct impacts caused by the project within its geographical boundaries. Since all the secondary and tertiary changes in the neighbourhood of the project are associated with but not directly attributable to the project, they are outside the purview of the SIA, and political institutions like the local governments and other government departments are expected to take care of these changes. But this does not happen quickly. As stated earlier, these changes begin to become significant only towards the completion of the project. The timing is important. Therefore, the realization of these consequences among the PAPs comes after the completion of the project. Therefore, the reflexivity and emergent new learning, and the action to bring about transformation in their social situation come after the completion of the project, and challenge its legitimacy. The discontent among the PAPs takes on different forms, from everyday form of resistance to an organized protest movement. Eventually, the socio-political system has to address this discontent among PAPs, irrespective of its nature. This results in legal and legislative changes over time.

The form and content of the environmental legislation are implicitly debated here. It is argued that environmental legislation should have a technological as well as a hermeneutic dimension. Currently, while the technological dimension is decided by various pollution standards, the hermeneutic dimension is implicitly dictated by instrumentally rational methodologies. What is argued here is that the hermeneutic dimensions should be dictated by the environmental critic as he[1] has a commitment to social justice, environmental wellbeing and moral economy. The environmental critics are the PAPs, who understand the rules of environmental adaptation, possess the environmental competence and propose a normative action plan that would restore environmental equilibrium. Therefore, the environmental critic's interpretation of the situation should be given as much importance as given to the scientific approach, in order to restore environmental equilibrium in the context of a development project.

---

[1] Though the enviornmental critic is addressed as 'he' in the text, the term encompasses both men and women.

Three

Methodology of Research

Theoretical development on the lines of a critical theory of environment is presented in the previous chapter. This chapter on methodology provides a link between the theory and the case studies related to various development projects that follow. A comprehensive theory indicates what to look for in the projects under review and the methodology proposes how to look for it and the tools to be used to collate information related to these projects. Real-life situations are in a constant state of flux and chaos. Examples of various trends in environmental sociology which reflect this chaos in real life are given in the following section. It is therefore extremely important to choose the right lens or methodology from among the available methodologies. A detailed discussion on the choices of various methodologies and their limits follows, in addition to the one I have selected to substantiate the theory. Here I distinguish between research methodology and methods of data collection. Thus, while the methodology has an ideological bias, the methods of data collection are considered, for practical purposes, to be ideology-neutral. The chapter concludes by restating the relationship between 'theory and practice'.

Developing an appropriate critical environmental theory is an exercise that spans my entire academic career. My doctoral dissertation explored the possibility of developing a critical theory of environment on the lines of Habermas' general theory of communication. I was guided in this direction by my philosophy professor and was able to develop the first level of a critical theory of environment: 'a general theory of environmental adaptation' based on the framework proposed by John Bennett, albeit with modifications.

At this stage, in the late 1980s, I got stuck at the question of who the 'critic' is and what role he plays in the further development of the project outcomes. The dominant methodology of that time, which guided the EIA studies, was rooted in positivism. It pointed in the direction of an environment protection agency or environmental scientists, or in the case of India, the Department of Environment in the Ministry of Environment and Forests (MOEF), as a critic. That was the time when the *Narmada Bachao Andolan* was at its peak and obviously the Department of Environment and Forests was not the dominant player in the project development. The *Andolan* and its supporters appeared as dominant players. The withdrawal of World Bank funding for the project was a major victory for the *Andolan*. Finally, the apex court in India, that is, the Supreme Court, had to intervene. The newly emerging trends in environmental sociology, as indicated in the following section, also pointed to the new things that were taking place in real life in the environmental sphere.

Trends in Environmental Sociology

Blaming the victims

Theorizing about the environment in India would be incomplete without accounting for the lack of environmental protest movements and the issue of routinized environmental degradation in regions like the vicinity of industrial estates, particularly industrial estates housing chemical industries (AIDAB, 1991b). What does one see? The surface and ground water, and waste sites, for example, in the shanty towns on the periphery of Hyderabad's urban life, face a very high risk of environmental pollution and degradation. In these areas, first generation migrants to the city are arriving in search of livelihoods as labour in urban industrial estates. Without the traditional protection of agricultural wage labour and subsistence access to common property resources, stable social relations and social capital that facilitate survival through lean times which still exist in the interior/rural areas, the pattern of moral selective neglect called 'passive resistance' by anthropologist Marvin Harris, is obvious in these communities surrounding the industrial estates. This pattern of moral selective neglect of the factories they work for is seen in the form of 'everyday forms of resistance' by the labour to industrial units manifested in the trend of showing up late, absenteeism and alcoholism, which are common. Communities which are themselves victims of severe social and institutional neglect, are blamed for allowing their physical environment to get polluted, as if this were an unnatural and inhuman act. Under circumstances of uncertain right to the lands that they live on, the pattern of selective neglect of their physical conditions of living due to visible environmental contamination and passive resistance to the neighbourhood factories that employ them, may be seen as active survival strategies for the communities living in the industrial areas. (Therefore, in some countries, the granting of 'property rights' to these residents is seen as one way of empowering the powerless who would then take responsibility for the care of their surroundings. These initiatives are part of the UN Habitat agenda consistent with the Millennium Development Goal.)

Physical environmental degradation becomes a routine in an environment wherein daily subsistence is at stake and bets are hedged. While the routinization of environmental neglect in the context of shanty town life is not hard to understand and quite possibly evokes empathy, its routinization in the formal institutions of public life is not easy to accept uncritically. The routinization of environmental degradation in formal institutions of public life, mainly the environmental protection agencies, occurs often. This leads to incomplete registration of environmental parameters of pollution by monitoring agencies. Often an environmental protection agency is looked upon cynically as one more green pasture for government officials to seek 'informal rents' from the industry. The traditional judiciary too contributes to the routinization of the indifference towards environmental degradation. It may no longer support the neglect of environmental degradation, but is bound up in procedures. The media takes cognizance of this situation only selectively.

These findings are consistent with the argument put forth by Scheper-Hughes (1989) in the context of poverty, and by Scott (1985) in describing everyday forms of resistance adopted by people who find themselves in hegemonic power relations.

Essentializing the displaced

In the context of development projects, the other issue of concern is essentializing the displaced. Human rights violation as a result of internal displacement is an exception rather than a rule. There are laws, bureaucratic organizations and standard normal procedures laid down by the state to carry out the resettlement and rehabilitation of the people displaced by any development project and people affected by natural disasters. Thus human rights violation occurs only under an exceptional social situation resulting in an internal armed conflict in the context of rural development projects.

In order to prove that human rights violation has taken place, the 'promoters of the human rights violation claim' have to project certain images of the victims to the international audience. This form of projecting the issue as a human rights violation is a political strategy that can get results such as project delays or re-negotiation of the resettlement packages in the short run. But in the long run, this process of strategic essentialism leaves certain categories of people worse off.

Innovative alliances in environmental struggles

More recently, the public sector aligning with a subaltern rhetoric to attain its own agenda is a new trend emerging in India. For all practical reasons, the public sector is fast becoming a marginal social group in infrastructure projects, and is threatened with extinction in the changing social order resulting from a development aid project. Under similar circumstances, public sector units use similar strategies to resist change and to modify the outcomes to make them more favourable to their own interpretation of reality with greater or lesser success.

Backlash against projects

More recently, there have been instances of an environmental backlash against the development projects planned in a region, for example, against the power plant in Dahanu, in Palghar *taluka* in Maharashtra in 1998, or over the location of a new airport in Mumbai city at the initiation stage of the project, again in 1998. In both these cases, there were fairly aggressive demonstrations against the development project, resulting in state action and finally a calling off of the project initiation itself. This is not necessarily a desirable outcome or a permanent status quo, though it may depict the initial victory of the people to reclaim their lands. A return to basics will ensure only subsistence for the people and not improvement in the quality of life for the future PAPs. The fact remains that if these sites have been selected for the projects, it is because they meet other environmental requirements.

Withdrawal of the promoter at this stage implies that the state government agencies are not willing to give their full support for various reasons. One reason for this may be political. Another reason could be that there is enough slack in the capacity of the existing systems which can be tapped into by more efficient exploitation of the existing capacity so that the delay in the project would not affect the economy adversely. Eventually when the need for a new airport or power plant pushes the state to promote a 'new project', these would be the same sites where the projects are likely to be initiated. This is because initial feasibility studies have identifed these sites from among at least two other options on the basis of various other environmental parameters. After a delay of, say 20 years, eventually when the projects have to be implemented, the environmental parameters that make these sites so attractive for the project would not have changed. I have known of a water augmentation project in the pipeline for over 25 years. At that point, the larger 'public good' that justifies the need of the project would outweigh the losses to the community. The question is, would the community then revert to its strategy of resistance and protest and hope that the project never happens, or would it be prepared to make the transition from a semi-agrarian to an urban economy? Historically, the PAPs have always 'reacted' to a project; with enough time would they be 'proactive' in their efforts and actually support the project? Would they be in a position to provide a concrete action plan, with cost estimates and stipulate conditions under which they are willing to support the project? We need to wait and see.

These protests, leading to delays in project initiation, could be interpreted as warning signs for a proactive policy that would incorporate the interests of the PAPs as an ongoing effort throughout the project duration, instead of a one-time Social Impact Assessment (SIA) study, as it exists today.

Inconsistencies

My own experience with the PAPs on the various projects I was involved with, was no different. As a consultant, I carried out the EIA, and particularly SIA, of various development projects and the projects were approved on the basis of these reports. The various environmental parameters like ambient air quality, and flora and fauna, were monitored during the construction of the project and after project completion to ensure that they were within limits. In case of SIA, there were no set parameters within which the impacts were considered 'within limits'. The only parameter was the setting of the land price (which is currently determined on the basis of future land use instead of current land use) for the land that was usually acquired for the project by the revenue department of the state government. The baseline data on the socio-economic profile of the PAPs could be documented but the social impacts of migration changes in the local economy and land use patterns could not be anticipated very precisely. The only information available was on construction labour needed for the project at the construction stage. Actual immigration to the area and associated infrastructure requirements of roads, power, water, sewage, etc., could not be anticipated and the local government had neither the financial resources nor the human resources to initiate such improvements. There was always the risk of an over-estimation of these needs. So local authorities usually followed the 'do nothing' option, sometimes in spite of the project promoter's willingness to contribute to this cause.

Once the project was initiated and project implementation was well into the completion stage, the role of the PAPs was crucial. All the SIAs for the projects carried out by me over the decade kept bringing me back to the role of PAPs in reshaping the project outcomes. Some of these outcomes were more dramatic as in the case of a violent protest, while in the case of others, the outcomes were more subtle, but the fact was that the principal actors reshaping the project were PAPs. The local authorities took their clue and filled in the gap. The agrarian studies programme at Yale University that I was visiting, led me to a different direction for the answer. The thesis of moral economy of the peasants, proposed by Scott (1976), who was the director of the programme, had a great influence on my work. It provided me with a framework that would put the human agency at the centre without being deterministic or ideologically biased. The use of moral economy/ecology claims by the PAPs as a discursive strategy to assert their perception of the environmental impacts of the development project, was quite innovative and such discourses had always existed among the PAPs in spite of the 'official claims' of the SIA. Being an anthropologist by training, I was used to listening to people 'talk'. These talking claims assert a reality that was biased in their favour and the action component was unique to the Indian context. They knew no one could punish them for 'talking', and if they were better organized and motivated they were able to access other social resources like the help of NGOs or other academic organizations. Often, they would use legitimate democratic means like *morchas* to protest against the project. The legitimacy of this form of protest is rooted in the historical context of the Indian freedom struggle. Various novel forms of *dharna*, fasting for *satyagraha* and *morcha* to the state capital were actions legitimized by none other than Mahatma Gandhi himself, in the Indian context. These allowed the PAPs to voice their discontent without challenging the legitimacy of the political power and without being branded as 'criminals'.

I had to modify the basic argument of moral economy to apply it to the PAPs who were predominantly peasants or agriculturists from semi-urban areas. PAPs were individuals who were reflecting on their changing situation due to the project. Their reflexivity, and their creativity and actions arising from this reflexivity, were responsible for bringing about social changes that were more favourable to themselves. But the two dominant paradigms of environment, the sustainable development approach or the dependency approach, were not able to identify the 'individuals' as agents of social change, and their discourse and related actions were never given any importance. The PAPs were passive recipients of changes, and the credit went to the policy implementer, or the emergent community leaders and NGO leaders, and ideology, in the two paradigms, respectively.

The Bridge

How does the critical theory framework link up with the real life situation? Or to rephrase the question, what would be the appropriate 'lens' or methodology that would tie up the theory and the case studies together? The critical theory of environment proposed here accepts the primacy of the socio-cultural over the techno-economic spheres in understanding the outcomes of the various development projects listed here. The socio-cultural sphere in the context of development projects, involves broadly three categories of actors: the PAPs, the promoters of the project, and the various decision-making and implementing agencies and departments, of the local, state or Central Governments. As is obvious from the case studies presented subsequently, there is a wide range of contexts in which these projects take place. The projects presented here have been selected for their unique outcomes, as each reflects the unique way in which each of these three main categories of actors have played their roles, and yet there is an underlying common theme that can be explained through the use of the theoretical framework. The question therefore is: What should be the appropriate scientific methodological framework that would help us clinch the relationship between 'theory and practical outcomes'? In order to answer this question, we need to first define what we mean by 'scientific' and then choose from among different scientific methodological approaches the one that is most appropriate for our theory.

What It Means to be Scientific

While carrying out real world research, should we be scientific? To take a step back, what do we mean by a scientific approach? Adopting a scientific approach refers to an attitude to seeking of knowledge: to systematically, sceptically and ethically carry out an enquiry (Selltiz et al., 1970). The main reason for working this way—systematically, being explicit about all aspects of your study, and opening up what you have done to scrutiny by others—is likely to lead to better quality and more useful research. Given the nature of studies of phenomena by natural sciences, the kind of methodology used—observations, quantification and law-like generalizations—leads to prediction and control of natural phenomena. Such a methodology is neither desirable nor feasible for undertaking research on human subjects. Human beings are capable of empathy and an inherent understanding of their actions. The acts they perform are meaningful to them. They use a logical framework, given a situation to arrive at these meanings and acts (Jarvie, 1972). Therefore, the methodology of natural science will not lend itself to an understanding of this basic nature of human action, and hence will always be capturing only partial truths of the subjects.

The assumption here is that the 'craft skill' or techniques of data collection and analysis of the collected data are assumed to be a precondition for carrying out research (Schutt, 2001), and the researcher has adequate training in it.

Positivistic View and Its Critique

The standard view of science is derived from the philosophical approach known as positivism (Robson, 2002). August Comte and Hebert Spencer were proponents of logical positivism with an emphasis on value-free evidence, hard facts and prediction in policy development by government and other organizations. Here causal explanation is a central aim and can be established through empirical regularities or constant relationships. In this standard view, science, including social science has explanation as its central aim. If you can relate an event, observation or other phenomena to a general law, then you have explained it. Developing universal causal laws from empirical regularities or constant conjunctions is thus the primary aim of research. The methodology is assumed to apply independent of the nature of science, be it natural or social science.

However, this methodology, though used for over a century, has not resulted in the production of any scientific laws in sociology or anthropology. One important reason for this is the nature of reality that is studied in social science. What the observer sees is not determined simply by the characteristics of the thing observed but the characteristics and perspective of the observer also have an effect on it (Jarvie, 1972).

The critic of the standard view questions the assumption that only observable phenomena should be the subject matter of science. It is impossible to distinguish between the language of observation and theory or facts and value. There is no one-to-one correlation between observation and theory. Instead of rejecting the philosophical doctrine completely, there is a move to re-conceptualize the view of science that provides an adequate representation of what a scientist does and a more promising basis for social science.

Relativistic Views and Rejecting the Extreme

The philosophical relativism maintains that there is no external reality independent of human consciousness; it is all in the minds of the people (Robson, 2002). Reality cannot be defined objectively but only subjectively. The extreme position states that all reality is only subjective and there is no reality independent of the subject. But common sense tells us this is not true. Hence, if we are to recognize the role of common sense as an adjunct to our thinking about research, full relativity as an idea needs to be put aside. The relativistic view is based on the foundation that the real meaning of social behaviour can be captured only by qualitative research. Objectivity in research through standardization and distance does not guarantee objectivity in quantitative methods. Therefore, there cannot be an objective reality as different cultures and societies would have different conceptual systems that make sense of the social reality. Nor is objectivity necessary as long as the biases of the research are put up front. The respondents are treated not as objects but as equal partners in research. The philosopher of science, Paul Feyerabend, views science as just one cultural tradition among many. Thus, even when qualitative research is given primacy, it does not reject empirical methods aimed at standardization. It accepts quantitative research as one among different cultural traditions. But such an extreme position is at odds with the world as we know it, as the world exists independent of the observer.

Within social science, there are influential relativistic approaches: constructivist, naturalistic or interpretative. They are all variants of qualitative research as distinct from quantitative research typical of the positivist tradition. They view reality from the eyes of the participant. The importance of viewing the meaning of experience and behaviour in context and in full complexity is stressed (Robson, 2002). The role of language is emphasized and the research process generates a working hypothesis rather than immutable empirical facts. These emergent accounts of reality are not accorded a privileged position; they are equivalent to other accounts.

Post–Positivistic and Constructionist Currents

Post-positivism recognizes that the theories, hypotheses, background knowledge and values of the researcher can influence research. However, there is still a commitment to objectivity and that reality can be known only imperfectly and probabilistically because of the researcher's limitations. They can find salvation in the critical realist approach (Robson, 2002) developed here.

The constructionists believe that reality is socially constructed. Therefore, the task of the researcher is to understand the multiple social constructions of meanings and knowledge. Therefore, they use research methods such as interviews and observations, which allow them to acquire multiple perspectives. A sophisticated realist approach can provide a framework for this approach too.

Emancipatory Approach Guided by Critical Realism

Marxism action researchers and many feminists share the concerns of the critical approach. Their central criticism of both positivist and constructivist researchers is that they are relatively powerful experts researching relatively powerless people, or the traditionally marginalized people. They find ways to overcome this imbalance in power. One way is to facilitate emancipation of the affected people and their views of understanding the world. Gender studies focus on issues related to women, while ethnic studies focus on issues related to castes and tribes. Since the three main groups of actors involved in the project are the project promoters, who are global players, the bureaucrats and technocrats involved in mediating for the project between the promoters and the PAPs, and finally PAPs, who are relatively marginal groups in these studies, I therefore recommend adoption of methodologies that would provide a historical understanding of each one's perspective. Such an enquiry will therefore have to be embedded in historical reality, as well as provide both a subjective and an objective understanding of the people involved (both quantitative and qualitative) with an emancipatory interest.

Plans for Real-World Research

Here I have focused mainly on the power imbalance between the three loosely defined groups of social actors involved in the development project: the PAPs, the promoters, and the various levels of government agencies involved in development projects in the context of its impacts on the physical environment in which the project takes shape. It is fairly well established from the case studies that historically indigenous ethnic groups have not enjoyed the same power and privileges as those enjoyed by the national level promoters of the project or the state agencies. The concern here is for understanding and improving the lives and relations between different PAPs, in particular, and the ethnic groups they belong to in a specific context, and the promoters and facilitators of the development projects. The purpose of this ecological inquiry is to understand the various kinds of relationships that evolve between the indigenous ethnic groups and particularly the PAPs, the project promoters and the state agencies, which would facilitate the emancipation of the 'victims' and an understanding of their views and actions in relation to the other two.

Realism provides a model of scientific explanation, which avoids both positivism and relativism, and has the potential of incorporating the features of an emancipatory approach. The example of gun powder is used to explain the principle of realistic explanations. Does gun powder blow up when a flame is applied? Yes, if the conditions are right. It does not ignite if it is damp or if the mixture is not right, and so on. In realist terms, the outcome of an action follows from mechanisms (composition of gun powder) acting in a particular context (the particular conditions which allow the reaction to take place). Understanding the action mediated by the mechanism that results in the outcomes in a context is how a realistic explanation is arrived at, in everyday life. At the heart of realism is the assumption that reality exists independent of our awareness of it, and this is taken for granted when one considers the everyday world of the physical objects around us. Realism acknowledges values and knowledge is seen as a historical and social product. Social science is a search for fundamental structures and mechanisms of social life (Harre, 1981).

Thus, the task of science is to invent theories to explain the real-life world, explanations concerned with how mechanisms produce events. The guiding metaphors are of structures and mechanisms in reality rather than phenomena and events. Laws are statements about the things that are really happening, the ongoing ways of acting independently of existing things, which may not be expressed at the level of events. The real world is not only complex but also stratified into different layers. Social reality incorporates individual, group and institutional social levels. The concept of causation is one in which entities act as a function of their basic structure. 'Explanation' implies showing how some event has occurred in a particular case. Events are to be explained even when they cannot be predicted.

Critical realism is the methodological approach I have taken in the case studies where the emphasis is on locating the events in a social, institutional and historical context, and on explaining their occurrence as an outcome of the actions of various individuals and groups, with each of them acting rationally to optimize their own interest. Here I make a clear distinction between methodology of research and methods of data collection. This methodological approach does not discount any method of gathering data, including the explanations given by the actors and empirical data-gathering methods. Thus an explanation of the outcomes of the event begins where giving the reason of the actors and empirical evidence, ends.

What is the implication of adopting this methodological approach to theory? Theory thus does not have predictive powers but it defines the parameters or the broad framework within which social action takes place, in everyday life. The various events taking place in a project during its completion, are elaborated by using this methodology in the subsequent chapters. They validate the theoretical framework as a convenient common framework to understand this complex reality wherein the multiplicity of events would otherwise prove to be beyond generalizations.

One of the advantages of realism is that it allows us to take on board some of the attractive features of the relativist position. Realism can acknowledge value, and because there is a reality to which reference can be made, there is a basis to choice among different theories. Realities do not aspire to the universalistic claims of positivism but see knowledge as a social and historical product that can be specific to a particular time and culture or situation. It is the task of science to create theories that aim to represent the world. The activities of people in society constitute a complex set of interacting things and structures at different levels. The task of a social scientist is to establish their existence and properties through both theoretical and applied work. Studying people is very different from studying inanimate objects in laboratories. The movement is from a close controlled situation to an open fluid one. Realism permits new integration of subjective and objective approaches in social theory. The subjectivist approach emphasizes that action is meaningful, and that reflexivity is involved in human actions. However, it tends to deny an objective character to social reality. The objectivists emphasize the reality of society but deny the causal role of an agency. The new integration argues that social structure is, at the same time, the relatively enduring product and also the medium of motivational human action.

For realists, explanation is constructed in terms of mechanisms, which can follow any of the theoretical designs mentioned here: embeddedness, or open and closed systems. Embeddedness implies that human actions can be understood only in terms of their place within different strata or layers of social reality. Open and closed systems imply that scientific laws in a realist analysis are about the causal properties of structures that exist and operate in the world. Explanation follows outcomes in an open system of organized complexity, while limited predictions are possible in closed systems.

Critical realism thus provides the rationale for a critical social science which critically analyses the social practices that it studies. Critical realism as a methodology, understands the social reality, and suggests means by which the social equilibrium, albeit at a higher level of satisfaction for the participant actors, can be restored. It provides a third way between positivism and relativism, and also helps fulfil the emancipatory potential of social research. Thus it acknowledges that positivism is discredited but, at the same time, avoids a divorce from science, implied by a throughgoing relativist approach.

Methods of Data Collection

At this stage, I would like to differentiate between data collection methods and methodology. The data collection methods can be considered, for all practical purposes, to be ideology-neutral and different methods can be used for collating data simultaneously. Thus, for different contexts, different methods will be needed. For example, for capturing the 'talking claims' made in the local discourse of the PAPs at a given time, the qualitative participant method of collecting data is the most appropriate method. The historical-qualitative techniques are most useful for understanding the complex social relationship that the PAPs have among themselves and with the state agencies, while the quantitative empirical data involving structured schedules is the most appropriate tool to capture a 'snapshot' of the socio-economic status of the existing PAPs (Croswell, 2002; Punch, 1978; Schutt, 2001). Thus all the data collection techniques are adopted depending on the context for the case studies presented in the following chapters.

Relationship between Theory and Practice

An understanding of the environmental impacts of development projects begins with a comprehensive theory about the human–environmental relationship. The proposed critical theory of environment consists of the techno-economic and the socio-political dimension and the outcomes of each, and is aimed at restoring environmental equilibrium, at the physical techno-economic and socio-cultural levels, by using a critical theory framework. It begins with the premise that evolution in the adaptation of humans to their environment, is through techno-economic (development) projects towards higher resource-consuming instrumentalities, with the stated objective of being economically viable, environmentally sustainable and beneficial to local communities. But bargaining for the spatial location of a particular techno-economic development project takes place at the socio-politico and cultural level. Specialists ensure environmental sustainability, at techno-economic levels through laws and procedures, while the socio-cultural equilibrium at the project site is largely ignored.

But very quickly, the disruption in the socio-cultural sphere asserts itself through the PAPs to facilitate restorative action. Human beings, including the PAPs, by virtue of their 'universal ecological competence', have the ability to reflect on their past actions, become environmental 'critics' and suggest remedial actions to restore environmental equilibrium in the socio-cultural sphere. Thus, the onus of critics shifts away from being specialists to human beings affected by the development project. Their self-critique leads to enlightenment and new learning.

The enlightenment is the realization that in order to ensure their socio-cultural survival as a distinct ethnic and social group, they do not have the choice of ignoring the project-related development taking place in their neighbourhood. They have to 'engage' with the project in order to ensure their socio-cultural survival, because however painful the engagement may be, the price of 'letting go' the project is much worse. The new learning implies the realization by PAPs that there are as many realities as people and that therefore they must adopt a reality that is most favourable to restoring their socio-cultural equilibrium. They should adopt the appropriate action to change the reality in their favour. The actions they use are drawn from their unique social histories. The fact that action occurs after the implementation of the project does not make it any less legitimate, and therefore environmental policy should ensure ecological justice, based on the PAPs' moral claim of 'survival first'.

This paradigm described in detail in an earlier chapter, provides the framework to understand the events that occur from the initiation of the project to its completion for the six different projects reviewed here. The methodology proposed as critical realism allows for the collection of quantitative and qualitative interpretative data on all aspects of the environment, which includes physical and socio-cultural historical aspects. All the projects involved the three main categories of social actors, namely PAPs, the project promoters and the state agencies. Following the methodology of critical realism, the details of these three categories of social actors are provided in the historical socio-cultural context by using qualitative data and to the extent possible, empirical data. Each narrative of the project begins with a broad historical and policy context within which the project takes place, which also includes specifics like the background about the location of the project, description of the physical environment and socio-cultural groups that live within it. It is followed by the socio-economic profile of the PAPs including quantitative details. These details of the more PAPs' socio-economic, cultural and ethnic background are also captured to the extent possible for the promoters and the government institutions involved. All this helps in locating the PAPs, the promoters and the government agencies in a particular socio-economic and cultural context in relation to one another in the triad. The point of entry of the researcher is explicitly stated. The actual events that take place over the span of the project are described in detail. This includes the 'official view' and the local narratives of the PAPs. The point of contestation and the outcomes of the project are presented subsequently. A brief link with the theorizing is explained at the end of each chapter. The individual projects presented here can be categorized into three different types, namely tourism projects, energy infrastructure development projects, and urban and industrial projects; the alliances and the resultant outcomes between each of these three groups of actors have led to unique consequences. While the consequences are unique, the outcomes can be explained and understood well within the parameters predicted by theory.

The following six chapters present various development projects with their environmental impacts by using this methodology. The PAPs, project promoters and various government agencies involved are unique to each of the case studies and yet the theoretical and methodological framework is able to unify this diversity. The concluding chapter ties up the loose ends, establishes the common theoretical framework that runs through these individual projects, and draws certain generalizations from the six development projects presented in the following chapters.

Four

Environmental Protest, Locality and Modernity*

The promotion of an amusement park as a tourism development project is the focus of study here. Tourism projects are generally considered as non-polluting and sustainable forms of economic development. They therefore do not require detailed Environmental Impact Assessment (EIA) studies. The amusement park located at Gorai was an exception and the Environmental Ministry of the Central Government got involved in it, instead of a local municipality, to address their issues. The causes and the outcomes are reported here. The following study is based on a retrospective analysis of an environmental protest movement against the construction of an amusement park, organized by people living in the park's neighbourhood. The park is a private enterprise located some 20 km away from the city of Mumbai in the Gorai Islands.

The Community

The Gorai Islands are a cluster of islands consisting of Marve, Manori and Gorai villages. They are described in the *Gazetteer of Bombay Presidency* (1920) as quiet seacoast villages, inhabited by fisherfolk

---

*This chapter is based on fieldwork carried out in Mumbai during 1996–97, supported by the Indian Council of Social Science Research, New Delhi. The support is gratefully acknowledged. Earlier drafts were presented at the Center for South Asian Studies, University of Pennsylvania, and at Ripon College, Wisconsin, during my Visiting Fellowship in the Programme in Agrarian Studies, Yale University, in 1997–98.

I was the project director of the ICSSR, New Delhi funded project titled, 'Amusement Parks Environment and Social Protest', from January 1996 to June 1997.

and horticulturists. They are linked with the mainland by a narrow strait in the northern part of the islands and are separated from the mainland by the Manori Creek. The population of these islands in 1920, according to the Gazetteer, was only 320; the islands population according to the1991 Census was 2,750. The three main caste groups inhabiting these islands today are the Kolis, Bhandaris and Dodhis, which, up to 15 years ago, were mainly dependent on fishing, rice cultivation, and coconut palm horticulture for subsistence. The religious composition of the group is of interest here: while the Dodhis and the Bhandaris are mainly Hindus, more than 85 per cent of the Kolis are Christians. Ninety-eight of the 100 families studied were born on the islands. All the groups are literate, and the islands have two schools located within their territories. Today, even though they retain a rural ambience, these localities can no longer be called villages. They have developed as a satellite town to the mainland of Mumbai. The communities have businesses in Mumbai. Some commute to the mainland for jobs, while others have trade relations with merchants in the city.

Before the Park

The coastline of the islands was always a recreational area for the urban dwellers of Mumbai. Even today, the beaches are used as picnic spots for Mumbai dwellers, mainly during the summer. The main visitors are students from the colleges of Mumbai and other picnic-goers. A few shacks along the beach belonging to the Kolis cater to the needs of these picnic-goers.

The Park

The Esselworld amusement park was commissioned in 1989, built on 67 acres of the total 753 acres belonging to Esselworld Enterprise, within the islands. Formerly a wasteland, this land was sold by auction by the Bombay High Court in 1981 for just 205 million rupees (Manohar, 1993). The landscaped park has 30,000 trees of 33 different varieties, planted on it by the Esselworld Enterprise. Construction for the park, which began in 1984, cost a total of 235 million rupees. The money was borrowed by the resident and non-resident Indian (NRI) promoters from various financial institutions, including the Tourism Finance Corporation of India, State Bank of India Capital Markets, and Twentieth Century Finance Markets Limited. The park had 23 'rides' when it opened in 1989, and a few more have been added since. It attracts 45,000 visitors daily, and about 3 million visitors annually. Each adult visitor is charged 150 rupees per visit (Tak, 1992). A boat service owned and operated by M/s Enterprise Holdings operates between the park and Manori Creek to transport the park visitors.

The Esselworld amusement park on Gorai Islands is targeted as a leisure activity to promote weekend tourism. The target population for the amusement park is visualized to be the urban upper-middle-class and middle-class residents of the city of Mumbai. The average monthly income of the visitors was between Rs 2,500 and Rs 3,000 according to a survey of visitors conducted for the Environmental Impact Assessment in 1988. The setting up of the amusement park is quite visibly a symbol of the way in which capitalism-driven development projects—in this case, tourism—may negatively affect local communities. Interestingly, since tourism is seen by the state as a non-polluting activity, without any negative physical or social environmental impacts, no impact assessment is deemed necessary.

Locale of Study

Gorai was a sparsely populated group of islands where peasants and fisherfolk lived at subsistence levels. The economy took care of the basic food, fuel, fodder, shelter and water needs of the community. Although the community had commercial transactions with the city of Mumbai, it continued to be sparsely populated. This is partially because of lack of access, and partially because it is covered by the rules of Mumbai Metropolitan Regional Development Authority (MMRDA) which designate it as a 'no development' zone. The islands can be accessed from the mainland only by crossing a creek. The only other approach road to the islands involves a detour of some 40 km through Bhainder at the nothern tip of the islands. Bhainder is outside the Mumbai municipal limits. Second, since it is a 'no development or green zone', multi-storeyed constructions and polluting industries were prohibited on the islands.

Among the three main caste groups inhabiting the islands, the Kolis are mainly dependent on fishing; some own mechanized trawlers, while others work on these along with the trawler owners. Kolis mainly live along the coast. Some of them traditionally rent out their cottages during summer to weekend tourists from Mumbai, shifting their residence from the coast to Manori Creek during the monsoons. They build temporary shelters and fish in the estuary of Manori Creek, mainly for home consumption, as the market for fish during this season is slack. This is their main source of income during the monsoon season that lasts for four months.

The Bhandaris are horticulturists and grow coconut palm gardens through well irrigation. They also tap *todi* or sap from the *tadgola* palm trees, which is sold on the mainland, in both its raw and fermented forms. Some of the Dodhis and Bhandaris own small rainfed agricultural lands, which they cultivate only during the monsoons. The main crop is paddy, grown mainly for home consumption. They also own some draught animals and small animals. The 753 acres of land at Gorai, which was owned by the state government till 1981, was like all other barren lands, and people had free access to it. They grazed animals on this land during the monsoons, dried fish there during summer and used this land as an approach road to their farms. Very poor families collected firewood there during the summer. Certainly, the land had no negative impact on the local economy.

When the ownership of the land was transferred to Esselworld Enterprise in 1981, it was accompanied by other changes that were detrimental to the local economy. First, the cost of Rs 2.5 million quoted was determined according to the prevalent value of barren land, and not based on the intended use value of the land as an amusement park. Second, in order to establish total control over their real estate, the new owners built a compound wall around it. This ensured that the local communities could no longer use the resources from the land. It also obstructed the local inhabitants' easy access to paddy fields on the other side of the amusement park. After the park became operational, the promoters asked the municipality to provide them with some additional lands for parking facilities for their visitors. This was granted, and land was given on a long-term lease to the park promoters. The additional land given on lease for the parking facility was originally a shallow pond that collected rainwater during the monsoons. This sweetwater pond was used during the monsoons for washing clothes and for the use of animals. During summer, when the pond dried, it was used by the local communities for drying fish. Conversion of the land into a vehicle parking area was achieved through levelling and resurfacing of the land, thus severely affecting its earlier uses.

Gorai Islands, as stated earlier, are shared by different communities living fairly harmoniously with each other. There is a reciprocal exchange among neighbours, especially of drinking water, which is always a scarce commodity on any island surrounded by the sea. Sweetwater is found on the top layer of the soil along the coast. Sweetwater in the dug wells of coastal regions requires careful handling. Over- extraction results in salt-water intrusion from the sea, rendering the water source brackish forever. Water was always exchanged free of cost among neighbours on the Gorai Islands and access to dug wells for drinking purposes was always given, even in the bad monsoon years.

The park also resulted in secondary growth in the area as the outcome of a change of ownership of other private lands in the surrounding areas. Locally owned lands were sold to the urban elite for construction of weekend homes. The first thing that the new absentee owners did was to put a compound wall around their estates and appoint an estate manager. This severely affected the reciprocal exchange, especially of drinking water, among neighbours. In addition, the amusement park appointed a private contractor to provide for the drinking water needs of the 45,000 daily visitors. Drinking water is delivered by tankers to the park where it is given primary treatment before being provided it to the visitors. The contractor buys the water from the surrounding surface water sources like ponds and dug wells.

Thus, what was taken away from the local communities was their access to common property resources such as water, fuel, wood, grass, and small timber, and access to their own lands. Esselworld Enterprise is able to extract huge profits from its investments through entry fees and other surcharges for about 3 million visitors per year. Esselworld managed to escape entertainment tax for the first two years. The financial sector institutions have recovered their investments. The state government also benefits through the taxes it collects from the enterprise. But for the local communities, there was disruption in the pristine natural environment of the islands. The average Goraikar (as the residents of Gorai call themselves) had to accept a forced change in lifestyle, from being peasants and fishing folk, to being self-employed small businessmen, selling soft drinks and snacks along the approach road to Esselworld. They are now exposed to conspicuous consumption by the tourists; their women are vulnerable to the indecent behaviour of drunken tourists. The tourists drive recklessly on the narrow roads of Gorai, endangering the lives of the local residents, and the road surface has deteriorated further. Residents also face frequent electricity failures. But the most important extraction that seriously threatens their survival is a loss of access to their drinking water supply, as stated earlier, partially due to their loss of access to neighbourhood wells and partially due to the amusement park, which promotes a market for drinking water. A commercial market is now available to individual well owners for selling their drinking water supply to the water contractor. Water is therefore no longer a free good available on reciprocal exchange.

The state government took no action to prevent this from happening. Within the scope of the EIA mitigative measures, it did insist that the park promoters make drinking water provision for visitors to the park, but it did not insist that the source for the supply of drinking water be located outside the Gorai Islands. The local communities have approached their political leaders and elected representatives for providing a piped water supply, but it would be extremely expensive to lay pipelines on the islands from the existing water sources. These reservoirs are a few hundred kilometres away and do not have surplus capacity. In fact, the water problem is part of a larger, unplanned 'builder'-driven development of the Vasai Virar area of the Mumbai metropolitan region, which will require both new water sources and political will. Meanwhile, Gorai residents have to depend on tanker-delivered drinking water supply during the three months of the summer, three times a week.

Thus, the three claimants to the land breached social obligations to the original inhabitants in different ways. The state did not ensure that the traditional rights of the original inhabitants were protected in any way, and rather appeared to be protecting the rights of 'other citizens' by giving them special concessions. The new landowners, Esselworld Enterprise, have unleashed market forces beyond the control of the local economy. The only option that the original inhabitants have is to join the market or be left out. Even when they join the market, without the active support of the state, they can participate only at marginal levels, as small self-employed businessmen. Furthermore, the elected representatives of this constituency in the local government could not ensure the protection of the rights of local inhabitants. They could not even ensure adequate drinking water supply. The best they could do is to make temporary provision for water in the event of extreme water shortage.

Environmental Changes

The promoters had procured this land on Gorai Islands with the intention of developing prawn fishing. In fact, the idea of setting up an amusement park came later, the plans for which were approved only in September 1983. Discontent against the amusement park among the local communities started as early as 1983–84 during the construction phase of the amusement park. The park was constructed by reclaiming land from the surrounding mangroves of Gorai Islands, and involved a considerable landfill operation. The park covers 67 acres, with 5 km of internal road; 300,000 trees were planted on a mangrove swamp and a 3 metre-wide and 160 metre-long jetty was constructed into the Manori Creek area. This required a substantial labour force during the construction phase. The promoters hired labour through labour contractors. Local people were not even hired as manual labourers on daily wages. The explanation offerd by the promoters was that the park was a time-bound project and the construction had to be completed within 18 months. The park consists of 27 'rides' and there are plans for creating a marine park with windsurfing and water-skiing facilities. Once the amusement park became operational, Esselworld hired 130 employees at entry level for office jobs and other operations. Not one of these employees was from the islands, even though there were enough young people living there who were suitably qualified for the jobs.

A ferry boat service began operating to transport tourists from the Mumbai side of Manori Creek once the park was commissioned in 1989. Seven boats, each making 12 to 15 trips, cross the creek every day. This contract was given to a sister company of Esselworld Enterprise, and not to the local Fishworkers Co-operative Society, which had for long been operating a ferry boat service in the creek and had the resources to buy new boats if given the ferry contract.

The intensified operation of the ferry service has significantly altered the local ecology. The most important ecological impact, according to the Kolis, is on the productivity of Manori Creek. The creek had historically provided subsistence fishing during the monsoons when open sea fishing is closed for the local fisherfolk. Now, due to the reclamation of sea for the park, the spawning activity of the fish in the creek has been prevented and over the last few years, almost no fish has been caught there. The Kolis' claim remains unsubstantiated, however, since without adequate baseline data, it is very difficult for a marine ecology study to attribute the reduction in the productivity of an estuary to a single cause.

There is statistically significant change in the ownership of land, boats, animals and vehicles by the local communities (Bapat, 1997). The number of people owning land, boats and animals has declined. The reduction in land-ownership is due to 'outsiders' buying land and using it as beach houses. The number of autorickshaws has increased, while the number of *tongas* has decreased. Similarly, employment has shifted from the primary to the service sector (Bapat, 1997). The spin-off from tourism has generated employment in the service sector as small self-employed businesses provide cheap snacks and drinks to the tourists on their way to the amusement park.

Infrastructure facilities have not improved significantly since the operation of the park began. The area suffers from an acute drinking water shortage. The approach road to the park has not been widened nor maintained, because of a dispute between the then Gram Panchayat of Meera Bhayander and the Greater Bombay Municipal Corporation (GBMC) over the maintenance of the access road. In spite of a 2800 MV sub-station set up by the Bombay Suburban Electric Supply Company, power failure in local households and extreme voltage fluctuation during peak hours are very common (Bapat, 1997).

Articulation of the Protest

Beginning in 1987 and continuing through 1990, local discontent culminated in a media campaign against the park in both the vernacular and the English press. News items pointed out the inadequacy of the ferry service, the inadequate and unsafe drinking water supplied to the tourists, and the high prices of food items within the park, and criticized the park's exemption from entertainment tax. The park promoters claimed exemption from the entertainment tax on the grounds that they were providing an educational service to urban children, but this was rectified two years after the park became operational and the promoters had to pay back taxes to the government.

Local leaders had, from time to time, approached the park promoters with their grievances but were politely ignored. Thereafter the local church became the nodal point for organizing an informal protest. As the opposition to the park intensified, the promoters were no longer polite. Finally intimidation and violence were used against the local communities. In due course, the protest against the park became better organized. The manner in which the local actors built up local resistance into an environmental problem is of interest here. This was the time during the late 1980s and early 1990s, when other environmental social movements like the *Narmada Bachao Andolan*, and the Kerala fishworkers' agitation were gaining momentum. It was easy to get media attention if the issues were articulated in terms of the negative environmental impacts on indigenous populations. This was a successful strategy, as the vernacular and the English press gave this social movement almost continuous publicity over the next three years. The movement addressed the following issues: (*i*) reduction of drinking water due to its over-extraction by the park for its visitors; (*ii*) creation of the parking area for the park out of government (common usage) land, which was a sweet water lake during the rains and served as drying grounds for fish in summer; (*iii*) loss of productivity of the Manori Creek due to the activities related to the amusement park; (*iv*) loss of easy access to privately owned lands due to the park boundary walls; and (*v*) loss of fuel wood due to privatization of 753 acres of government lands resulting from the sale of this land to the park promoters.

Opposition to the park culminated in a *morcha*. The *morcha* was taken to the *mantralaya* (the seat of power) in Maharashtra, and in 1989, a memorandum was submitted to the then Minister of Urban Affairs. One hundred and fifteen people were arrested on their way back from the *mantralaya* after they burned a bus owned by the park. Twenty per cent of the people from the local communities actively participated in the agitation, while almost everyone living on the islands supported it.

Articulation in environmental terms provided the protesters with a bargaining position, and focused media attention on the issue. Although technically they could not stake claims to the resources owned by the state and sold to a private enterprise, casting the conflict in environmental terms allowed them to stake moral claims to these common property resources, especially water.

State Response

Since the agitation challenged the legitimacy of the state by articulating the issue as one of moral economy, the state could not overtly take an anti-agitation stand, but ordered an Environmental Impact Assessment (EIA) report as a means to reinstate its legitimacy. Interestingly no environmental clearance had been deemed necessary at the beginning of the project because, according to the Development Control rules of the GBMC, amusement parks are a permitted activity within a green zone. Therefore, only a 'consent application' to the local municipality is required for getting clearance for the project. However, given the capital investment made on the project, the Ministry of Environment and Forests had to be involved since all projects costing beyond 50 million rupees require Central Government clearance before the construction phase of the project can begin.

The EIA which is expected to consider the impact of a project within the boundaries of the project and to list the ecological and environmental impact on air, water and land due to the project, casts environmental issues in a particular framework of cost-benefit analysis. The impacts are quantified and measured within the boundaries of the project. Mitigative measures also apply only to impact within the project boundaries. The EIA report related to the park accepts that certain trees in the mangroves were destroyed during construction of the jetty. It also lists the precautions taken by the promoters for solid and liquid waste disposal, and the safety and health precautions for the visitors in case of accidents (EIA Report, 1989). The report was submitted to the Ministry of Environment and Forests and approved in 1989, shortly after the park had opened to the public, and since social or ecological impacts of the project beyond the boundaries of the park are considered outside the EIA procedures, the EIA provided the state with the necessary means to de-legitimize local environmental claims.

Comparison with Other Movements

The form of articulating grievances against the park by the local inhabitants has both parallels and significant differences with other two environmental protest movements mentioned earlier, namely, the National Fishworkers Federation in Kerala and the *Narmada*

Bachao Andolan. The former was an agitation, organized by a clergyman, against large mechanized trawler fishing near the coast of Kerala, which received wide media coverage between 1984 and 1986. The *Narmada Bachao Andolan*, in the central part of India, received almost uninterrupted national and international media attention for almost nine years (see Baviskar, 1997).

Both agitations share some common features. They are agitations led by social-minded outsiders. They mobilized the 'small' people against the mighty state or international institutions and, most importantly, they provide moral legitimacy to the claims of the local community over their natural resources.

The groups of people at Gorai, by contrast, are not peasants, and not all involved in agriculture. But the issue they raised is a moral issue of the right of the group to protest against environmental degradation that affects their subsistence economy and threatens their survival. This has proved to be a successful strategy. The state, the Church, the World Bank, as the case may be, could be forced to a negotiating table by such an agitation.

There were also parallels between the fishworkers, agitation in Kerala and the local fishing community, both Hindu and Christian of Gorai. The local fishing community was, by many counts, conservative and traditional. Like Tom Kocherry, the leader of the Kerala agitation, a local official of the church at Gorai was involved in efforts to form co-operatives, establishing the Machimar Co-operative in Gorai early in 1974 to help fishworkers get loans for trawlers, etc. Women were also active in the co-operative since, by the usual division of labour, they handled the marketing of the fish. Women therefore were mobilized early during the discussion and the agitation.

But there were also significant differences between the communities in Gorai and the fishworkers' agitation. The size and therefore the duration of the protest are factors here. The fishworkers' agitation in Kerala involved 120,000 households, as against a few thousand in Gorai and spanned two and a half decades from 1960 to 1984, as against a mere five to seven years in the Gorai case.

The ideological commitment of Kocherry, the leader of the Kerala agitation, was leftist though not Marxist. The ideology of the Gorai protest was not well articulated, but protest was focused on three issues. First was the destruction of the marine ecology of a single estuary, due to increased navigational use and landfill activities. Earlier there was only one boat, which carried people to the villages every two hours; now there were seven making 17 trips each. The second issue was the loss of access to agricultural lands and other common property natural resources, especially water, which had been adequate for the limited population of the islands before the park was constructed. Finally, the movement was being pushed—by virtue of the involvement of women in the struggle—to protest against adverse tourist behaviour, like eve-teasing and reckless driving. Tourism and gender issues did not quite fit the perspectives—whether of 'ecology' or of 'liberation theology'—of the Kerala fishworkers' movement.

It appears then that the environment tourism moral economy impulses that were to become prominent in the protest movement came from the people themselves. They are part of the diffused but widespread development of a mass-based Indian environmentalism that is arising out of the popular experience of capitalism-driven development projects—in this case, urban tourism.

Political Battles

The other environmental protest movement, the *Narmada Bachao Andolan,* is also significant by way of comparison here as a political battle over access to resources, projected as a basic conflict between the state and the people (Singh, 1997). In the present case, Esselworld has received popular support as represented by the numbers of visitors coming to the park every year. There is therefore an important issue of conflict between not only the state and the people, but also between different sections of people, that is, between the recreational needs of Mumbaikars and the subsistence needs of Goraikars. The question is, whose needs should be prioritized? And what should be the legitimate means of fulfilling them? Both the subsistence needs of the local inhabitants for water and the need of the urban dweller in a congested city like Mumbai for easily accessible recreational places are equally important, but the subsistence needs of local people should receive priority and active support by the state against capitalism-driven development projects.

The other related issue is that of the right of local people to the profits generated by developmental activities in their neighbourhood. The local people do believe they have a right to the developmental activities taking place in their neighbourhood, and make various kinds of claims. They wanted a reserved quota in the employment generated by the park and exclusive rights to the spillover services generated by the park, like the ferrying and transport contracts to bring tourists to the park, and the contract to deliver water. They wanted part of the profits made by the park to be ploughed back into community development programmes like education and health services. Last but not least, they claimed that the natural habitat should be preserved on a sustained basis. They made what they considered to be legitimate demands to all the three claimants: the state, the park promoters and the elected representatives.

As against this, only individual property rights, and the right of access to individual properties, were considered legitimate and taken cognizance of by the park promoters and indirectly supported by the state. The state, on the other hand, took cognizance of the environmental impact on the estuary, as claimed by the movement leadership. It also supported the demand for a reserved quota in the local employment generated by the park. The elected leaders could only informally pressurize the amusement park promoters to negotiate with the local community, but were successful in persuading the local municipality to provide tanker water to the community.

Informal negotiations took place on four issues. The first was a 10 per cent reservation of jobs within Esselworld for the Gorai residents. This was a promise made (and only partially adhered to) by the promoters. The local people were selected only at entry levels on a temporary basis, and fired at short notice so that they could never claim 'permanent status'. The Machimar Co-operative Society was promised that they would be given the contract to ferry the tourists to and from the park. This did not happen as tenders were invited for the contract in which they did not qualify. The agriculturists were earlier promised that photo passes would be issued to them for granting them access to their lands through the park compound. This promise was not kept. The management offered to buy their farms at a mutually agreed price of Rs 125,000 per acre. The owners who opted for it were given Rs 25,000 up front, and the rest was to be paid in four instalments. These instalments are still pending. The management also promised a donation to one local school and later to a health facility. But the movement participants could not decide on the school to receive the funds, so no funds have been disbursed.

The only circumstances under which these demands were respected was when the protest movement was fully organized, as indicated by the show of strength in the form of the *morcha* organized to the Mantralaya by the movement leadership. When one of the informal leaders of the protest was transferred by the church in 1991, the organized manner in which the protest was conducted broke down. The community could no longer continue to exert the required social pressure to ensure that the promises were fulfilled. In the absence of social pressure, the amusement park promoters could not care less. The state also did not intervene to push for the informal demands that emerged out of the negotiations, as the demands had no legal status.

Like the Narmada controversy, the present case involves conflicts between different branches of the state, the various ministries at the centre, between the Central and state governments, and between the state and regional authorities. The relevant conflicts are highlighted here.

The conflict between the Ministry of Environment and Forests (MOEF) and the Tourism Department in regard to coastal areas is very obvious here. The MOEF requires the implementation of the Coastal Regulation Zone (CRZ) in coastal areas, disallowing any construction of more than 30 to 40 ft high within 200 metres of a high-tide mark. It is silent about landfill in an estuary or a mangrove, which totally destroys the marine ecology, and large-scale reclamation, as in the present case, is not anticipated by it. The Tourism Department, on the other hand, promotes construction of tourism facilities, including five-star hotels, along the coasts and beaches.

Gorai Islands comes under the Mumbai Metropolitan Region Development Authority (MMRDA), which follows urban planning norms and zoning regulations, similar to the development plans followed by cities elsewhere in the world. The zoning regulations require that different areas within the city be marked into four zones: industrial, commercial, residential and green zones, depending on the type of development planned for that region. The development control (DC) rules of the MMRDA allow non-polluting activities, like amusement parks, in the green zones. But the draft development report is not legally binding and is considered only as a guiding principle at the discretion of the political leadership.

The J.B. D'Souza Committee, appointed by the former Chief Minister, S.B. Chavan in 1986, drew up a Draft Development Plan for MMR. The secretaries of the Urban Development, Industries, Housing, Judiciary and Environment Departments prepared a Draft Plan. The Secretaries' Draft, which had agreed in principle with the then

Prime Minister, Mrs Indira Gandhi's directive, laid down rules to mark 200 m from the high-tide mark as free of structures. Gorai Islands come under the 'no development zone', which allows only certain types of non-polluting development activities, while 30 to 40 feet of structures could be permitted according to the Report in under developed areas like Mudh, Marve, Manori and Gorai.

Subsequently, when Mr Sharad Pawar became the Chief Minister in 1989, he sought to promote beach development as top priority, with a view to encouraging tourism. He chose to ignore the Draft, which was under consideration for final action, as, according to him, it was only suggesting a guideline to be followed. The result was the construction of the Esselworld Amusement Park.

The different alliances formed by the state are of interest here. The state government partially supported the demand for tourism by supporting the Esselworld Enterprise. The state also partially supported the demand by the local community for a review of the scheme's impact. Formally it ordered an EIA, and informally it pressurized the promoters of the project to open informal negotiations with the community leaders. Thus, in the process of promoting economic growth through tourism, the state maintains an apparently neutral stand which works in favour of the promoters (De Kadt, 1979).

Global Influence

By not supporting the traditional or customary rights of the local inhabitants, the state supports individual property rights of development promoters and the rights of national citizens over those of local inhabitants (Appadurai and Holston, 1996). The balance of power is tilted in favour of large development projects and individual property rights.

Global ideas and development in various forms are at work here which over-ride the rights of local inhabitants. Conceptually, the idea of an amusement park on the lines of Disney Land in the USA as an ideal leisure activity is a global concept: artificially developed environments with amusement 'rides', is the ultimate in the commercialization of leisure. These rides in the form of giant swings, giant wheels, roller coasters and roundabouts, are based on an appeal to the infantile and the emotional, in human nature. The need for this type of leisure is an artificial need, stimulated and spurred in a systematic large-scale manner, mainly by the media and this demand, which is beyond rational human need, is satisfied through capitalism-driven development projects in the present context of financial cities like Mumbai.

The development of Mumbai as a financial capital, on the one hand, results in the generation of money and wealth, while on the other, it finds its expression in a homogeneous and monotonous society. Time spent at work is considered as time wasted from life while time away from work, or leisure, is equated with liberation. The commercialization of leisure has given rise to half a dozen such amusement parks in the Mumbai metropolitan region in the last decade, with Esselworld being the first. This trend represents an integration of leisure into a totality of economic phenomenon of the city of Mumbai.

The popularity of the park represents a reinforcement of this global trend in recreational tourism the world over. Accumulation of wealth in the city of Mumbai allows for surplus discretionary cash in the hands of people of all ages, but especially among teenagers and young adults, the target groups of these amusement parks. The park is promoted as a hide-away from the city to teenagers and, as a place for family recreation by offering special family discounts including those for senior citizens during the peak season.

Funding from non-resident Indians(NRIs) and other financial institutions, and various concessions given by the government, endorse this trend in tourism. The idea of promoting tourism as a 'green', non-polluting industry that brings economic benefits to the local communities as a 'win-win strategy' is a concept supported and promoted by national and international agencies like UNESCO (De Kadt, 1979).

Evaluating the environmental impact of the project, exclusively in terms of the physical environmental impact on air, water, land and people (national citizens) within its physical boundaries, to the exclusion of local inhabitants residing within its neighbourhood, is a dominant global trend in the conservation and preservation of environment. In the present case, the state's perception of the environmental impact, earlier mandated by consent application and subsequently by EIA, is narrowly defined as an impact on the physical environment to the exclusion of the social environment. The direct or indirect non-economic impacts on local communities resulting from the project are not considered worthy of formal recognition by the state.

Without state support and formal recognition, in the long run, the local community is unable to sustain social pressure through continued organized protest to ensure that promises made by project authorities are met. This results in 'everyday forms of resistance' by the community (Scott, 1985).

Although the Maharashtra government had adopted a resettlement and rehabilitation policy as early as 1986, the policy technically does not apply to projects that do not involve the physical displacement of households. The post-project switching to other bases of livelihood is not considered worthy of resettlement efforts. The issue of tribal identity does not apply in this case either, as none of the communities involved are tribal communities. The Kolis here are Son Kolis and not Mahadev Kolis who are listed as scheduled tribes (STs).

Talking Claims

After the *morcha* by the protesters and the informal negotiations with the promoters, the church official actively involved in the protest was transferred in 1991. The social movement has since been dormant, but there is evidence to suggest that non-harmonious relations exist between the amusement park promoters and the local community. This evidence takes three forms: (*i*) the local discourse of the affected people in the form of narratives; (*ii*) acts of pilferage when the occasion permits; and (*iii*) increase in police control.

The local narratives, almost five years after the formal agitation, are extremely interesting. People tell such stories as a way of constructing a reality that is biased in their favour, as against the 'official' version that is published in reports. The stories constitute part of the discursive strategy that is a crucial component of the process of negotiation (Fortmann, 1994). They serve to bolster people's confidence in their own claims, thereby legitimizing their claims. By repeating the stories, they are re-asserting their version of the reality, as against the official version.

One hundred different houses were visited and people were asked to describe their perceptions about what has changed since the amusement park came into existence. In 10 of these, people were too nervous to discuss Esselworld. Among the remainder, the wife of a local restaurant owner said, 'The water from the reservoirs and the local wells is taken and sold to Esselworld. The road between the creek and the village is not lit at all and accidents have increased. Our village youth find jobs as autorickshaw drivers, but our children and girls are not safe [from the tourists]'. When asked about the agitation against the Esselworld, her neighbour, sitting nearby said, 'We all took part in the agitation against Esselworld being set up. Later we took *morchas* even for tap connections. Our elected representatives visited us after that, but nothing has happened since'. When asked about the benefits from Esselworld, another fisherman said, 'The floating jetty put up by the Esselworld is a good aspect, as we do not have to wade through water to reach our boats'. In another house when questioned about the infrastructure facilities, one woman said: 'Phone connections to this place came soon after Esselworld. But till January this year (1996), the lights used to go off every second day because of Esselworld. The electricity still goes dim in the evening. We have complained to the MSEB (electric company)'.

In another house, the two sons and husband and wife were very vocal about the economic impact of the park. The son said: 'Our condition has not improved. There is a basic lack of facilities—our houses are not secure (referring to the recent land transfers to "outsiders" by local people). Employment chances have increased but they are on a temporary basis, and prices of all commodities have shot up as compared to the city (Borivali)'. Another person owning land to which access was made difficult after Esselworld put a compound wall around its property, said, '*Morchas* were taken as Esselworld has taken over our agricultural lands. They promised us a road to our lands. Photos were taken but no passes have been issued, and later nothing was done. Gorai is well-known now, but no one, not even the government, is bothered about its (Gorai's) problems'. 'The other road access from the back to our lands is not proper. It is difficult to walk or take our carts there since it is muddy and sticky, but we do not want to sell our lands because it is our only source of livelihood during the monsoons'. Another person with him stated, 'Esselworld has promised to provide basic facilities and develop the place. Nothing has happened. They promised lights for the *padas* (residential settlement of the village). They took signatures also, and said they would make the houses *pukka*. All false promises, nothing has happened'. Another owner of a *tonga* said, 'I had a *tonga* business which was destroyed because of Esselworld. We protested against the free Esselworld buses coming here, and were jailed. Yes! Unemployment chances have increased'.

Another fisherman said, 'During the monsoons when we stay in huts along the creek on the outskirts of Esselworld, we do not have any water to drink as the only well in that area has gone to Esselworld'. On the same subject, another one said: 'The road built near the creek by Esselworld has affected our fishing activity during the monsoons. Little or no fish can be caught in the creek water around Esselworld'.

People in Kulvem, a settlement of Gorai, said they were affected in two ways: 'The Esselworld parking area (previously which was government-owned land) used to be a place to dry fish during summer and a *vihir* (well) during the monsoons. Now it is all gone'. The other issue related to the loss of access to a common property resource, that is, firewood. One woman stated, 'There is a problem in getting firewood after Esselworld has come, since the forest area has diminished'. Many stated, 'We fear from tourists. Women do not feel safe. There is drunken and reckless driving, and our animals and children die'. Most importantly, one woman said, 'So far it has not benefited the village in any way. The entrance fee is too high and people in the village cannot afford it. Our children cannot go there while only rich people can take their children there even by making them miss school'.

The general sentiment is summed by the outburst of the man, who said, 'Esselworld is a heavy project with huge investments. The management is supported by the Central Government. What can an insignificant Goraikar do? People should join hands. Gorai village should get political support from the present government. It is doubtful if the government will support people. I do not think the solution will be found, because no government has the stability. The process will continue'. The general feeling is of a breach of trust by the government, on the one hand, and by their elected representatives, on the other. Esselworld is treated with great hostility and is not seen as trustworthy at all. It is also seen as the cause for all the evil in that region.

The narratives of the people affected by the amusement park can be broadly divided into narratives that are about individual injustice; narratives of physical and cultural harm caused to the community; and narratives of failed promises. The main narratives are about how they have failed to benefit from the employment generated by the park. Often an individual will begin by talking about his/her experience of how they managed to get employment for less than a year in the park, and how they were subsequently humiliated and fired from the job. Other names are then mentioned with similar instances. The narratives concerning the physical, cultural and ecological impacts of the park refer to traffic, tourist behaviour, the decrease in fish catch, and the water and fuelwood crises. Since the spillover benefits of 'making

Gorai famous' and the economic benefits to self-employed entrepreneurs are of considerable significance, the expression of discontent is subtle.

There is also considerable fear in the minds of local people when speaking against the park, which they describe as being due to 'terrorism'. There has been an increase in the regular police force posted near Esselworld for security reasons. Before the park came into existence, local people, and especially the Kolis, had opened some small restaurants serving food and drinks to the weekend tourists. The reaction of one restaurant owner is representative: 'Gorai has become famous. More tourists come here now than before. But they do not come to the restaurants any more; all that we get is policemen harassing us for running illegal businesses'. The owners rent their cottages to couples or families for a weekend, an arrangement that had existed much before the park came into existence. But now the local cottage owners along the Gorai coast complain about police harassment. They claim that the police trouble them and threaten to arrest them on grounds that 'illegal' activities are taking place in the cottages.

Evidence of pilferage recently caused an indefinite strike among the park employees. It was reported that pilferage of the property of the Esselworld had been taking place for a long time in connivance with the local people. Recently, the management caught one of its employees red-handed while he was transporting the stolen items outside the Estate. The reported theft, which caused a labour strike, could be one such form of resistance by the discontented local employees/people.

Conclusion

The protest movement in Gorai has had some achievements. It was successful in its ability to empower the local communities to articulate their demands in their own terms. It was able to organize the local community comprising different castes and occupational statuses over a common issue by articulating the environmental (secular) dimension. The movement leadership was able to exploit the contradictions and tensions in the various levels of the government bureaucracy to bring the local issue to national attention for redressal through the EIA. By raising the moral economy issue, they were able to pressurize the local government to bring the amusement park management to the negotiating table. During this informal negotiation, the park promoters had made commitments on various issues, but the protest movement failed to sustain the social pressure on the promoters, and the commitments made by them were not honoured. Nor was the movement able to address the larger issue of limitations of the EIA or the Resettlement and Rehabilitation Acts in their present forms. Thus, the emergent picture of a partially successful protest movement tells a complicated story. Although it is based on a moral economy issue, the protest also covers a wide range of other related issues, such as local cultural, political, material and economic issues.

The critical theory of environment provides the most comprehensive framework for understanding the impact of this amusement park. During the planning phase of the project, the investment funding from major financial corporations for the project is important. It helped create the necessary consciouness that the project would bring about rapid economic growth in that region which has suffered in spite of its proximity to a major uban metropolis due to its geographic constraints. The initiation of the project was smooth as the land was given by the state with an assumption that it would be developed as per the Development Control rules pertaining to 'green' zone or 'no development' zone. Although initially the land was given for developing prawn fishing, its subsequent change in use to an amusement park was consistent with the Development Control rules.

As the project progressed during the construction phase and finally during the operation stage, the local community, which had hoped to get some employment and petty tourism benefits from the project did not benefit substantively. The moral economy argument is helpful for understanding the community response. The changes in the distribution of risk that results from a change in regime from government to private entrepreneurs results in the breach of a stable exchange of resources. The moral issue here is not how much of the 'surplus' or, in this case, profits were generated and taken away by the corporation, but what is left for the survival of the original inhabitants technically defined as the PAPs. They did not benefit by the sale of lands, and they did not have access to the employment generated within the park. When they protested against this exclusion, they instead suffered a backlash against their resistance to the project in the form of harassment and coercion by the local police force against the petty tourism businesses they practised, and against the small food-related businesses they set up. The drunken behaviour of the tourists and the introduction of fast driving vehicles were some of the other adverse impacts they suffered. But more severely, the drinking water shortage on the islands as a result of overdrawing of surface water was the impact that affected their survival. This 'survival first' principle motivated the emergence of an organized protest in the form of a *morcha*, which culminated in the promise of a piped water supply to the islands at the operation stage.

But organized protest is exceptional. Non-harmonious relations and coercion still continue without protest, under similar circumstances (Scott, 1976), as seen in the local discourse among the affected people in the form of narratives, in pilferage when the occasion permits, and in increased police control. All these are symptomatic of PAPs, who are critical of these changes, trying to reclaim their land and their economy to ensure that their identity, their economic survival and their future are safe in the face of a politically strong, private corporation. Since the case study clearly reveals the violation of social obligations by the state and local governments as well as by private enterprises, the moral claims of the PAPs cannot be ignored.

Five

National Parks, Land Alienation and Tribal Livelihoods*

The Sanjay Gandhi National Park, formed in 1983, straddles the two urban centres of Mumbai and Thane. This park is located some 32 km away from the island city of Mumbai. Declaration of the national park by the State Forest Department has caused significant hardship to the people living in the core area of the national park. But there is absence of an organized social protest. This is not to be confused with the absence of resistance by the community. Their attempts to reclaim their lost customary rights to the natural resources, is of interest here.

Protected Areas

The process of formation of national parks as protected areas, for the purpose of the conservation of wildlife, other scientific and public interests, is an indication of the dominance of interest representing scientific rationality over the subsistence needs of the inhabitants, who are economically and socially less powerful. Here is a case study wherein the national and international agendas of elite and economic gain, are given primacy by the state, over the claims of the local communities to the natural resources.

Close on the heels of the Stockholm Conference of 1972, the elite environmentalists consisting of wildlife amateurs as well as members of the scientific establishment and academicians, successfully brought pressure upon the then Prime Minister, Mrs Indira Gandhi, to create

---

*This chapter is based on the fieldwork carried out in Mumbai during 1996–97. I am grateful to the Indian Council of Social Science Research, New Delhi, for supporting the project.

a network of national parks and game sanctuaries and other protected areas (Baviskar, 1997). The 1974 Wildlife Conservation Act passed by the Government of India firmly placed India on the world map of environmental legislation. It was among the first environmentally oriented Acts to be passed by the newly formed Ministry of Environment of the GOI (Chakravery, 1996). The 1972 Stockholm Conference deliberated on issues of development and environment. It was then established that environmental concerns should be of equal concern to developing countries as well, in their pursuit of the development agenda. Politically, the then Prime Minister actively supported the environmental agenda. Therefore, the environmentally oriented elite were successful in lobbying for the passage of the Act. Historically, the creation of these conservation areas received only positive media attention.

In India the exact number of protected areas (PAs) is not clear, as different sources quote different figures. The current PAs comprise 70 national parks, 416 sanctuaries (Shekhar, 1998) and 512 protected areas (Kothari et al., 1996). They cover a total land area of 140, 200 sq km and 4.26 per cent of the total land area of the country. This can be contrasted against five national parks and 126 sanctuaries in 1975 (Shekhar, 1998). But in spite of the phenomenal increase in the number of PAs, rarely does one read a negative report about the impacts of the national parks on native populations. In India, unlike in the West, wildlife areas are habitats for humans and animals alike. But the declaration of national parks since the mid-1970s onwards, has rarely resulted in any organized protest against such a declaration.

The subsistence claims of the local residents adversely affected by the PAs have rarely found a voice in the mainstream media, till recently. It was mainly the pro-conservationist lobby of the elites that found a voice in media and international conferences. There are reports of interference in the conservation area by the 'natives'. The conservationists believe that the attempts to stake claims to the benefits of forest resources by the natives, have a considerable nuisance value in the efforts to conserve the endangered species (Daniel and Serao, 1990).

Conservatives among the elite NGOs, dedicated to the cause of conservation of the wildlife believe, that the problem of interference faced by the PAs, is a law and order problem. The more liberal conservationist believes it to be a problem of ignorance on the part of the local communities. The solution therefore is to educate the local communities. The educational approach to conservation argues for persuading the local communities to make the rational choice of conservation. If they can understand the future value of wildlife and its conservation, as against the present value of the consumption of natural resources, they will support the wildlife or the endangered species.

Over the past few years, social activists among the environmentally-oriented NGOs have voiced some discontent related to the constant harassment of the people by the local forest officials in and around the PAs. Social activists working among the communities residing in and around the PAs have raised issues of the rights of these communities to natural forest resources. The *Jangal Mitra Bachao* rally is one such instance, of attempts to raise awareness about this issue among the various policy makers, wildlife conservationists and people in general. The rally was organized by ecologically-oriented NGOs in support of the communities living in the protected areas (Dwivedi, 1997). But the leadership of this rally was mainly urban middle class. Systematic and scientific studies of the crop and livestock damage caused by wild animals in protected areas are rare and of very recent origin. Shekhar (1998) has attempted to quantify the extent of crop damage caused by the wildlife. He identifies measures adopted by local communities to protect crops and tries to determine solutions to minimize the damage as suggested by the local people.

More recently, there is increasing realization among the conservationists that wildlife or habitat conservation may be only one possible goal, among the various goals pursued by different stakeholders residing in and around the PAs (Clark and Wallace, 1998). What is required is a negotiated settlement among the various conflicting goals. But this understanding among conservationists is limited and applied only to wildlife conservation in developed countries like the USA and Australia. Even today, organized protest by people and communities living in and around the PAs in India is rare.

Background of Park at Borivali

The Sanjay Gandhi National Park (SGNP), as it is now called, which is located in the northern part of Mumbai city in Borivali division, is one such protected area and is the focus of discussion here. It partly lies in the Thane district (58.64 sq km) and partly in the Mumbai suburban district (44.45 sq km). Presently the park extends over an area of

103.09 sq km, piecing together the land of the following classification. Of this, an area of 5.75 sq km is set aside as a recreational zone known as Krishnagiri Upavan and 10.38 sq km is assigned as a buffer zone. This recreational zone houses a lion safari, children's mini train, crocodile park and the Kanheri caves, Mahatma Gandhi Memorial, a deer park, panther enclosure, and a boating and information centre. The land was acquired from different sources and consolidated into the national park.

Historically, as per the provision of the Bombay National Park Act 1950, the Krishnagiri National Park was formed covering an area of 19.2 sq km and the park management was under the Department of Parks and Gardens of Bombay State. Prior to 1950, these forests belonged to the Inamdars and Khot or the local landlord who exploited them for commercial gains. In 1969, these lands were brought under one management by transferring them to the forest department, and a special sub-division was created, which was upgraded to a full-fledged division in 1972. In 1977, it was transferred to the state-run Forest Development Corporation and it has been back with the State Forest Department since 4 February 1983. It was renamed as the Sanjay Gandhi National Park and was declared as a game sanctuary for the leopards in the core areas.

Thus till 1950, the park was commercially exploited for timber by the private forest owners and the Forest Department itself. There used to be stone quarrying activities within the park boundaries. There were temples and tribal settlements inside the park. One agro-based factory was allowed to operate within the park boundaries. This park was thus never a wilderness but a habitat for various human beings, including the tribal groups called the Warlis and Mahadev Kolis and non-tribal Dodhis. Historically, they all enjoyed customary rights to the collection of minor forest produce, people from outside visited the temples and caves on special occasions, and non-forest-based commercial employment was generated due to quarrying and the factory (Bharati, 1992).

National Park Formation

The ecological transition in the lands that initially belonged to the revenue department took place as the result of a new consciousness towards wildlife conservation that was emerging in the mid-1970s among the national elites. In 1974, the GOI passed the Forest Conservation of Wildlife Act whereby it declared a few forests as conservation parks. The Borivali forests, covering an area of 86.96 sq km, were notified as a national park. It came under the Conservation Act in 1983 (vide government notification no. PGS/1081/131724/F5, dated 4 February 1983) and was renamed as the Sanjay Gandhi National Park. As per the Conservation Act, the park followed a particular pattern of zoning (Daniel and Serao, 1990). Out of the balance area, 5.74 sq km is set aside as a recreational zone and the remaining 10.38 sq km is assigned as a buffer area, while the rest is declared as a core area. The forests and hills form a part of the Western Ghats, a long chain of mountains in the western part of the country.

The main objective of the park management is conservation and preservation. Conservation of the fauna and flora of the forest, and its unique geological, historical and archaeological features is the key commitment of the management. The protection and promotion of key watershed areas and promotion of tourism by throwing open certain areas to the tourists for aesthetic, educational, scientific and recreational purposes are the subsidiary objectives of the management.

Thus the main objective changed from economic exploitation of the forest and its lands as a resource, to conservation and preservation. Historical land uses linked with economic exploitation, mentioned earlier, are now unlawful. These land uses are now identified as problems faced by national parks, while new forms of development permitted within the policy, such as recreational tourism, become legitimate. This has resulted in two types of action taken by the park management, namely actions taken to promote the new objectives, and actions taken to de-legitimize the historical land uses of the park area.

The result is that over 3 million people visit the park every year and an average of 8,000 to 10,000 every day (Bharati, 1992). They are charged an entrance fee of Rs 4 per adult and Rs 2 per child, and vehicles are allowed into the recreational area and charged on a wheel basis.

Actions taken to de-legitimize the historical land uses of the park area include relocation of the agro-based factory, closure of the quarrying activities for which a case is pending in the Bombay High Court, and relocation of tribal *padas*. Only about 130 families that owned leased lands in the national park were identified for relocation purposes in 1983 in Kuthal village in Thane district. They were given lands, temporary houses made of tin and a sum of Rs 75 as relocation allowance.

Local Community

As per the 1991 Census, the park area houses 970 tribal families. The main tribal groups inhabiting these forests are Warlis and Mahadev Kolis and non-tribal Dodhis. Even now they continue to live inside the park boundaries in spite of relocation attempts by the park authorities, as mentioned earlier. They are mainly dependent on fishing, cultivation, small game hunting and basket weaving, for subsistence.

Even today, all the groups live in huts made of mud and straw. They plant vegetable gardens in their yards in front of their dwelling houses during the monsoons. Marketing of the surplus provides them with additional income. Their other sources of monetary income are the sale of firewood, liquor, fruits and other minor forest products. Most other tribal communities living in the Western Ghat forests share a similar lifestyle. The forest even today provides them with ample resources for survival.

The religious composition of the group is of interest here. All of them follow the 'tribal religion', have their own gods and their own rituals, and, at the same time, broadly follow Hindu festivals like most tribal communities in western India. Ninety-two of the 100 families studied were born in the forest. All the groups are illiterate and the Social Welfare Department has sponsored an NGO, which has recently opened schools and provides primary healthcare facilities.

Before the declaration of these lands as protected areas (PAs), these lands were controlled and exploited by the State Revenue Department. The department economically exploited these lands for their natural resources and was supporting the livelihood of these tribal people directly and indirectly. Directly the forest contractors and the stone quarry owners found it convenient and cheap to hire tribal labourers for the exploitation of resources. Access to benefit streams arising from other land-related common property resources in the form of firewood, small timber grazing, hunting, fishing and collection of non-timber forest produce like roots, tubers, fruits, flowers and leaves, free of charge ensured the survival of the tribal communities during the lean season and in the event of a slack labour market.

The Crisis

When ownership of lands changed from the Revenue Department to the Department of Wildlife and Forests, all this changed. When the Forest Department took over and declared it as a PA, the only social obligation that it recognized towards the inhabitants of the forest was the individual property rights to agricultural lands held by the tribal households. It neither identified nor acknowledged their traditional or customary rights to the benefit streams arising out of the natural resources belonging to the land that was enjoyed by the tribal group as a whole. They therefore tried to relocate only those with individually owned leases to lands and ignored the rest. This resulted in the disruption of the traditional rights and loss of access to resources needed for the survival of the community, in addition to the loss of employment opportunities that the commercial exploitation of these lands ensured historically. The moral issue here is not how much of the surplus from the lands, or in what form (as in the present case) is taken away by the various claimants, but what is left for the survival of the peasant or tribal, in this instance. This change proved to be life-threatening to the tribal communities. As stated earlier, the benefit streams arising out of the lands ensured the survival of the tribal community in the lean years. This pattern of ecological exploitation forms a basis, which defines their primary identity as a tribal. They were morally justified in resisting it. But the resistance did not result in a revolt or an organized social movement.

There is a breach of social obligations by three claimants in this situation. First, the earlier landowners (in this case, it happens to be the State Revenue Department as all barren common lands are owned by the state); second, the new landowners, in this case the State Forest Department that became the new owner of the land after it was declared a PA; and third, the elected representatives to their constituency, in the local, democratically elected government. There is a breach of trust by the government revenue officials who took away the land titles from these families without adequately providing for their survival. The forest department has not respected the customary rights of the tribal communities. The identity and survival of the community are inextricably linked with these customary rights.

The fact is that the 1974 Wildlife Conservation Act has created havoc in the lives of the communities residing in and around the protected areas. The Act allows for the state government to declare a forest area as a protected area. The model of a protected area follows a universal pattern wherein the central area is declared as a core area and is surrounded by a buffer zone. While the buffer zone allows some human activities, the core area is to be kept absolutely free of human interference. In order to achieve this, all the communities residing in the core area are displaced and continue to have limited access to benefit streams from the buffer zone. While displacing the communities in the core area and being totally insensitive to the needs of these communities, the Act is quite sensitive to the financial needs of the regulating authority. In this case, the Forest Department may develop a recreational zone in the buffer zone in order to promote eco-tourism. Such economic activity is intended to generate revenue for the support of the wildlife management of the Protected Area Act, 1974.

But the economic loss due to the loss of traditional rights of the local communities is ignored. The concern expressed by the groups of people, about the depletion of water, degradation of land and other changes in ecosystems affecting the traditional patterns of natural resource exploitation do exist and are dominant in the local discourse of the affected people in the PAs. These PAs are generally located in rural areas and the local communities, either within the boundaries of the PAs or in areas surrounding them, suffer as a result of lack of access to these areas. The anthropogenic pressures in the PAs are mainly due to benefit streams related to natural resources within the PAs (BNHS, 1994). These relate to hunting and fishing as well as the grazing of domestic animals and collection of other non-timber minor forest products. There is some assertion of these traditional rights even at the local level of discourse among these communities and it is linked with issues of identity.

Transformative Action

Revolt is an exception and it happens only under the right conditions. The possibility of a revolt in this case was very slim. In this case, the number of tribal people affected by the change, that is, 970 families, was very small. The declaration of the national park and the related displacement were immediate. This did not give the tribals much time to organize. Although the social relations within the different tribal communities are fairly homogeneous, the class difference between tribal communities and other caste groups is very sharp. In addition, there is a history of exploitation of the tribal communities by other caste groups. These factors further deterred organized protest. The population is ecologically vulnerable and changes leading to reduction in the access to the benefit streams from the natural resources threaten their survival. The outcome was immediate.

They initially took what was offered and migrated but soon discovered that migration did not ensure survival. The alternate lands provided for cultivation were full of boulders and stones, and could not be cultivated immediately, and no non-agricultural employment was available during the lean season, which resulted in considerable hardship for the relocated families. They all returned to their original *padas* within one year of their relocation. They were allowed to occupy their houses only temporarily, but they have not been allowed by the Forest Department to reclaim their agricultural lands. Thus they have lost their lands to the Forest Department for good.

Before displacement, they were able to generate enough food grains like *wari*-rice, maize and even paddy through rainfed cultivation of a few acres of lands, when they still owned leases to these lands. This was supplemented by milk and meat from a few domestic animals, fish, small game and vegetables grown or collected by them. Even edible oil was manufactured locally from *mahua* fruits.

Since displacement, they used different survival strategies. Social banditry is reflected in their continued defiance of the forest rules and restrictions against the collection of forest produce. They continue to brew liquor in their homes. This activity is now called bootlegging by the state and is legally banned. They had always brewed liquor by using *mahua* flowers, but now their access to *mahua* had become difficult, so they switched to other types of raw material. This led the state to declare this activity as illegal. The firewood for brewing that they formally collected was now identified as timber smuggling, by the State Forest Department. They resisted the forced migration to Kothal village as is indicated in their 'running back to their homes'. The strategy of renting of their houses to outsiders ensured them steady economic returns on a resource, which they knew they will be allowed to hold on to only temporarily, namely their house plots.

Non-Revolt and Self-Help

But non-harmonious relations and coercion may exist, without revolt, under similar circumstances (Scott, 1976). Evidence of non-harmonious class relations and coercion can be gathered at three levels: first, in the local discourse among the impacted people in the form of narratives, second in the form of pilferage when the occasion permits and finally, in the increase in police control.

Linked with the breach of social obligation are issues of tribal identity as represented in the assimilation and preservation debate, displacement and resettlement of the tribal communities affected by the PA, and discourses at the local and official levels that indicate forms of resistance put up by the community. Finally, there is the issue of leadership for social protest. The leadership for protest, when borrowed from outside the community that is adversely affected, often leads to tensions among the leaders and the community as very ably documented by Dwivedi (1997), and a similar problem exists here.

State Action

In this instance, the various conflicts between different branches of the state, such as between various ministries, or between the Centre and state governments are missing. The usual tensions across state departments allow for social space for formation of alliances between the various groups of people or people's organizations and state institutions. For example, in the case of the *Narmada Bachao Andolan* and the Ministry of Environment and Forests, the agitators' decision to throw in their lot with the *Narmada Bachao Andolan* (Singh, 1997) is one instance wherein they could exploit the inter-departmental tensions to their advantage.

In the context of protected areas, the state appears as a monolith. The forest department is quick to declare the displaced communities trying to reclaim their customary rights over natural resources as encroachers. The punitive powers of confiscation and arrest, given to the forest department are implemented promptly. Even the judiciary and the local municipality support the forest department and the police in taking actions against 'encroachers' in the PAs. Thus, here the state seems to behave as a single entity in the environmental elite interest and against the customary rights of the local communities.

The state, goaded by environmental NGOs like the Bombay Environmental Action Group (BEAG), legitimizes the stand of the SGNP authorities and endorses it from time to time (Balaram, 1998). The proponents of the BEAG subscribe to the view that the park is a green lung for the city and helps maintain the environmental balance. It provides a respite from the noise polluted metropolitan city. A natural habitat for various kinds of fauna (the rusty spotted cat is a rare species) and flora, it needs to be preserved. It is a haven for bird watchers.

In 1993, the park authorities, along with the help of the municipal authorities and the police, destroyed huts along the borders and a municipal official was killed in the encounter. On 7 May 1997, the High Court Bench of Bombay High Court passed orders to evict the encroachments from the national park areas of slums and quarrying activities. A time-based action plan was to be suggested by the park authorities to achieve this within 18 months, that is, by 7 November 1998. The Maharashtra government assured the court that it would do so.

The interview with the then Deputy Conservator of Forests summarizes the dominant narrative about the national parks including this one. According to him, the national park had to be vacated by the *adivasi*s in order to 'prevent any adverse impact on the environment and the wildlife'. As per the process of eviction, he said, 'We gave them notices one year in advance, though legally we had to give only 30 days' notice, and verbally informed them about the alternate place in Kothal'. Regarding the status of the land, he said, 'The *adivasi*s were tilling lands owned by Aarey milk colony on six monthly leases for which they were paying taxes in kind to the Aarey milk colony'. Moreover, the *adivasi*s staying in SGNP were not recognized by the Revenue Department. They were just a 'colony of migrants'. Thus, there is no revenue document to prove their ownership of the lands. As regards compensation, the official stated, 'The land in Kothal was given free, even when they were not the official owners of the agricultural land that was taken from them. It belonged to the Aarey colony. Besides the place in Kothal, is a tribal village in a tribal belt. This was considered while giving the lands. Also, there is no question of loss of access to forest resources since there were forests adjoining the alternate place given in Kothal '. Besides, according to the deputy conservator, 90 per cent of the *adivasi*s have been employed in the forest department.

The tribals are ambivalent to the state. The state appears multifaceted through its institutions (Guha, 1989). If the state has deprived them of their subsistence, that is, cultivation, it also appears benevolent through its development activities. Since 1992, an NGO (CCD Trust, n.d.) has adopted these *padas* for community development, health and education purposes, with support from the State Tribal Welfare Department. They have helped them get ration cards, healthcare and educational facilities in their neighbourhood. The state maintains a duality, by culturally legitimizing that the state is good, just and compassionate; if it does not appear to be so, it is due to the inefficiency and greed of the local bureaucrats. So while they continue to resist the attempts of the local bureaucrats to relocate them and to delegitimize their subsistence livelihoods, which are dependent on the surrounding forests, they continue to believe in the omnipotent government.

The state bureaucracy appears to be simultaneously the most invisible and yet the most visible in its domination of the local communities, in this instance of declaration of protected areas. In case of the amusement park, the physical changes accompanying the transfer of ownership of the land are very visible. Land is marked, compound walls are erected, the rides are put in place, etc., while in the case of the declaration of a protected area, there are no obvious physical signs of change within the ecology of the area. There are no compounds or fences in place. The boundaries separating the core area and the periphery are invisible. The forest department knows it through its record book. There are no obvious physiological changes in the natural habitat as a whole except where areas are marked as recreation zones. Yet the state department that controls it is very visible through its bureaucracy. The punitive measures for infringement of the boundaries are severe for people who are poor while the organized criminals like the slum lords or the sandalwood smugglers get away.

At present, the dominant discourse about the park begins from the time of declaration of the park. There is no mention about the displacement and resettlement of the people living within the core area. The creation of the park resulted in the displacement of 970 families in 1983. Today there are only 449 families still living in the park.

The park-related discourse highlights the scenic beauty and picturesque landscape and identifies it as a priceless asset. It is said to cover four types of habitats ranging from mangroves to the evergreen forests of the Western Ghats. It is called the 'green lung' of the city. It is identified as a home for many endangered species and its significant zoological value is elaborated by the forest department (Bharati, 1992). In short, it is rare, unique and worth preserving.

Since the formation of the park, the forest department has identified problems of a different kind. A shrinking prey base and rise in the number of wild animals is one such problem, while the other is the encroachment of people. The state legitimizes the dominant discourse of the park authorities and endorses it from time to time through action. For example, in 1993, the park authorities, along with the help of the municipal authorities and the police, destroyed huts along the borders and a municipal official was killed in the encounter.

Talking Claims

Evidence of the continued non-harmonious class relations and coercion can be gathered at three levels: first, at the local discourse among the impacted people in the form of narratives; second, pilferage when the occasion permits; and third, an increase in police control.

The local narratives constitute a way of constructing a reality that is biased in their favour as against the 'official' version that is published in reports. The work of the stories here is to create and maintain an often localized discourse in the context of which the other parts of the struggle proceed. The argument is that these stories constitute part of the discursive strategy that is a crucial component of the process of re-negotiations (Fortmann, 1994). Why are local stories/narratives important? They are, because stories are oral manifestations of a local discourse seeking to define and claim 'local' resources. They serve to bolster people's confidence in their own claims. The local narratives are a form of legitimizing their claims. By repeating the stories they tell each other and others, they are re-asserting their version of the reality, as against the official version, in this case, that of the forest officials. They are important because they articulate a reality, which is different from the official version of the story. After all, there are multiple versions and interpretations of a reality depending on who is talking. The problem, of the narratives to be specific to the listener, is recognized here. The status of the researcher as an 'outsider', which may cause certain narratives to dominate, exists, and is recognized as such, but is beyond the scope of this chapter.

One hundred different houses were visited and people were asked to describe their perceptions about what had changed since the amusement park came into existence. Twenty-six households narrated their experiences of displacement and relocation, as mentioned earlier. Thirty-seven households printed out at great length how the park did not benefit them at all. This reflects the local level discourse in contrast with the official version stated earlier. There is considerable fear in the minds of the local people to speak against the park and 14 households refused to respond to these questions.

The park is a PA and so no vehicular movement is permitted inside the premises after dark. There are no street lights, hence the *pada*s could be accessed only during the day. The vehicle could reach the *pada*s earliest by 11 a.m. Therefore, by the time the researcher could reach these *pada*s, all the able-bodied working males and females had already left for work. Those interviewed were therefore mainly women. A female research assistant thus proved to be very helpful.

Non-Benefit, Harassment Narratives

The main complaint was related to insecurity due to the presence of leopards in the area (Seidensticker et al., 1990) and harassment by the forest officials. 'Officials in the park prevent us from collecting wood for our houses', said a Warli woman. 'We are not allowed to extend our houses. We face the threat of eviction and the threat of panther attacks; there was no fear from the jungle before', an old Katkari man said. 'We are troubled by the forest officers. They prevent us from collecting firewood, and do not let us build our homes; there is no security and we can be thrown out of the park—we are at the mercy of the forest officials. They have just taken away our light connections', lamented another Thakar woman. These electric connections are illegally purchased by the tribal people from across the boundary at considerable personal cost. 'Light connections are cut off, we are stopped from collecting firewood, (tap) water connection to this area has just come, but we do not get it'.

In a group interview, women said different things. 'We have lost our lands. We face threat from the forest by way of animal attacks, inflation and financial insecurity is what we face now.' 'They prevent us from keeping domestic animals like sheep and goats, and prevent us from extending our houses.' 'They destroy our kitchen gardens, and prevent us from collecting firewood. If we do collect some, they confiscate it and demand fine from us.' 'It takes some four to five hours to collect all the twigs and branches from the deep forests and to bring them home.' 'They have taken lands. Before the park, we could do some cultivation and sustain ourselves. Everyday, forest officials come out with new rules to curb our freedom. Now they are talking about throwing us out again. They say they will give land at Dahisar, who knows whether they will really give us anything.'

A lot of respondents talked of financial insecurity and inflation as the major problems that they face now. They are finding it increasingly difficult to collect products from the woods and sell them outside and so they are forced to 'buy' everything from the market. Without assured monetary income, they find it very difficult to survive.

Following are the benefits, or rather, 'non-benefits', from the park formation: Eleven families perceived panther attacks as threatening. Twelve families identified confiscation of firewood and prohibition of house expansion as major problems. Five families felt that water availability is a major problem.

'The park has not benefited us in any way. We have not got jobs in the park, whoever has got it—most of them are on a temporary basis', said an unemployed youth from the hamlet. 'We are troubled by forest officials. After 6 p.m., no vehicle is allowed in the park boundary. During medical and other emergencies, we face problems,' said his friend, from another hamlet. 'Buses come till the Kanhery Caves but we cannot use them as the fares are too high' said a man working as a labourer in a nearby industry. 'Earlier we used to provide/sell drinking water in earthenware pots but now Bisleri (mineral water) has taken over,' said another woman. 'Firewood sale is also a source of livelihood but we cannot sell it now as the officials confiscate it'. A Warli widow said, 'We have jobs in the forest department now, but we are financially insecure since these jobs are temporary. My husband used to work in the forest department but I still haven't got his pension'.

Political Action

Fifteen persons from different families participated in some form of political action. Different people, mainly men, mentioned the different actions in which they had participated:

Last year, we went on a *morcha* led by Vithal Lad of the *Shramik Mukti Sangathana* against the threat of eviction of *adivasi*s in the Park.

Just before the municipal elections last year, Hemendra Mehta, the corporator, promised us bore well at Chinchpada. Nothing has been done.

We face the threat of eviction even now. We sought Ram Naik's help three to four years ago, when they were planning to throw us out of here. We went to Azad Maidan on a *morcha* then. The outsiders who stay among us are also victims; they are here because they were thrown away from somewhere else and have come to our shelter.

I am on the *adivasi* committee for better facilities and to fight future evictions.

There is a lack of basic facilities here. We agitated for bore wells (for drinking water), and though we were promised these wells, nothing has happened.

Resistance

Given their lack of education and access to the urban employment market, the tribals continue to pursue their traditional occupations, wherever possible. They continue to create *wadi*s during the rainy season for growing vegetables. They still collect the minor forest produce by bribing local guards. Those among them who can afford to do so continue to get illegal connections for electricity and try to build more permanent structures. All these new constructions and agriculture activities are routinely destroyed by the forest bureaucracy as and when they find time. The cost of damages caused by leopards has to be paid to the people and this is done, albeit grudgingly and after a lot of delay, by forest officials.

Thus the tribals have lost their agricultural land, over the past 10 years. The only form of subsistence livelihood known to them was cultivation, employment as wage labourers in timber and mining operations and collection of minor forest produce, which they could sell in the local markets. These were denied to them by the formation of the national park. The forest management believes that 'they cause tremendous damage and disturbance to wildlife habitat all around' (Bharati, 1992: 10).

Lacking education and access to the urban employment market, they were forced to look for some steady source of income. The response to this survival crisis was a sub-letting of their huts to 'outsiders' and in the process alienation of the tribals from their own houses. The result is that there are a total of 494 huts belonging to the tribals with 1,200 tibals and 1,700 non-tribals residing in them. This has aggravated the problem of rehabilitation and these *padas* are now clubbed together with the other encroachment problems faced by the park authorities.

Years after the formation of the park in 1983, the locals continue to build permanent houses, get electricity and water connections, try to cultivate the *wadis*, hunt, brew liquor, etc. Their numbers have reduced in proportion to others. They are especially targeted for development but they have survived and continue to resist any attempts to be physically displaced from their lands.

Conclusion

Sanjay Gandhi National Park, which aimed to promote the protection of wildlife, was slated to be a leopard sanctuary. Its formation was motivated by the environmental conservation struggles in other developed countries in the 1970s to conserve wildlife in its natural habitat. The recreational zone in the park caters to the promotion of weekend tourism. The target population for the national park is the urban middle class residents of the city of Mumbai. The setting up of the national park is quite visibly a symbol of the way in which a handful of elites are able to dominate the state agenda. This vision of conservation in developed countries does not have to take into account the fact that the wilderness constitutes habitations for people, as it dies in India. In this instance, only a small number of 480 families has survived in the region after 25 years.

By backing the claims of these pressure groups, the state is ignoring the rights of the original inhabitants or the tribal communities to their livelihoods. Since the original inhabitants did not have land titles for their habitation and the lands they depended on for their livelihood, the state department was able to disregard the claims to a livelihood based on the local ecology, thereby negatively impacting the tribal communities. Thus the state agencies have become a direct agent of exploitation and the state power holders have become exploiters.

In other situations, wherein new environmental movements take place, the intra-state disputes provide for a social space for articulation by the affected group. But in this instance, the state comes up as a monolith against the interests of the small marginal groups. The only choice the group has is to resort to everyday forms of resistance.

What was taken away from the local communities was their access to common property resources, such as fuel wood, grass and small timber, and access to their own lands. What the state was able to extract was exclusive economic profit from their declaration of the PA. But what was left for the local communities after the various claimants made their claims is of interest here. The local communities lost everything. They lost their lands, and their customary rights, and now they are threatened with the loss of their status as tribals, as they are clubbed with encroachers and would have to fight their battles as such, with the rest of the 'encroaching' groups.

Thus, to conclude, the dominant motivation for the ecological transition, in this case, the setting up of a wildlife conservation park, was international interest in the conservation of wildlife. With a promise of the safety of wildlife and of a new life for themselves, the original settlers were shifted to houses nearer the cities. The crisis of not being able to integrate into an urban way of life because of their socio-economic disadvantages as tribal persons became obvious to most relocated people, fairly quickly. Very soon, within a year, the social disadvantage of being tribal, unskilled and illiterate in an urban environment, forced them to return to their original place of residence in the jungles.

The tribals quickly learnt and realized that their only chance of survival was to reclaim their way of life and to retain their cultural identity. There was also a realization that as a small group with no access to resources, the only way they could survive was by not resisting the state agencies subversively. They therefore adopted a strategy of passive resistance as a result of which they were able to get the patronage of the state agencies and the Social Welfare Department, which, with the help of an NGO, has started the process of providing education and health services to the tribals.

Thus, the strategy of passive resistance resulted in transformative action, which ensured their survival, and their right to retain their identity and re-assert their claims as original inhabitants. Therefore, the fact that they continue to survive as a tribal group, continue to pray to their gods and continue to resist domination by the forest officials through everyday forms of protest, is in itself an important achievement.

Six

Aierawat (The White Elephant) and Other Stories*

Environmental struggles result from a crisis among the social groups who feel marginalized, forcing reflexivity and critique of the dominant claims made by a development project. These are predominantly PAPs. But a new social group that is fast emerging on the horizon is that of public sector employees. This group, similarly disillusioned by the dominant rhetoric of economic growth and technological efficiency, is constructing new forms of resistance and actions, resulting in social change that is favourable to their perception of reality, with a greater or lesser degree of success. This group is well-organized and unionized. Its members have, due to historical reasons, a lifetime guarantee of employment and pensions, without it being linked exclusively to productive efficiencies or accountability to their consumers. In the new economic order that is based on efficiency and rationality, such job opportunities would disappear and private 'rent seeking' opportunities will not be available. A remarkable resistance is offered by the public sector employees who know exactly what they stand to lose in the changing social order towards more private sector entry into what were originally public sector monopolies. A new turn of events in the recent history of India is taking place as a result of a well-organized and unionized public sector that is threatened with annihilation by the recent push towards more economically rational and technologically efficient private infrastructure development projects that have been coming into the country over the last decade. The pressure to 'perform or

---

*An earlier draft of the chapter was presented at the Ninth International Conference on Maharashtra at Macalester College, St Paul, Minnesota on 6–10 June 2001.

perish' is resisted by this social group very efficiently by using similar techniques of resistance as used by PAPs, through self-reflexivity and construction of new social realities that are more favourable to them. In the process, they often use subaltern claims or rhetoric of the new environmental struggles to their advantage. Two such case studies are discussed in the book. The first is the case of the Dabhol Power Project and the collapse of its parent company, which was used by the Maharashtra State Electricity Board (MSEB) to postpone power sector reforms. The second, discussed in the following chapter, is the case of a coal washery project that used subaltern claims to resist the introduction of 'software' in the form of more rational accounting practices linked with the new technology, accepted only the hardware component in the form of new machines and chose to maintain the status quo—coal mafia and all.

The Project

The study is based on a retrospective analysis of an infrastructure project that was commissioned in 1992. The Government of India, in the flush of economic liberalization, took a strategic decision to liberalize the power sector by opening up power generation to private companies. The assumption was that the inherent problems within the power sector (inefficiencies in the recovery of dues, power losses, theft, etc.) could be solved by increasing production without addressing the inherent inefficiencies of the public sector power companies. In a bid to deploy a 'fast track' power project and to attract private investment in power sector generation, it approached Enron, then a giant in the power sector, to set up a power plant in India.

With the help of Bechtel, Enron formed the Dabhol Power Company (DPC) to construct an 826 MW (gross) and 740 MW (net) combined cycle power plant in the state of Maharashtra. Bechtel Power Corporation constructed the facility and General Electric (GE) company supplied the equipment. DPC would operate the plant. The electricity thus produced was to be sold to MSEB under a 20-year power purchase agreement (PPA) with a counter-guarantee by the Central Government. The necessary environmental and financial approvals and clearances were granted to the project and construction of the plant began in 1996, targeted to be completed in December 1998. It commenced commercial operations in May 1999.

The Dabhol Power Project is a joint venture of Enron, which owns 50 per cent of the project, the MSEB, which owns 30 per cent, and General Electric Capital Corporation and Bechtel Enterprises Inc., which owned 10 per cent each in Phase I. In 1996, Enron was one of the largest independent developers and producers of electricity in the world.[1] Dabhol was seen as Enron's flagship project in India. Phase I of the project was valued at $1 billion. Various international financial institutions provided US$ 150 million while the US Export-Import Bank provided US$ 298 million, based on Industrial Development Bank of India's (IDBI) projections. IDBI was also the lead arranger for a rupee loan provided by Indian financial institutions, equated to US$ 96 million (constituting less than 1 per cent of the capital). The remainder of the project cost was funded through owner's equity in the proportions of 80 per cent by Enron, and 10 per cent each by Bechtel and GE Caps.

The construction for the second phase of US$ 1.87 billion, which was planned with a generating capacity of 1,624 Megawatt (MW) to begin in May 1999, was to use natural gas. It was scheduled to begin operating in late 2001. During this phase, the ownership was shared among Enron (80 per cent) and Bechtel and General Electric 10 per cent each. MSEB had the option to acquire 30 per cent of Enron's interest.[2] Preliminary site preparation activities were under way by 1993 and the Phase I commenced operations in May 1999.

The Locale of Study

Enron opted for the most economically developed state of Maharashtra to locate the power plant. Since the plant was based on oil and compressed natural gas (CNG), it was situated on the western coast, some 190 km south-west of Mumbai along the south bank of the mouth of the estuary of River Vasisthi. To summarize, they set up a new power company called the Dabhol Power Company (DPC) to build and operate a thermal power plant to generate electricity. It had the capacity of generating 2,245 MW of electricity. The capital investment

---

[1] www.enron.com/corp/pressroom/releases/1996/141. dekho. htm, dated 2 December 1996.
[2] www.enron.com/corp/pressrom releases/1999/ene/financerelease.html, dated 6 May 1999.

as per 1994 prices was Rs 80 billion. Two American companies and the World Bank jointly held the capital stock. The power plant was planned in two phases—the 765 MW Phase I was to be completed by 1996 and used oil as a basic fuel, while the 1,480 MW Phase II of the project, due to be completed by mid–2001, used liquified natural gas (LNG).

DPC was located at Guhagar, and the seventeenth century Maratha port of Dabhol from which the project derives its name, is on the opposite bank, and is located in Dapoli *taluka* in Ratnagiri district. The local people relate the Maratha army's supremacy over the sea with great pride. This is about 50 km away from the Maharashtra Industrial Development Corporation (MIDC)-promoted newly industrialized region of Lote Parshuram in Chiplum *taluka* of Ratnagiri district.

The land use in the surrounding area of the project site was essentially rural. The 10 km radius from the project area was dominated by subsistence rainfed agriculture, mango horticulture, coconut and arecanut gardens, and trawler fishing in the open sea. The four main ethnic groups in the region are the Kunbis, the Kolis, the Muslims and Brahmins. The Kolis are involved in deep-sea fishing and usually market their fish in the Mumbai markets. The Kunbis and Brahmins have a long history of migration to Mumbai and Pune areas. The Kunbis are engaged in agriculture and work as tenants or labourers. The Brahmins usually own the horticulture orchards and areca and coconut gardens. Most of the able-bodied young Muslims even today are in the Middle East. The local economy is a 'remittance economy', with the implication that social networks extend beyond the national boundaries.

The more seriously affected were five villages surrounding the project site. These included Anjanwel and Katalwadi-taraf-Anjanwel, both located near the sea and populated dominantly by Muslims. Mauje-Anjanwel, Veldur and Charatwadi-taraf-Veldur predominantly consist of the fishing community. The other villages of Ranavi and Guhagar *taluka* are predominantly agricultural.

Environmental Impact Analysis

The project site occupied 277 hectares out of the 2,778 hectares of land of the five villages mentioned above. The land was to be acquired by MIDC and transferred to MSEB. The DPC was not directly involved in any of the land procurements. In fact, DPC took pains to project itself as a benevolent multinational corporation (MNC) coming into the backwaters of a Third World country. It offered to settle the land claims by giving ex gratia payments for lost lands, which were very few.

The project planning stage overlapped with the rapid EIA stage, wherein the basic statistics related to the socio-economic conditions of the PAPs were being established. There was one major design element that needed a local input—location of the jetty needed for unloading of the liquefied natural gas (LNG), the main fuel for the second phase of the project. LNG was a major component in the project as it promised to lower the operating cost of the plant and to prevent environmental pollution as it was a 'clean fuel' and would emit no pollutants but only water and carbon dioxide, unlike coal which may have volatile matter, thereby creating environmental contaminants hazardous to plants and animals. At the same time, LNG was a highly inflammable and hazardous substance that needed special precautions during unloading. An exclusion zone of 500 m was needed to be maintained wherein no ship movement could be allowed during the unloading operations. Also, the storage facility, though located in underground tanks, needed a similar exclusion zone of 200 m. The local port was an attraction for the site selection, as a port in an estuary of a river would allow for protection of the ship during unloading operations from the high sea winds and other turbulent weather conditions.

But the old port was blocked by a sand bar under the sea that would have to be cut and a channel created for big ships to come into the port that would extend into the river bed. This would involve an additional cost to the project. The 500 m exclusion zone would mean that the entire town of Dabhol on the other side of the river, and the five villages mentioned earlier would have to be resettled completely. This was a serious issue, as the funding for the Sardar Sarovar project on the Narmada river was withdrawn by the World Bank at about this time. A similar environmental back lash against the project was something that the DPC was keen on avoiding.

Therefore, during the final planning and design stage, the plan to locate the unloading jetty in the river estuary was dropped and the jetty is now in the open sea. The storage tanks were located on the barren lands of the plateau with no habitation in the vicinity of 200 m, so that relocation of people was not an issue. The project boundaries were also re-negotiated to avoid disturbing some ancestral graves of the local people.

The second major socio-economic impact of the project was related to the construction phase when an estimated construction labour force of 4,000 was expected to come and stay during the 18 months. The plant was using state-of-the-art technology and needed skilled labour that was not locally available and would have to be brought in from outside the locality. The potential impact of 4,000 mostly single male adults in the form of construction groups of the contractors, in villages with a 4,700-strong population, would be tremendous. The social situation was even more volatile as the majority of adult males had migrated to other cities and towns in search of jobs and single women-headed households dominated the social profile. As the project progressed, the local inhabitants did not perceive these villages to be 'safe'. But the responsibility for the accompanied changes in the neighbourhood could not be passed on to the project. Heavy machinery was brought in by sea and unloaded at the jetty. No local internal roads were used during the construction phase as the need for maintenance of approach roads to the project was minimal.

A rapid and a comprehensive EIA was conducted as part of the clearance process needed for locating a power plant in that area, which involved an 18-month period, starting from March 1993 (EIA Report, 1993). This involved a year-long monitoring of weather conditions and a rapid SIA, in addition to a more detailed SIA, if needed. With the site of the jetty re-oriented towards the open sea, no major resettlement and rehabilitation issue was involved in the project.

Thus, though the DPC was the cause of the socio-economic changes taking place in the neighbourhood, technically all the associated changes due to a 'boom-town' effect on the neighbourhood of the project could not be blamed on the DPC.

Conceptual Framework

Culture and cultural identity are re-negotiated by the social actors, in the face of certain problems, to reinforce their claims. This is part of the discursive strategy to strengthen the appropriate image needed to reinforce their claims in a particular context. Culture then acts as a common pool resource from which images of appropriate identities can be drawn, to best fit the image needed to strengthen the bargaining power for negotiating with the 'other' in contemporary times. Culture is thus a common pool resource that allows social groups to accumulate multiple images of cultural identities. This common pool resource is being constantly increased and expanded by accumulation of new information and re-interpretation of the old.

Thus, cultural identity most appropriate to the context is socially constructed by using certain important ideologies. Ideologies have constructed new identities as in the case of Phule and Ambedkar. The traditions that they have 'invented' have affirmed a distinctive culture. This emergent ethnicity cannot be collapsed into caste or class categories (Heredia, 2000). In the present case, the commonly shared ideology between the MSEB and the local environmental protest is anti-globalization and anti-economic reform. Both the public sector undertaking and the local communities feel threatened by the emerging global order. They used the three dominant local images of the Maharashtrian identity as a discursive strategy to counter the claims of 'default' made by Enron when it evoked the sovereign counter-guarantee earlier in 2001. These images of Maharashtrian identity were:

1. Maharashtrians have always been able to take on foreign powers, be it the Moghuls, the British, or in this case, Enron, head on.
2. Maharashtrians are a hardy race able to take on challenges of the physical environment, as well as of foreign powers. A person frequently invoked as a proof of this is *Swatantraveer* Savarkar.
3. Maharashtrians are able to resist any attempts to control their resources and suppress their identities as being morally right. The moral righteousness of Tilak, when he faced the Mandale imprisonment, and said, 'There is a power higher than the biggest court in this world where I will be found innocent', is often quoted.

While the process of a private power company beginning production is an apparently economic one, the discursive strategies of organizations like the MSEB, at different points in time, create the space for the emergence of new cultural identities. The public sphere then becomes an arena wherein the culturally defined identities are constantly being re-negotiated and re-defined in the context of new economic challenges thrown up by the contemporary process of globalization. This holds true for apparently secular organizations like public sector power companies in the context of an overtly economic crisis.

The promise of economic growth by a multinational company is given primacy by the state over the claims of the local communities to their natural resources. The only exception is when the MNC starts pushing its 'own' agenda for protecting its own economic interests and proves to be difficult to deal with, for the state. The state uses local claims that are articulated in terms of a 'moral economy' to counter the discourse on economic rationalization forced on it, by the MNC. It is then that the local communities' discourse, rooted in its ethnic identity, of that particular MNC being exploitative of the local subsistence-based economy, and being anti-development, is picked up and articulated at the state level. By doing so, the public sector is able to catapult a local issue that is internal to the organizational crisis, into an international issue of exploitation of the 'poor' by the 'rich'.

In this case, it allowed the Maharashtra State Electricity Board (MSEB), in particular, to stall the economic reforms needed in the power sector. The power sector in Maharashtra is riddled with financial losses caused by power 'theft' and subsidies given to various consumers. Increasing the supply of electricity was seen as a 'soft option' as against the 'hard option' of power sector reforms. Bringing down theft or transmission losses meant disrupting the status quo, as everyone, including the politicians and the bureaucrats/technocrats, benefited from the lax regime. To use a hackneyed analogy, pouring more water into a leaky bucket would buy more time and delay the need to repair the bucket. Thus bringing in DPC was seen as a way to delay the reforms. MSEB signed a PPA (Power Purchase Agreement) with the DPC. This PPA agreed to buy all the power generated by the plant at 68 per cent plant load factor. This is the breakeven point for Enron wherein their cost equals the price of producing electricity. The per unit price of electricity produced by DPC was fixed at 4.75 paise per unit by the PPA. This plant load factor is a reasonable norm for a thermal power plant but not for a gas or oil-based power plant that can operate at higher efficiencies. The plant load factor for the LNG plan is well over 90 per cent. Thus, producing more power would lead to reduced per unit cost, given that the cost was decided. There is therefore no reason for the company to produce at 98 per cent efficiency. If the plant load factor is increased to 98 per cent, which an LNG-based power plant is capable of doing, the per unit cost would come down to 2.45 paise from 4.75 paise. But this is still higher than the current tariff of 2.15 paise. Thus the power purchase agreement locked in the MSEB to buy power from DPC at a price higher than their existing tariffs, without having the option of buying it from cheaper sources first. MSEB used this PPA to put the blame for the current crisis in the power sector on DPC and to consequently delay the reform process. The Power Sector Regulator,[3] on the other hand, was able to see an opportunity within this crisis to push for reforms so that the Central Electricity Board (CEB) could actually buy the surplus power from DPC and sell it to deficit states at 'reasonable' prices, and resolve the crisis in the power sector.

The moral threat to local ethnic identities, in this case, the 'imagined Maharashtrian community' (Anderson, 1983) was evoked to substantiate the claims of MSEB. The local media is supportive of these claims. That Enron was responsible for the bankruptcy of the MSEB (Damale, 2001; Iyer, 2001), became headline news in the local vernacular press as well as the national press after the revoking of the counter-guarantee by DPC. The media also accused the DPC of dragging the MSEB to bankruptcy.

Risk Perceptions

In the present context, the arrival of Enron posed a moral threat to the local communities, as well as to local agencies such as the MSEB and the state government. The three main players, namely the local community, MSEB and DPC, perceived their respective risks very differently.

Enron as a global player was drawing on its global experience of infrastructure development in the Third World. Until DPC, the largest power project they had built was a 780 MW project in Latin America. They were operating eight other power projects operating all over the world at the time of negotiating for the Dabhol project. Their experience with infrastructure projects in the global context made them very aware of the potential for the delay of a project,

---

[3]Personal interview with Mr J.J. Bajaj, Chairperson of the Central Power Regulatory Commission, on 7 February 2001, New Delhi.

through popular environmental social protest movements. The *Narmada Bachao Andolan*, popular environmental protest movement and the withdrawal of the World Bank from the project, had just occurred in India. They were therefore very keen to guard their flanks against environmental protest movements or agitations.

The second risk which they perceived as being very real was a political risk. They were very worried about the political risk in signing the PPA with one set of politicians and then the opposition getting elected and their PPA being revoked or re-negotiated (McKechnie, 2000). Both these were 'expensive' options. In every meeting during the EIA, they never failed to ask this question. The only answer was the history of the state. Until February 1992, the Congress (I) was the incumbent political party. Unfortunately for them, the next elections were won by the Shiv Sena–BJP coalition (Hanssen, 1996), and true to their fears, the PPA was the first casualty. The public image they wanted to project was that of a benevolent player, and they were willing to make side payments to people who had lost lands and to make some funds available for the social benefits of the local communities.

The other equally strong message was based on Enron's work culture of doing it right (sticking by the rules) and doing it on time (project schedules). Economic efficiency and economic rationality were the two cornerstones for their projects. They were here to do no one any harm and yet not allow the local culture, of inefficiencies and project delays, to influence them. The constant rhetoric highlighted the need for timely completion of the project right from the EIA stage. They did stick to the schedules and they did go by the book in evoking the sovereign counter-guarantee.

This challenged the perception of the local identities of the Maharashtrian community about themselves, when the PPA was revoked by the DPC.

MSEB's Risk Perception

The total existing power generation capacity within the public sector Maharashtra State Electricity Board at the time of commissioning of the DPC was 2,000 MW. Like all other state electricity boards, MSEB (World Bank, 2001) is plagued with the problems of power theft and inefficient collection of dues. This is because of wrongly targeted subsidies and inefficiencies within the organization. Bringing more power into the system was slated to be a solution to the systemic problems of the state electricity board. It was easier to do this, and did not require any major structural change within the organization. Therefore, even when the DPC power was to be more expensive at 68 per cent plant load factor which was agreed upon, it was not discounted as a solution. As observed earlier, the per unit cost of production of the current coal and hydropower plants worked out to be 2.15 paise per unit and the cost of the thermal power after the PPA was to be 4.75 paise (Ramachandran, 2001b). It was very clear that the power generated by the DPC would be more expensive. But no demand assessment study by MSEB was done to indicate the need for the project. The assumption was that doubling the capacity of production would actually lead to an increased demand for power, irrespective of the cost.

The dominant rhetoric of the MSEB was that the operation of the power plant in the neighbourhood would be a critical factor for the economic and industrial growth in that region, especially the new industrial area in Chiplun, the neighbouring *taluka*. With power being available, a boom-town effect was expected in the next five years. This would mean that the average *Konkani* would no longer have to run to Mumbai to get jobs. The cost of the power was never seen as an issue. The assumption was that if the quality and reliability of the power supply improved, the buyers would not resist tariff hikes. High investment, improved quality and higher tariff, was the mantra suggested by the World Bank, though in this case, even the World Bank had criticized the choice of fuel and size of the project. The World Bank had warned that Dabhol is not the least cost option for power development in Maharashtra in the early 1990s. The power generated from LNG instead of coal would be much more expensive. The size of the project of 2,015 MW was too large to pay the price fixed for base load operations to Enron. Thus, these two factors combined would place a heavy financial burden on Maharashtra (Iyer, 2001).

Thus, MSEB did not really perceive the PPA and the doubling of the cost of purchase of the power as a very serious threat to the status quo. But the dominant rhetoric was that if the sovereign government was providing a counter-guarantee, then it had no fear of default, because the government would always bail them out. Therefore revoking of the counter-guarantee and litigation that would follow were never seen as a serious threat by the organization. On the other hand, having more power production capacity was seen as helping them to buy time to further delay reforms.

The Local Claims

At the time of the EIA studies, the local people were ambivalent about the project. They did see the immediate benefits of changing land use from agricultural to industrial since most had relatives in Chiplun where lands were acquired at four to seven times the prevalent electricity costs. The local Muslims were not interested in these changes, but the Kunbis saw opportunities for service sector employment. Industrial employment and land prices at industrial rates were a major expectation of the local communities. A local college teacher stated, 'If a big company is coming into my neighbourhood, I should train my sons to that calibre of education before I can stake claims for employment in the company'.

But this rhetoric quickly changed to hostility immediately after the land acquisition for the project took place. After the 1995 elections and the completion of Phase I of the project, the local protest became more articulate. The land was acquired by the MIDC for the DPC, and the local rates were given on the basis of current land use as per the older Land Acquisition Act. As the project was heading towards completion, it became pretty obvious to the local residents that there were very limited jobs on a contractual basis within the power plant. Only 150 highly skilled employees would be on the staff of the power plant on its completion. Even the entire 4,000-strong labour force required for the construction phase of the plant was brought in from outside by the contractors. Thus, only the spillover benefits of the project were coming the way of the local residents.

Moral Economy

The moral economy argument put forward by James Scott (1976) is helpful for understanding the impact of this power plant on the local people. Various risk-sharing arrangements may evolve over time to ensure survival. Tracing the changes in the distribution of risk that results from a change in regime from an agrarian subsistence economy to an industrial commercial regime is of interest in this situation. A change in regime occurs when government-owned public lands are bought by private companies for industrial use. When the lands are barren and public, they offer certain inputs to their subsistence economies in the form of fuel, wood, fodder, etc., and do not pose any threat to their health, livelihoods or natural resources. The arrival of a power plant in the neighbourhood changes all this. A power plant attracts industrial labour and threatens local livelihoods. The public land becomes privately owned, so access to this is denied to local people, and additionally, the pollution that it causes threatens their natural resources and health. The changes in the distribution of risk result due to a change from an agrarian horticulture regime, based on public barren lands, into an industrial regime based on private property (lands). This often results in the breach of a stable exchange that threatens the survival of the local communities, in this case, the PAPs. Under the right conditions, the sustained deterioration of natural resources without the provision of adequate alternatives, may result in a revolt or an organized protest movement. The moral issue here is not how much of the surplus is taken away by the various claimants, such as the state or the power plant, but what is left for the survival of the PAPs. Thus, the arguments for the emergence of an organized social protest movement in the neighbourhood of the power plant are the 'survival first' principle and subsistence ethics used by the local communities.

There is breach of social obligations by three claimants in this situation: first, the earlier landowners (in this case, the state, as all barren common lands are owned by the state); second, the new landowners, in this case, the land-ownership rests with the state and is only leased to DPC; and third, the elected representatives of the constituency in the local, democratically elected government, who actively supported the local claims when in the opposition. Later, when they became a part of the ruling coalition, their language changed, and their support was withdrawn.

When the ownership of the land was transferred to DPC in 1992, it was accompanied by other changes that were detrimental to the local economy. First, the cost of land compensation quoted was according to the present value of barren or agricultural land, and was not based on the intended use value of the land as a power plant. Second, in order to establish total control over their real estate, the new owners built a compound wall around it. This ensured that the local communities could no longer use the resources from the land. It also obstructed the local inhabitants' easy access to their neighbours on the other side of the power plant. The plant also stimulated secondary growth in the area. This resulted in the change of ownership in other private lands surrounding the plant. The new arrivals were much more enterprising and thrived financially as compared to the local people.

Thus, what was taken away from the local communities was their access to common property resources, such as fuelwood, grass and small timber, and access to their neighbours. DPC Enterprise was able to extract huge profits from their investments, by guarantees of a 16 per cent rate of return to Enron (Ramchandran, 2001a). DPC managed to cover the risk of default through a Power Purchase Agreement (PPA) initially for the first two years, and subsequently, for the life of the project. The financial sector institutions have recovered their investments. The state government also benefited by gaining clout in the system. But what was left for the local communities to deal with was disruption in the pristine natural environment of the coastal town. The average *Konkani Manus* (as the residents of that area call themselves) had to accept a forced change in their lifestyle, from being peasants and fishing folk, to being self-employed small businessmen, selling consumer goods and renting shops along the approach road to DPC. They are now exposed to conspicuous consumption by the tourists and other professionals, whose number has increased in the area as a result of these changes; their women are vulnerable to the indecent behaviour of drunken tourists and the migrant labourers settling in that region. The road surface has deteriorated further. Residents also face frequent electricity failures. But the most important extraction that seriously threatens their survival is a shortage of drinking water supply and sewage disposal facilities, partially due to the power plant, which has led to emigration. The municipality has not been able to raise resources for increasing supply to the town or for creating new infrastructure to take care of the additional sewage.

The state government took no action to prevent this from happening. Within the scope of the EIA mitigative measures, it did insist that the plant promoters make provisions for sanitation and drinking water for their labour camp during the construction phase. However, it did not insist that the source for the supply of drinking water be located outside the plant limits so that others could access it later. The local communities have approached their political leaders and elected representatives for providing piped water supply to new settlements outside the town, but it is expensive to extend the pipelines to the areas surrounding the town from the existing water sources. The barrage is a few kilometres away and the existing capacity needs to be augmented for which the local municipality does not have resources. This will require both new water sources and the political will to tap them. Meanwhile, residents have to depend on private wells and tanker-delivered drinking water supply, during the three months of the summer, three times a week.

The original inhabitants living in the villages and town surrounding the project area before the project felt betrayed by the state government as the latter made no provisions for reservations in the jobs that were created in the power plant by Dabhol Power Company. Comparisons were made with the Jawaharlal Nehru Port Trust project, where one person from every displaced household was given employment in the port, which was a public sector project. Instead, the land was acquired under the old land acquisition act by the state and handed over to the DPC to reduce the capital cost of the project, which was interpreted by the local people as the government supporting DPC interest. DPC did not offer any financial assistance to the original inhabitants to help improve the infrastructure facilities or skill development option in a newly booming market situation. A speculative market for land was already booming by this time, other small industries had arrived and commercial and service sector growth was exponential. The only option the original inhabitants had was to join the market forces or be left behind. Even when they tried to join the market forces without active support from the state government, they could at best participate at marginal levels as small self-employed businessmen. The elected political representatives were not in a position to demand special rights for their constituencies they could at best provide water tankers in case of acute drinking water shortage.

The only spin-off of the arrival of the DPC was generation of employment in the service sector. Small self-employed businesses sprung along the road to the power plant and the demand for autorickshaws significantly increased, compared to animal carts. The size of land holdings reduced as well, and were converted from agricultural to non-agricultural use like housing colonies or market complexes (EIA Report, 1993).

Infrastructure facilities have not significantly improved since the operation of the plant began. The area suffers from an acute drinking water shortage. The approach road to the plant has not been widened or maintained, because of lack of resources with the municipality of Guhagar. Power is not a problem. Telephone connections have increased.

But revolt or organized violent protest, according to Scott (1976), is an exception and happens only under certain conditions. Non-harmonious relations and coercion may exist, without revolt, under similar circumstances. Evidence of non-harmonious class relations and coercion between the power plant and local communities can be gathered at three levels: first, in the local discourse among the affected people in the form of narratives; second, pilferage when the occasion permits; and finally, an increase in police control.

Talking Claims

After a *morcha* was organized by the protesters and informal negotiations were held with the promoters, the political leaders actively involved in the protest during 1993–95 became a part of the ruling coalition. The social movement has since been dormant, but there is evidence to suggest that non-harmonious relations exist between the power plant promoters and the local communities. This evidence takes two forms: *(i)* the local discourse of the affected people in the form of narratives; and *(ii)* increase in police control.

The local narratives are extremely interesting. People tell stories as a way of constructing a reality that is biased in their favour, as against the 'official' version that is published in reports. The stories constitute part of the discursive strategy that is a crucial component of the process of negotiation (Fortmann, 1994). They serve to bolster people's confidence in their own claims, by legitimizing their claims. By repeating the stories, they are re-asserting their version of the reality, as against the official version.

Twenty-five different houses were visited and people were asked to describe their perceptions about what had changed since the power plant came into existence in 1995. A few of the people were too nervous to discuss DPC. Of the remainder, the wife of a local restaurant owner said, 'Our village youth find jobs as autorickshaw drivers, but no one works in the plant from here'. When asked about the agitation against the DPC, her neighbour sitting nearby said, 'We all took part in the agitation against DPC. Our elected representatives visited us after that, but nothing has happened since'. When asked about the benefits accruing from DPC, another fisherman said: 'The open sea jetty put up by the DPC is unfortunate. If they had put the jetty in the estuary of the river, the sand bar currently blocking the deepening of the Dabhol harbour would have been cleared for big ships. Dredging the harbour would have really developed that area but now what use is DPC to us?' In another house, when questioned about the infrastructure facilities, one woman said, 'Telephone connections to this place came soon after DPC. Nevertheless, until January this year (1995), the lights used to go off every second day. What use is a power plant if we cannot get lights?'

In another house, the family was very vocal about the economic impact of the plant. The son said: 'Our condition has not improved. There is a basic lack of facilities—our houses are not secure (referring to the recent land transfers to "outsiders" by local people). Employment chances have increased but they are on a temporary basis, and prices of all commodities have shot up'. Another person owning land nearby claimed that access to the land was made difficult after DPC put a compound wall around its property, and said: '*Morchas* were taken as DPC has taken over our lands but nothing was done. Dabhol has become famous now, but we are not even known and we have to suffer. Not even the government is bothered about Guhagar's problems'. Another person with him stated, 'DPC promised to provide basic facilities and develop the place. Nothing has happened. They promised technical schools and hospitals. All false promises, nothing has happened'. Another owner of a *tonga* said, 'I had a *tonga* business which was destroyed because of DPC. We protested against DPC and were jailed. Yes! Unemployment chances have increased'.

The other issue related to loss of access to common property resource was firewood. One woman stated, 'There is a problem in getting firewood after DPC has come, since the already scarce forest area has diminished further'. Many stated, 'We fear outsiders especially since our husbands are away. Women do not feel safe'.

The general sentiment is summed up by the outburst of a man, who said, 'DPC is a big project with huge investments. The management is supported by the Central Government. What can a lone *Konkani* do?' The general feeling is of a breach of trust by the government, on the one hand, and by their elected representatives, on the other. DPC is treated with great hostility and is seen as not being trustworthy at all. It is also seen as the cause for all the evil in that region.

The narratives of the people affected by the power plant can be broadly divided into narratives that are about individual injustice; narratives of physical and cultural harm caused to the community; and narratives of failed promises. The main narratives are about how they have failed to benefit from the employment generated by the plant. Often an individual will begin by talking about his/her experience of how they managed to get employment for less than a year in the plant, and how they were subsequently fired from the job. Other names are then mentioned with similar instances. The narratives concerning the physical, cultural and ecological impacts of the plant refer to traffic, the decrease in fish catch, and the water and fuelwood crises. Since the spillover benefits of making Dabhol/Guhagar prominent and the economic benefits to self-employed entrepreneurs are of considerable significance, the expression of discontent is subtle.

There is also considerable fear in the minds of the local people when they speak against the plant, which they describe is due to 'terrorism'. There has been an increase in the regular police posted near DPC for security reasons. Before the plant came into existence, local people, and especially the Kolis, had opened some small restaurants serving food and drinks to the weekend tourists. The reaction of one restaurant owner is representative: 'More tourists come here now than before. But they do not come to the restaurants any more; all that we get is policemen harassing us for running illegal businesses.' They claim that the police trouble them and threaten to arrest them on grounds that 'illegal' activities are taking place in the restaurants.

The Protest Movement

The local community organized into a formal protest movement very quickly. By 1994, they had formed an association that called itself the *Enron Virodhi Manch* (literally translated as 'an association to oppose Enron') and has the support and backing of the National Alliance of People's Movement. The National Alliance was formed by activists like Medha Patkar of the *Narmada Bachao Andolan* and Thomas Co Cherry of the Kerala fishworkers' agitation, and others who came together to help organize the local environmental protest movements (Omvedt, 1993) against globalization and economic reforms. They organized *dharnas* and gained constant media focus from both the vernacular and the national press. They invoked the images of the hardworking *Konkani Manus* exploited by the multi-national corporation in their own backyard.

Given the constant situation of social ferment, supported by environmental activists, the police presence in that region has increased. Especially since the beginning of this year, when the counter-guarantee clause was evoked, the number of social protests in the form of *dharnas and morchas* against DPC even in Mumbai have increased. There is a *chowki* at Guhagar where very few policemen existed before, but now there are twice the number and the local small traders complain of harassment by the police.

Unexpected Ally and Political Battles

During the initial part of the commissioning of the power plant, the PAPs were resisting the power plant, while the MSEB, which is the local power utility company, the Government of Maharashtra and even the Central Government overtly or covertly supported the power plant. The Central Government's counter-guarantee for the Power Purchase Agreement is a proof of this. But as the white paper of the Maharashtra government (Government of Maharashtra, 2002) indicates, the state went bankrupt by 1990.

Political battles are usually projected as conflict between state and the people (Singh, 1997). But here is an instance where the state agency is using the local people and their perception of threatened local identity, to fight DPC. At the same time, MSEB has allowed another Indian company, that is, Reliance, to hawk its power to a third party (De et al., 2001), because the PPA allows a 750 MW plant to do so. DPC was not allowed the same privilege.

However, conscious efforts were made by the DPC to ensure that land acquisition or environmental issues did not become a cause for an organized environmental struggle. They even willingly changed the original LNG unloading facility draft plan, which may have involved resettlement and rehabilitation of the five villages named earlier and considerable disturbance to the Dabhol harbour at the time of unloading.

DPC covered its political risks quite effectively through the PPA with MSEB being backed by a sovereign guarantee. The Corporation obviously negotiated with the Pawar government quite effectively, as between January 1993 and February 1995, there was no political backlash against the project. When the government changed after the March

1995 state elections, the Shiv Sena–BJP coalition came into power partially on the promise of 'throwing Enron into the Arabian Sea' by Bal Thackeray, the founder of the Shiv Sena, and partially because of an effective strategy of 'vernacularization' adopted by the alliance (Hanssen, 1996). Enron's Mumbai representative called on Bal Thackeray. 'The meeting was behind closed doors and one-to-one and instead of scrapping Dabhol, the deal was "re-negotiated"' (Iyer, 2001). From November 1995 to May 1996, when the deal was re-negotiated, no Central Government counter-guarantee was forthcoming. So when the Central Government changed in May 1996, with the 13-day old Vajpayee government falling on the thirteenth day, minutes before the government was resigning, it issued a counter-guarantee (Ramchandran, 2001b. Thus, when on 6 February 2001 *(Business Standard,* 2001b) DPC invoked a state guarantee for about Rs 1.5 billion of the December bill, and Rs 690 million of the total November bill of Rs 790 million, it accused MSEB of repeated default since early 2000. DPC was fully prepared to drag the Centre to the London Council of Arbitration if they refused to pay.

The MSEB's claim that Enron was responsible for making a prosperous state, bankrupt was backed by the state government. But the state government's plea to the Centre to bail them out, was not entertained *(Business Standard,* 2001c). The Godbole Committee report also suggested re-negotiations of the PPA, in its interim report. The Maharashtra government has to appoint a committee to look into issues like the cost of power and the use of power by DPC on the basis of these recommendations.

Whenever convenient, MSEB and the state government used the local claims to their advantage and against DPC. The local struggle was kept alive for years to keep the pressure on DPC and, from time to time, it was allowed to escalate to agitation levels whenever the state required it to do so. The *Enron Virodhi Manch* organized the most vocal state-wise agitation against DPC in the months of February and March 2001 mainly in Ratnagiri and Mumbai.

MSEB, GoM and the Power Sector Reforms

Mumbai area is served by three power utilities. MSEB was set up in 1960 to generate, transmit and distribute power to all consumers in Maharashtra excluding Mumbai. MSEB is the largest SEB in the country. The generation capacity of MSEB grew from 760 MW in 1960–61 to 9,771 MW in 2001–02, while the customer base grew from 107,833 in 1960–61 to 1,40,09,089 in 2001–02. MSEB has a strong generation capacity base. In spite of poor quality coal, its thermal power stations achieved an all-time high by increasing its power availability to 86.49 per cent and plant load factor to 74.34 per cent in 2001–02. Currently, the MSEB has locked horns with the Maharashtra State Electricity regulator on the one hand, to allow it to raise its tariffs to meet the increased costs of electricity due to the Power Purchase Agreement (PPA) signed with the DPC. At the same time, given the vulnerability of the DPC, it is trying to wriggle out of the PPA. DPC is stuck with an expensive power plant that they would have to get rid of due to the financial situation of their parent company. MSEB is thus using the subaltern rhetoric to win its battles with DPC and the regulator to escape power sector reforms. Pouring more water into a leaking bucket is seen by MSEB as a viable solution.

The state of Maharashtra and the MSEB are both financially in a bad shape. Up to the 1990s, the state experienced a high growth rate. However, it has seen a decline in growth rates in recent years. The average annual economic growth declined sharply from 7.8 per cent between 1985–86 and 1994–95 to 5.3 per cent during 1995–96 to 1999–2000. While the losses of MSEB in 2002 are to the tune of Rs 15 billion, the revenue is Rs 12 billion. MSEB is plagued by heavy transmission and distribution losses of 39.4 per cent. The LT/HT ratio is 2, leading to heavy transmission and distribution losses at the last mile. This is because the power sector as a whole is in a bad shape in India. Jumping onto the bandwagon of the environmental protest movement was a strategy that bureaucrats and technocrats within the MSEB used to distract the attention of the regulator and policy makers from the reform agenda. They do not believe that the measures taken by the GOI to open the sector to competition would bring in efficiency, but rather do just the opposite. These groups typically argue that the government has been mainly responsible for the poor state of the power sector. A coalition of vested interests consisting of sections of politicians, SEB workers, private contractors and consumers gradually took over the control of the sector. These vested interests bled the sector for personal and political benefits at the cost of larger public interest and financial viability of the sector. These groups fear that the proposed privatization and reforms would lead to a further adverse impact on consumers and the economy as these reforms offer an increasing role to the private sector and further erode the ability of consumers and people to control the affairs in the sector. The process of inviting independent power providers, which has been mired in controversies, on account of environmental impacts, violation of human rights and adverse economic impacts, is cited as example in support of their argument. They therefore resist reform. The trade unions in Maharashtra are not an exception and the Dabhol controversy has provided them with the much-needed tool to slow down the power sector reforms in the state, albeit with the help of the already existing environmental protest movement and the call to protects local identities.

There are multiple claimants to the Dabhol power plant, including the NTPC, the domestic lenders, foreign lenders, the government of Maharashtra and the Central Government.

After Enron declared its bankruptcy, the Bombay High Court scuttled a move by the Enron group of companies to move the New York courts to oversee the disposal of 2,184 MW of power plant in Maharashtra, claiming first charge on assets and arguing that assets cannot be part of the bankruptcy proceedings. NTPC will now be running the plant though under the control of the court receiver. The Maharashtra government wants the PPA to be re-negotiated before it evacuates the plant. It is also demanding higher plant load factor and lowered interest rate, to bring down the operating cost of the plant, and the price, including tax relief for MSEB. The plant has been lying idle for 18 months. It stopped producing power since May 2001 and the cost of the project is Rs 120 billion. The cost of delay in starting the plant is Rs 25 million per day. By May 2003, the two-year mark, the interest was Rs 18 billion, due to the plant shutdown.

Conclusion

MSEB held the conviction that the additional power production was a solution to the power sector crisis in the state of Maharashtra. With this conviction, the public sector company supported and promoted the setting up of the LNG power plant. But the major structural crisis of a bankrupt state, unable to support non-viable fiscal deficits of the power company landed the power company into a crisis. Instead of tackling the systemic issue that resulted in the crisis, the public sector power company decided to postpone the issue. They used the new language of subaltern rhetoric of the environmental protest movement that already existed, with the help of the mass media, for postponing the power sector reforms within the state a bit longer.

The changing alliances in the state are interesting. Earlier, it was the DPC with Enron, Bechtel, GE, Indian foreign investors (FIs) and the MSEB pushing for the project, against the PAPs. Then, with the completion of Phase I of the project, when MSEB could not pass on the cost to consumers because the regulator refused to oblige, the new alliance between MSEB and the FIs from India emerged to further postpone the reforms. The technocrats, bureaucrats, labour unions and Indian financial companies, all stand to benefit from this delay and are waiting for the kill.

Seven

Cultural Imperatives of Technology Transfer*

This is another case study wherein the public sector bureaucrats in the mining sector were able to stall the social transformation threatened by a development aid project by using the subaltern rhetoric very effectively. Development aid projects that involve technology transfer never completely fail. The success of the project is determined in terms of the goals that the project is able to achieve and is, in turn, determined by the local culture and social context. Technology is considered as 'neutral' in nature. Hence any technology transfer through a development aid project by a donor country to a host country is cast in terms of technological efficiency. However, every aid project has a social development component with implicit social goals. The case study demonstrates how the project manager of an Indian public sector undertaking and his team were able to have their own agenda pushed through in a development aid project at the feasibility stage by 'successfully' drawing upon the local narratives.

Technology transfer (TT) through bilateral aid project is of special interest to sociologists and social anthropologists because it is a situation for potential social change. The key issue here is: What is

---

*I wish to thank the Australian International Development Aid Bureau (AIDAB) for giving me this opportunity to study the Moonidih washery in such detail. The views expressed in this chapter are my own and in no way reflect AIDAB policy. An earlier version of the chapter was presented at a conference on 'Problems and Challenges of Technology Transfer, In-house R&D and Indigenous Technology for Indian Industry for the 1990s', 24–26 January 1996, at the Indian Institute of Technology, Mumbai. I found the comments from the audience very useful in revising the arguments.

I would also like to thank Eric Worby and Robert Stalling for providing me with conceptual insights, and other colleagues at Yale University for their suggestions.

the social goal of the TT policy? There is a hierarchy of goals: one is to maintain the social status quo within the host country and to implement the technological dimension of the project alone, which is the most desirable for the host country. The second goal is a social change agenda that is acceptable to the host and the donor country alike, a compromise solution. The final goal is promotion of the social agenda of the donor, as professed in the Memorandum of Understanding (MOU) signed between the two friendly nations, which is dictated by the donor country. Thus there are no failures in an aid- related TT, and 'success' is a relative term determined by which of the goals the project is able to achieve and is, in turn, determined by the local culture and the social context.

Here is a case study of a coal washery in Dhanbad, Jharkhand. The local economy of Dhanbad can best be described as an 'enclave economy'. The work culture within the public sector undertaking is characterized as an 'indulgence pattern' and the social control of the 'coal mafia' cannot be ignored. Given that the said washery needed new machines and was cash strapped, the technology transfer through development aid by the Australian government was an attractive proposal. But the development aid package also had a 'social development agenda' dictated by the donor country that threatened to disrupt the socio-cultural status quo. In the present context, the Indian project manager was able to 'successfully' draw upon the local narratives to counter the social development component of the aid project.

Technology Transfer Policy

In India in the early stages of industrialization, even in the 1980s, the emphasis of the policy was on technological 'self-sufficiency'. Foreign direct investment (FDI) in India and non-equity arrangements in the form of technological collaborations with trans-national corporations were permitted only on such terms as were determined by the government to be in the national interest. As a general rule, the government gives first preference to the acquisition of technology against a one-time lump sum payment. Second preference is given to arrangements involving the payment of royalties while third preference is given to equity participation, preferably with an Indian partner. Foreign direct investments (FDI) unaccompanied by technology transfer are discouraged.

More recently, the government has decided to permit FDI in new ventures in preference to the outright purchase of technology. It has also permitted FDI in existing companies in high technology areas. Further, in the 1980s, two exceptions were made to permit portfolio investments by investors from OECD (Organisation for Economic Co-operation and Development) countries and NRIs. In the 1980s, and particularly since 1984–85, India has adopted an open door policy to FDI (United Nations, 1992).

There is a lively debate on the impact of liberalization, and especially technology transfer, to Indian industry, with a special emphasis on labour and labour markets (Tulpule and Dutta, 1995). While all these debates focus on the impact on labour, they do not directly consider the socio-political and cultural dimensions of technology transfer, because TT is perceived to be value-neutral. But it is precisely these dimensions that determine the fate of any project related to TT. This is the focus here.

Technology transfer through aid

TT done through development aid assistance, is a special case of TT involving a financial component and a social development component, as perceived by the donor. It has a small aid component, but a large portion of long-term, low interest loan given by the donor country, (with the condition that the equipment and machines necessary for the TT be purchased from the donor country), and a matching component from the host country. The social development agendas include issues related to 'women in development', 'community participation', 'environmentally sustainable development', etc. These aid packages are channelled through an 'aid agency' of the donor country, which appoints project managers, and is implemented in the host country by an industry or an agency identified by the host country. A Memorandum of Understanding (MOU) to this effect is usually signed between the respective countries.

In the present case, the MOU was signed between India and Australia under the development assistance agency, AusAid, earlier known as AIDAB (Australian International Development Aid Bureau).

Case Study

Under the development assistance programme designed to foster broader economic co-operation between Australia and India, it was decided to proceed with the proposal involving the introduction of Australian coal fines benefication techniques in classification, extraction, separation and controls, and improved management practices in order to achieve more efficient coal operation and utilization. As per the policy of development aid assistance in Australia, three components with a definite social agenda were included in the MOU. These were 'community participation', 'women in development' and 'environmentally sustainable development' (AIDAB, 1992a).

The proposed location was the Moonidih coal preparation plant (washery) in Dhanbad, Jharkhand, operated by Bharat Coking Coal Limited (BCCL). The estimated cost of the project is Aus $4 million. The implementing agency on behalf of the Government of Australia was Australian International Development Assistance Bureau (AIDAB), which sub-contracted the project management function to an Australian company. On behalf of the Government of India, Coal India Limited (CIL) was the implementing agency with participation from Bharat Coking Coal Limited (BCCL).

Historical Background

During the Nehruvian era, the Damodar Valley Project and associated development in the region of Dhanbad were the results of an Indo-American venture and were cast as the Indian equivalent of the Mississippi Valley Project. But since the onset of the Cold War, the American interest and aid waned, and Australians slowly replaced them in the steel and coal sectors.

Moonidih coal washery is attached to the Moonidih coal mines in the Jharia coalfields of the Dhanbad district of Jharkhand. It therefore shares the common features of the other coal fields of that region. The coal fields of India are characterized by the development of an 'enclave economy' (Rothermund, 1978). An analysis of the economy shows that the enclave developed in Dhanbad due to three main reasons: that is, the prevailing feudal structures, the British managing agency system and the colonial system of long-distance labour recruitment.

The prevailing feudal structure precluded an adequate response to the challenges of the new economic activity and placed severe constraints on the development of the region. In Dhanbad, *zamindars* were essentially absentee landlords and the tenants were the effective controllers of the lands and employed the local landless labourers on their farms. When coal mining started in the district, the coal companies inserted themselves into this structure. They became, in a sense, sub-surface farmers and did not intervene with the surface farming as far as possible. Unlike the earlier coalfields wherein mining companies acquired landed rights in order to convert peasant holdings into service tenure for miners, the quick expansion of the mining operations in the Jharia fields of Dhanbad necessitated a different approach to the recruitment of labour. The peasantry was treated with indifference by the mining company and villages were disturbed only when they blocked the way for railway sidings and pit-heads or when they were later affected by the subsiding of the soil when empty inclines collapsed. Thus coalfield enclaves included quite a few villages whose straw hut and green terraces provided a striking contrast to the grimy mines next door (Rothermund, 1978). The Moonidih mines and the washery also have these paddy fields adjacent to the washery. These fields are now being exploited by the coal mafia as will be highlighted later.

The second reason for the development of the enclave economy in Dhanbad was that the British managing agency system was geared to a restricted market and to making huge profits with minimum capital investments. Both the feudal agrarian systems and the colonial manifestation of capitalism in the managing agency system were of a narrow restrictive type, and mutually reinforced each other in maintaining the enclave character of the coalfields and the backwardness of its rural hinterlands. As a result of this colonial legacy, coal utilization became a quasi-monopoly of the railways, and steel and power plants owned by the state. These quasi-monopolies later proved to be detrimental to the opening up of coal markets by the price decontrol mechanism.

The third determinant that stifled the regional development was the colonial system of labour recruitment. The labour recruitment system depends on the captive worker who is bound by a contract indenture and advances, and is thus deprived of mobility. Most labourers fled from rural poverty and captivity only in order to submit to new servitude under tough 'raising contractors' who made profits by exploiting their labour force as much as possible (Rothermund, 1978).

Labour Unions and the Coal Mafia

Before nationalization, the industry was characterized by a multitude of relatively small mines and only a few large-scale modern mines. In most of the mines, only 50 per cent of the workers were listed on a permanent payroll. The others were employed as temporary or contract labourers and thus deprived of benefits. Any attempt to organize labour met with limited success because of this (Rothermund, 1983). In 1967, the award of the Central Wage Board which guaranteed minimum wages was to be implemented by all the mines. As an incentive for its implementation, the coal prices were decontrolled by the government. But this move could not be implemented effectively because the decontrolling of coal prices did not work, due to the quasi-monopoly of the railways and the steel plants, which vehemently resisted the increase in prices. Thus, in the process of trying to force the mines to implement the award, the trade unions were reduced to a 'forum of case pleaders'. The contract system was used to break the workers' movement.

In 1970, the Contract Labour Abolition and Regulation Act came into force. Simultaneously, in 1972–73, the mines were nationalized. The new owners were faced with a flood of unauthorized induction. In addition, the contractors and trade union leaders had entered the names of contract labourers in the registers whom they were committed to employ in the collieries under them.

With the advent of nationalization, the labour contractors were replaced by another type of contractors who had fleets of trucks and dumpers for the transport of coal from pitheads to sidings, and so on. They formed their own unions. It is said that the upsurge of violence in the coalfields was an outcome of the struggle between the contractors, each of whom tried to establish his own sphere of influence among the workers. Whenever any one influential contractor-cum-trade union leader attempted to intrude into the domain of the other, shooting started. The murders and killings in the Jharia coalfields are thus alleged to be actually battles among the powerful contractor lobbies. In a Home Ministry study into the source of violence, it was discovered that the transport contractors of Bharat Coking Coal

Limited had formed gangs which operated by spreading terror and violence in the coalfields. Finally, BCCL is reported to have brought in its own fleet to substitute private transport and eliminate the mafia type of gangsterism.

But the nationalization of the mines helped implement the Wage Board award since 1975. As a result, the miners today earn much more than they previously expected and some piece-rated workers like loaders (general *mazdoor*) earn monthly wages totalling four figures (Rothermund, 1983). Thus, what is observed in the coalfields of Dhanbad, namely, mafia type gangsterism and terrorism, the simultaneous existence of paddy fields and mineheads, and the inability to organize labour into unions, are all symptoms of a larger systemic problem of the 'enclave economy' and the under-development of the hinterlands. Within this system is located the Moonidih coal washery, which is the focus of this study.

The Washery and Its Community

Plant setting

The Moonidih area complex consists of five units, including the underground mines, coal washery, captive thermal plant, long wall, and the mechanization training institution and area services. The washery is situated in the south-central part of the Jharia coalfields, about 12 km from Dhanbad and 2 km into the Dhanbad–Chas road (NH 32) from Pootki. It is surrounded by other coal mines of the BCCL at one end, and extend up to the river Damodar on the other side. The total area of the leasehold land is around 18 sq km and is surrounded by 16 villages having a total population of about 20,000 people. Education, water, electricity and roads are some of the facilities provided to these villages by BCCL (1992).

Technical profile

The coal washing operations are intended to separate pure coal from the run of mine (ROM) coal. It involves three stages. The first stage entails crushing of the ROM coal into a size acceptable to the machines in the coal preparation stage. Then this crushed ROM passes through various screens and centrifuges to separate different sizes of pure coal from the ash (middling). The coal fines are extracted by adding water, magnetite and surfactant, and settled in a huge siltation tank where the ash settles and fines overflow. These are recovered and dried in shallow open ponds (fines). The technology has not changed in its production and design. A major increase in efficiency is achieved through labour and time saving by using computerized numerical component (CNC) machines and bigger transportation equipment.

The washery was designed with the help of Polish technology in 1972–73. Its plant design was copied from Poland without accounting for the tropical climate of India, and with no captive power supply. It is situated in a seven-storey building to protect it from snow during winters. This makes the washery very dark and intolerable when the power is off, which happens quite frequently. The storage and loading facilities are also covered and suffer from the same problem. In addition, there are huge piles of muck caused by spillage due to the improper operation of the machines. It has a design capacity capable of processing 2 million tonnes of raw coal per year and was designed to accept up to 700 tonnes of the high quality coal from the adjacent underground shaft. The official statistics indicate that the normal operating rate for limited periods is between 250 to 300 tonnes/hour. The washery currently receives additional quantities of varying quality of coal from five other mines to supplement the Moonidih shaft output. This leads to further problems in operating the unit. There are piles of debris all over the buildings which make the already difficult access to the machines almost impossible.

Sociological profile

The washery is operated by 617 people. The principal reason for overstaffing was the post-nationalization labour surplus. At present, the washery staff comprises a workforce of 617 people, including 55 women employees and 30 officers. In Australia, on the other hand, the same sized washery is operated by four people with the help of computers.

All the 30 officers are males. Twenty-four of them are engineers, and 21 have engineering degrees, including seven who have postgraduate qualifications. The others have commerce degrees. The average age of the staff members is 38.5 years. All have an average experience of 10.6 years and all belong to the upper castes with the exception of seven officers who have not reported their caste. Fourteen of them are from Bihar and four from West Bengal, while the rest are from other states, but none are from Dhanbad district. They are all involved in supervisory work related to the garage, three maintenance units, one operations unit and a personnel department.

A 5 per cent stratified random sample of 32 workers was taken to obtain the profile of all the other employees who work in shifts. Most of them have worked for an average of 7.9 to 10 years in the washery. There are only 12.5 per cent new recruits who have worked for less than one year. Of these, 37 per cent have ITI certificates and more while 23 per cent are illiterates. The rest have had some schooling. While 41 per cent belong to the upper caste groups, 18.7 per cent belong to the scheduled castes (SCs) that traditionally moved earth, namely, the Mohato, Noniya and Moniya castes. The others belong to occupational castes. The average age of these workers is 40.2 years. Needless to say, there is a high and significant correlation between caste and education ($r = 0.428$ for 1 tailed significance of 0.008).

The 55 women employees of the washery have been working here for 5 to 10 years. Their average age is 37 years. They are all illiterate, except two women who have passed SSC and work as peons in the personnel office. They also happen to be Rajputs, while the others SCs. Eleven of the women have been working in the washery since nationalization. All other women are employed because their husbands died in harness and their children, being young, could not be employed. They all work in day shifts and are involved in cleaning the spillage from the operations. The minimum monthly wage of the piece-rated labourers was Rs 1,700 in 1992.

Work culture

What the workers and the management think of each other is reflected in the work culture of the place. The work culture can be described as following an 'indulgency pattern'. An indulgency pattern is a connected set of concrete judgments and underlying sentiments disposing workers to react to the plant favourably and to trust their supervisors (Gouldner, 1954). All workers were unanimous in judging the management as being lenient and considerate, and claimed that the latter allowed them a lot of time that was not supervised during working hours. Women employees were especially indulged. This is an important factor though not the only source of job satisfaction experienced by the workers, which motivates them to work, and express commitment to the washery, thereby generating loyalties and expressing preference for certain patterns of social relations rather than others. Both the officers and the workers were weary of union leaders. The six different unions and their leaders are believed to be constantly fighting with each other and rarely have the workers' cause at heart.

Thus the Moonidih washery is no exception to the enclave economy. Its management and labour are dominated by 'outsiders', coming from other districts. It has a multiplicity of trade unions and is characterized by infighting among various union leaders for control. It even has its own coal mafia. The washery is surrounded by paddy fields just outside its boundaries. Since this washery is operated by BCCL, it has its own fleet of trucks. Outside the boundaries are the trucks of the local mafia leader called the *Lala*. These trucks collect the coal fines that come out of various waste water outlets from the washery all through the day and night. These coal fines of washed coal are allowed to escape through waste water outlets and the adjacent fields operate as sedimentation ponds where the fines settle. After seven days, they dry up sufficiently so that they can be easily loaded in trucks. These loading operations are supervised by armed guards of the private contractor. This *Lala* has 3 armed guards and 10 trucks assigned for this operation.

Any intervention in the form of an outside agency intending to alter the existing machinery through replacement in the washery will result in the disruption of the status quo. This leaves the washery officers vulnerable to personal financial losses through the loss of 'rents', victimization by others if they support change, or the threat of outright violence.

Point of Entry

As part of the TOR, the Australian project management agency, in consultation with its counterparts in India, was stated to prepare a feasibility report. The brief was to conduct a washery audit as an input to the feasibility study in order to assess the present status of the washery, and to suggest improvements thereof, in co-ordination with its Indian counterparts.

The AIDAB had contracted out the project management function to an Australian company. Its team went to Moonidih to prepare a feasibility report. This report highlighted the present status of the washery by using the methodology of audits. The audits involved a total of 12 persons and five months of work, including two months on the site. Audits were conducted on seven different aspects of the washery functions. These included the operations, maintenance management, electrical systems, management functions, sociology/role of women, environment, and occupational health and safety. The technocratic hierarchy was replicated with counterparts on both sides of the teams.

Given the 'indulgency pattern' that encouraged a patron–client relationship, and that the Indian officers outnumbered the Australian staff 30 to 12, the perception of the Indian project leader was that the Australian counterpart was 'subordinate' to him (Ferguson, 1990), should therefore behave like a 'guest', wait to be showed around and depend on local help. Further, the Indian team leader expected his Australian colleague to inform him of every move made by him within the washery 'territory'.

The Australian team leader, on the other hand, believed that he was equivalent in status to the washery's general manager, and it never occurred to him to take permission or inform his counterpart beforehand of any of his movements or that of his team members. He refused every help, in the form of peons, typists and other staff offered to him and insisted on maintaining an independent office, and independent eating and living arrangements, away from the Indian staff of the washery. His logic was that he had to maintain a distance from the washery staff, as the feasibility report had to be 'unbiased and objective'. He might have to recommend measures that would cause disruption in the status quo and would lead to a conflict of interest if he took help from the Indian workers. This was interpreted as resistance and non-co-operation by the Indian project manager. This antagonism built up to such hostility that when the project finally wound up, it took the Australian project staff five hours to get a 'gate pass' to take their own computers and refrigerator out of the washery.

Even under normal circumstances, the work done by any 'outsider' without consulting the Indian project manager would have been viewed with suspicion. Given the social distance between the two team leaders, the work done by the Australian project manager became an issue of contestation. The insistence of the Australian project manager to trust the 'written word' in the TOR made him undermine the very important dimension of inter-cultural communication, which is so essential for the success of any joint venture. The Australian project manager's efforts to establish an equivalent and independent status at par with the washery's general manager, was the beginning of the breakdown of communication between the two agencies at the project level. A loss of trust and faith in each other at the initial stages of the feasibility study then pushed both the team leaders into extreme positions, leaving no space for negotiations or bargaining. The Australian project leader pushed himself and his team to rely on technologically efficient solutions and a scientifically correct analysis of the problem, while his Indian counterpart drew upon local narratives to counteract any recommendations made in the project design document.

Each of the claims made by the Aide Memoir (AIDAB, 1992c) became claims for contestation, especially the claims that involved 'soft' sciences like sociology, management and psychology. The reality represented in social science analysis is never absolute and always open to contestations. Multiple interpretations of the social reality are possible and the local actors can choose the narrative that is most representative of his or her claim.

The Audits

As stated earlier, audits were conducted on seven different aspects of the washery's functions. These included the operations, maintenance management, electrical systems, management functions, sociology/role of women, environment, and occupational health and safety. Thus the audits covered both the objective and subjective aspects of the washery. The objective assessment of the materials and machinery was covered by operations, electrical systems, and maintenance and environmental pollution control audits, in order to suggest improvements in the technological aspect of the project. The subjective dimensions were management practices, sociology/role of women, and occupational health and safety audits, which aimed to suggest improvements in work conditions and management practices. These audits were conducted in order to assess the present status of the washery and to recommend policy changes in line with the Australian policy related to development aid assistance.

The project design document related to 'women in development' (WID) and 'community participation' provided the general guidelines for this policy. The WID policy has a socially desirable component of promoting equal representation of women and equal opportunity for women in any project funded under development aid. It also covered welfare and social benefits like maternity leave and day care facilities to be made available to employed women at their workplace.

The social policy related to community participation and actively promoted better work conditions at the workplace through occupational health and safety aspects, and opportunities for human resource development through staff training and development, as an integral part of the development aid project proposal. The audits were thus required to note the WID dimensions of the project at the feasibility stage so that it formed an integral part of the project document. It also had to recommend strategies for the promotion of equal opportunities and development avenues for women.

All the 'official' documents of the audit were perceived by the washery's general manager as attempts by the Australian project manager to undermine his authority in the washery. The alternate narrative he could draw on to challenge this official version of the washery is thus of interest here.

Local Narratives

But before we proceed further, let us examine why people tell stories and why these stories are important. First, stories are a way of constructing a reality that is biased in their favour, as against the 'official' version that is published in reports, in this case, the Aide Memoir. The work of the stories here is to create and maintain an often localized discourse in the context of which the other parts of the struggle proceed. The argument here is that these stories constitute part of the discursive strategy which is a crucial component of the process of re-negotiation (Fortmann, 1994), or for legitimizing their claims to the understanding of the local reality. In this case, it was a strategy used by the Indian washery's general manager to put forth the legitimacy of his version over the official version of the Aide Memoir.

Second, local stories/narratives are important because these are oral manifestations of a local discourse seeking to define and claim 'local' knowledge. They serve to bolster people's confidence in their own claims. The local narratives are a form of legitimizing their claims. By repeating the stories that they tell each other and others, they are re-asserting their version of the reality, as against the official version. In this case, the 'official' version was documented in the Aide Memoir (AIDAB, 1992c), which highlighted the local staff's incompetence and technological inefficiency. The local narratives articulate a reality which is different from the official version of the story. After all, there are multiple versions and interpretations of a reality depending on who is making the interpretation. In the present case, these local narratives were important because they were used by the project leader of the host country to undermine the claims of the 'official' document presented by the donor country team leader. This represents a definite political strategy to achieve what the host team leader perceived as a threat to his power and authority, and subsequently, the status quo.

The problem that the narratives by social actors could be listener-specific is recognized here. The status of the researcher as an 'outsider', which may cause certain narratives to dominate, exists, and is recognized as such, but is beyond the scope of this book.

Since the three audits, namely, the sociology/role of women, environment, and occupational health and safety audits, covered the subjective dimension related to the perception of the local actors about their social reality, it would be interesting to know how the local actors perceived themselves. These local narratives of the women employed in the washery and living in the colonies, the officers and the semi-skilled and skilled labourers, are important. These were collected in the course of interviews by me during the fieldwork.

There were a total of about 600 wives and daughters of the employees, living in the colonies of the coal washery, and some were employed by it, as stated earlier. The dominant narrative of all the women was that of good housekeeping. They were interested in self-supporting economic activities at home in order to 'make some money of their own'. The wife of a fitter said, 'I like staying at home with my husband here (as against in a joint family in a village)'. Most of the women were semi-literate or illiterate with agricultural work as their only work experience. They visualized mobility in the form of not having to 'go out' to work as agricultural work is considered to be a drudgery in these parts. One woman said: 'I spend all my time taking care of my house and children, so I have no spare time to work outside'.

No woman wanted to work willingly in the washery, as it was perceived to be a dark, dirty and unhealthy workplace, and essentially a male domain. Even the officers' wives could not think of working in an office job there. Out of the 60 women interviewed, only two, one of whom was the wife of a welfare officer and another the wife of a fitter, were willing to work out of home. The latter said, 'I would like to learn typing and work away from home'. Twenty-seven of the 60 women interviewed wanted small capital to set up knitting and sewing machines at home. One said, 'Our daughters cannot be sent to the schools in a school bus here because the "(social) environment" here is so bad. But we would like to get some training for them and us, in sewing, knitting and cooking, which will benefit us'.

Of the women employed as *Kamin*s, only four were willing to speak out openly and revealed that they had aspirations for better work conditions. One said, 'I would like to work in an office like a peon'. Her friend said, 'I want a uniform, a washing allowance, a peon's designation and safety equipment'. An older woman said, 'All I want is that my son be given a job here'. The frustration of their work situation was stated by one who said, 'We are all stuck here, no one is moving up the category (unlike men). We continue to work here with the hope that our sons will get our jobs after us'.

As against this, the Aide Memoir, drawing from the experience of a lignite project in Thailand, also funded by the AIDAB, recommended the creation of new technical and 'office' jobs for women in computers, accounting and laboratories ('in Australia we have women working inside mines and they even drive dump trucks') with avenues for upward mobility and development. This recommendation could be a completely utopian idea in the present social and cultural reality of the washery's setting.

The narratives of the officers about their work and responsibilities are equally enlightening. They perceived themselves as responsible individuals pitted against bad technology. The goal of their existence was to keep the washery productive (and themselves safe from the mafia) in spite of poor conditions of equipment and machines. One officer said, 'My responsibility is running the plant, to somehow manage to keep it running is important'. They all perceived their jobs as primarily supervisory and not as 'hands on' management. The senior engineer described his work as: 'I collect reports from the plant related to failure/maintenance, solve difficulties and leave the plant only after it starts running'. The executive engineer described his job as: 'I inspect failure (in machines), identify the person for that work and ensure the supply for work'. The second executive engineer said, 'I see log books and identify problems, and give jobs to the foremen in operations and maintenance'. A superintendent engineer described his job as: 'I examine what is happening, identify what we should do, meet with the project officer, discuss with people and instruct them regarding the starting and running of the plant'.

Even the SWOT (strengths, weaknesses, opportunities and threats perceived by the group) analysis, conducted by the psychologist for this project, captures these narratives of the local knowledge and understanding of the reality as perceived by the washery's officials. The SWOT analysis is a technique developed by psychologists to understand the emergent group knowledge of their local reality in different settings including organizational settings. The SWOT analysis, involving four groups of officers, indicated the following facts. The strengths of the management perceived by these officers were the holding of open discussions about the problem, and a culture of co-operation in the organization. Manpower and resources were also seen as strengths. Some of the other strengths were the availability of 100 per cent residential accommodation and clearly stated job descriptions.

Limited power and centralization of power, lack of training and dedication, and the absence of motivation were seen as weakness within the culture. The shortage of spare parts and long lead time were seen as the technical weaknesses.

Opportunities in the form of future planning and developments were identified at the organizational level. Learning opportunities and support by seniors, career growth and job security, were seen as opportunities within the organization and the system.

The threats perceived by all officers were the existence of the mafia at the management level, union rivalry and the potential for victimization at the organizational level.

The solution to the present crisis was perceived by the officers as a technical one, according to which all the old equipment should be replaced, the quality and quantity of coal should be improved, lead time for spares should be reduced, and responsibility for the functioning of the plant should be fixed, clearly stated and manageable. Positive reinforcement for good performance should also be rewarded explicitly (AIDAB, 1992c).

The recommendations of the audit, however, projected the management practices as being inefficient and incompetent. The management functions and sociological audit showed that the maintenance department had a very large staff of executive engineers and other workers, but the workshop facilities were rudimentary or non-existent. The tools and spares available were extremely limited. The lead time for vital components was as long as 18 months resulting in the routine stripping of bypassed equipment. The mechanical and electrical functions of the plant indicated that less than 50 per cent of the machines specified for the tasks were currently functioning. Higher powered motors had replaced the design specification to keep the machines working (AIDAB, 1992c).

The health and occupational safety audit listed a large number of significant hazards due to broken stairwells, missing safety rails, unguarded moving equipment, exposed electrical contacts, and the absence of trip wires that start warning alarms or any functioning emergency stop system on conveyers (AIDAB, 1992c).

This perception of the working conditions happened to match the perception of the non-officer cadre of the washery project. A 'helper' working there said, 'The workplace is dirty and unsafe. There are no toilets and no cleanliness'. Another said, 'The work is permanent, the job is secure and wages are higher here'. A third helper suggested improvements such as, 'They should take better safety care, improve risky spots, stop coal spillage. The plant is dirty, dusty, dark with scrap (metal) lying about, there is no safety'. But in general, very few were willing to speak about the work conditions and the management but the words of a *mazdoor* sum up the general sentiments. He said, 'The workplace is dirty and unsafe but what can I say, I will be as they keep me'.

The environmental audit also stated that the ambient air and water quality indicated the total suspended particulate matter (SPM) and total dissolved solids (TDS) to be significantly above the stipulated limits. The SPM also contains high volumes of respirable dust particles. The TDS has a high volume of coal fines, and the biological oxygen demand (BOD) and chemical oxygen demand (COD) levels far exceed the standards. The noise levels in workshops and washery are also far above the limits (AIDAB, 1992c).

The environmental audit, which is apparently representative of an objective reality of the physical environment, at the end recommended measures that have a significant social implication, as is stated in the recommendations given below.

The operations audit included sampling of raw coal supplied to the washery, which was required for working out the details of design in the future. The maintenance management and electrical systems audit involved a complete assessment of all electrical and mechanical systems. It was found that the ROM coal available to the plant contains a high proportion of oversized lumps which create major problems and increase cost in the delivery, storage and reclaim systems. The breaking, crushing and conveying systems are poorly maintained. This results in major spillage, access, safety and energy consumption problems. This leads to inadequate liberation and inconsistent feeding of the coal separation systems. The separation plant is extremely congested and poorly designed. None of the measurement and control units are in operation. Less than half the equipment originally designed in the plant is in current operation. Most of the pipes and chutes are bypassed or put to use where they were originally not intended (AIDAB, 1992c).

Recommendations

AIDAB proposed that the preparation plant be constructed to accept 700 tonnes/hour of ROM coal and operate for a minimum of 6,000 hours/year, equivalent of 20 hours per day. It was proposed that the ROM coal be accepted from all mines, broken to 125 mm and transported by conveyor to Moonidih, and that new machines be installed at the crushing and pretreatment stage. A high proportion of superfluous and inaccessible equipment should be removed and the building should be opened to light and air.

Coarse clean coal, middling, fines refuse and dense media refuse should be recovered and transported by conveyors to the captive power plant. All solid rock waste should be crushed and used for landfills. All the water-based effluent, including total suspended solids, should be brought to the Pollution Control Board (PCB) standards and then released.

It was also recommended that a major series of training programmes be initiated at all levels to make the functioning of the new machines transparent and efficient. This was perceived to be difficult due to the low levels of formal education prevalent. Maintenance and training facilities should be established on a permanent basis. Women should be especially targeted for training programmes so that they get more opportunities for advancement.

All environmental regulations should be complied with. Thus, effective solid and liquid waste management would ensure that nothing escapes the plant boundaries. Since the implementation of the project would remove sources of profit for the local contractors, an effective and reliable security force would be required to ensure that the programme proceeds unhindered (AIDAB, 1992c). As stated earlier, the recommendations have a definite political and social agenda. It is recognized that there is a threat to the washery personnel, if these recommendations are implemented.

The Contestation

The recommendations of Australian project manager became an issue of contestation. Not only was the audit projecting the Indian management in bad light, it was endorsing the views held by the labourers. The recommended transparency and accountability in management practices could be interpreted as a revolutionary agenda. The management would be accountable to the workers instead of the workers being accountable to the officers. Installing of security systems to counter the backlash from the coal mafia, that the protection of the coal would generate, was something that could not be stated openly but was feared by all. The social and gender-related recommendations were seen as being utopian.

The Outcome

The results of the washery audit were presented by the Australian consultants before the Indian government officials including the BCCL officials. The chairman of the BCCL contested and debated each and every statement in the audit except for the statements relating to operations, maintenance and electrical system status. These in summary stated that 'all the old equipment should be replaced, the coal quality and quantity be improved, and the lead time for spares be reduced'.

All other recommendations pertaining to environmental management, the training needs of the plant personnel, management functioning, status of women, and the health and safety aspects of the audit, were aggressively disputed by the BCCL officials. The BCCL chairman was able to draw on the local narratives to de-legitimize the claims to these components, made by the official report of the washery audit. He was able to effectively convince at least his own seniors that the recommendations of the audit relating to these components were either utopian or impractical. He was thus successfully able to use a discursive strategy to re-negotiate the terms of the TT according to the dominant local discourse among the officers in the washery. This local discourse about the solution to the present crisis was perceived by the officers as a technical solution, that is, that all the old equipment be replaced, the coal quality and quantity improved, and the lead time for spares be reduced.

The net result was that the aid package was reduced to two years. This was the time required for installation of new equipment and machines in the washery. This was accepted in principle by the Australian government and Government of India. Since then, the project has been shelved.

Conclusion

So why is studying a failure important? It helps us to re-examine the assumption on which the development aid-related TT is based. The assumption of the TT is that the development aid project is apolitical in nature, an assumption that is seriously challenged here. Second, the belief that the donor country controls the project is questionable. The only choice it has is not to fund that particular project, but if it has decided to fund it, there is very little the donor can do without the co-operation of the host country agencies and social actors. The power balance is skewed and contrary to the belief of the managers of the project from the donor country, it is skewed, in favour of the host country (Ferguson, 1990), as in the present case. All technology transfer projects have a political, and social dimension that needs to be acknowledged. The insensitivity of the project manager to these political, social and environmental realities in the host country, and to take the MOU at its written word, would lead to the failure of the venture.

In the context of the critical theory, this consciousness was created by the technology transfer rhetoric. The promoters of the project adopted the dominant paradigm of growth, development and environmental efficiency. The crisis in the disruption of the status quo of the existing social order was severe enough for the public sector bureaucracy to be life threatening. This pushed them into reconstructing their own interpretation of the reality that would allow for the status quo at the social level to be maintained and perpetuated, this being a pre-condition for their survival. They used the local rhetoric to tilt the scales in their favour, a successful strategy to get the technology without upsetting the delicate balance or stalling the project altogether and, which helped maintain the status quo.

Eight

Limits to Pollution Abatement

The typical rhetoric of the people living in the neighbourhood areas, especially if the industrial area is carved out of a previously agricultural economy, is the claim that the pollution of air, water and land adversely affects agriculture and other related occupations. The popular assumption is that the environmental regulators are responsible for it because they are corrupt and that a 'proper and strict' implementation of the existing environmental legislation can lead to the mitigation of adverse environmental impacts.

The following case study conducted in 1998–99, indicates that 'Pollution Under Control (PUC)' is interpreted in common sense understanding as zero pollution. So any visible sign of pollutants is seen as a violation of the law. The truth is that pollution under control implies 'pollution within the stipulated standards'. This is a sanction to release pollutants in the environment within stipulated limits for the 'load of pollutants' considered as 'safe' for human and animal consumption. The event that triggered the investigation was a public interest litigation (PIL) lodged by the local NGOs from the district of Davangiri in Karnataka state.

The Event

In September 1998, there was a second major fish kill, the first one being in the Tungabhadra river basin in 1994. Overnight a lot of dead fish were found floating in the river basin and they continued to appear over one week's time. This created a major public outcry that was reported in the local and national papers, and local media. Finally, the Environment Minister of the state ordered an investigation into this incident and the local fisheries department had to carry out a detailed investigation into the cause of the 'fish kill'. The outcomes of the investigation were inconclusive. Simultaneously, a PIL was filed in 1998 against the industry by the local NGOs and the Kanataka High Court ordered the Karnataka Pollution Control Board (KPCB) to investigate into the allegations. Rallying around this obvious visible pollution load was the environmental social protest movement organized by the Tungabhadra Parisara Samiti (TPS), consisting of the affected people living downstream of the Tungabhadra river in the Harihar and Samaj Parivartana Samudaya (SPS) of Dharwad, against industries in the Harihar *taluka*. It is a social movement that is unique in several ways. It combines the issue of infringement of customary rights that threaten the survival of the fisherfolk, sheep grazers and issues linked with improving the quality of life of the people living in the villages along the Tungabhadra river in Harihar *taluka*.

The social groups that support this movement are mainly from the middle and upper middle, agrarian cultivator class. Typically, the families of the landowning classes have moved to the urban areas and the agricultural fields are managed by the landowner by employing agricultural labour. Therefore, not surprisingly, the leadership for the movement comes from the urban centres. The means of protest used by the movement are court litigation and sustained media coverage, including the local, state and national level media. The movement is over 25 years old and appears to be strongly supported by the agricultural lobby and has considerable clout in the state. This has led to a situation of social ferment and the community at this stage appears to have gained an upper hand over the industry. Through the protest movement, they have systematically targeted the industry in general, and in particular, Harihar Polyfibres of the Aditya Birla Group of Industries that produces viscose staple fibre from wood pulp. The Grasim Group, with factories located in three towns across India, produces 90 per cent of the total viscose fibre needed in India and a majority of it is exported. Since its inception in 1972 at Davangiri in Harihar, over the last three decades,[1] the industry has been targeted by the NGOs through various means of protest including public interest litigation. This study was carried out on behalf of the KPCB to investigate into the allegation of the public interest litigation (India Development Service et al., 1998).

---

[1] http://in.biz.yahoo.com/p/g/gras.bo.html.

Locale of Study

Harihar *taluka* is located 15 km from the now district headquarters of Davangiri district. It is situated at the centre of the Karnataka state about 230 km from Bangalore, the state capital. It is well connected by train and road to the state capital. Ninety per cent of its land is irrigated. The dominant caste group are the Lingayats, while some of the other groups are the Kurumbas, Naikas, Muslims, Adi Karnatakas, Adi Dravidas, Lambadis, and Raj-Gonds, a migrant tribal group (*Gazetteer of Bombay Presidency*, 1883) now settled in the *taluka* through government efforts. Lift irrigation and dam projects are the main sources of irrigation. Being irrigated, the lands are very rich and fertile, and at least two crops a year are grown on them. Thus, a landholder in this region is economically quite well off and therefore fairly literate. The main occupation of the Lingayat community is agriculture and trade. They own lands and shops in the towns. Kurumbas, a nomadic tribe, are now settled in the *taluka* and are involved in sheep and goat herding activity. They move from farm to farm to graze their sheep and goats on the paddy fields after the harvest. At other times, they graze them on common village lands and hill slopes. The Gangamatas and Naikas constitute the fishing community. They use fish traps and fishing nets to catch fish. Their womenfolk locally market the fish. Fish is sold at about Rs 25 a kilo and the average fish catch during a good season is about 35 to 40 kg per day. This volume makes fishing a viable occupation.[2]

Agriculture is the main occupation for most people in this region. The main crop is paddy. The other commercial crops grown in this area include sunflower, sugarcane and areca-nuts. There is shift away from agriculture and towards horticulture crops, especially areca-nut, in the district as whole. In the drier regions, the farmers are switching over to more remunerative crops like sunflower and cotton seeds and moving away from maize. There is a change in the cropping pattern where up to 30 per cent of the land under maize is now being converted from maize cultivation to cotton seeds and sunflower cultivation. This is because the maize price is not able to keep up with the high cost of irrigation in the Davangiri Koppal belt (*Indian Express*, 1998). The reasons cited for this are labour shortage and the spiralling prices of areca-nut. The industries in the region are mainly agro based.

---

[2]Personal interview with the Assistant Director of Inland Fisheries, December 1999.

Davangiri, a district town 15 km from Harihar, was historically known as the Manchester of Karnataka, and was famous for its textiles, and there were many cotton mills. Almost all these mills have now closed down allegedly due to labour trouble. Davangiri as a major textile town declined in the 1970s. There are various agro-based industries in the region such as vegetable oil extracting factories, rice mills, sugar mills, local dairy and brick making. All these industries thrive on paddy, its husk and stalk. Oil is extracted from the husk, it is burnt in the brick making and the stalk is used for stall feeding of cattle.[3] The urban industrial town has since developed into a major service centre and houses major educational and medical institutions.

There is rich history of co-operative movement in this region and the Harihar *taluka* alone boasts of 116 different co-operative societies. The first one was set up in 1944.

Table 8.1
The Nature of Co-operative Societies

No. of societies	Nature of society
28	Primary agricultural credit societies
38	Milk producers co-operative society
1	PICAD (Primary Credit Agriculture and Rural Development Bank)
1	Marketing society for rice mills
1	Urban bank
11	Non-agricultural credit society
17	Consumer co-operative society
2	Women's co-operative society
7	Sugar, fishermen, fruit growers, etc.

Source: 'Co-operative Societies in Harihar Taluka', 1999.

These societies have prospered and some even have a record of recovering up to 91 per cent of their credits. One co-operative credit society, the Vyavasai Sahakar Sangh Bank (VSSB) has developed into a full-fledged bank. Lift irrigation is claimed to be the major reason for the success of these co-operatives. Thus people have a history and capability of rallying around a common cause, organizing and sustaining a social movement.

---

[3] Personal interview with the Assistant Commissioner, Davangiri, December 1999.

Recently, the trend in the development of the district has started changing. It is now developing as a major educational and healthcare centre. There is an engineering, a medical and a veterinary college in the town. There are three major hospitals including a TB Hospital in Davangiri and there are 25 private practitioners and six nursing homes in Harihar town.[4] Lingayats, the dominant caste group, are agriculturists and traders. Davangiri is a major trading centre for agricultural products, cement and iron. After Shimoga, it is a major marketplace for areca-nuts.

Major Players

One former municipal councillor[5] believes that growth of Harihar town is a consequence of the development of two major industries. Before these industries came into existence, Harihar was a village in the shadow of Davangiri. Industries have brought higher levels of incomes, business, prosperity and urbanization of Harihar. The two major industries are Mysore Kirloskar and Harihar Polyfibres. While Mysore Kirloskar was established in 1941 and has brought economic prosperity and ancillary industries to the region, Harihar Polyfibres, which was established in 1972, had a very hostile reception from its very conception. The genesis of Mysore Kirloskar lay in the freedom struggle. They started producing lathes in the region to support the struggle for *swadeshi*. Since then, the management has promoted local employment and more than 50 per cent of the employees including the management cadre are local people from Harihar and the nearby areas. They believe in employee empowerment through education. They run three schools with about 2,300 students each. Of the 200 students who graduate every year, at least 20 go abroad after finishing their education. They have recently set up the Kirloskar Institute of Advanced Studies, which even has a website. The industry does not consume much water and at the end, the waste water generated is re-used in their gardens.[6]

---

[4]Personal interview with the *Tehsildar*, Harihar, December 1999.
[5]Personal interview, December 1999.
[6]Personal interview with the Industry Manager of Mysore Kirloskar, December 1999.

Although the polyfibre industry came into the region through the special efforts made by Mr Nijalingappa (ex-chief minister of Karnataka) and land, water and raw material, were made available at subsidized rates, it was always perceived with hostility by the local agricultural lobby. The polyfibre yarn produced by it, is in direct competition with the cotton industries. The tension began when the government decided to give an area of 400 hectares of village forest lands on a long-term lease to Harihar Polyfibre in order to help it create a captive eucalyptus plantation for the factory. The local people actively resisted this conversion of the commons and filed a PIL and the High Court granted a stay on the lease, in the early 1970s. Till recently, the forest department sold eucalyptus at Rs 50 a tonne. Since then, the price has been revised but it is still considerably lower than the market price.

Risk Perception by People, Industry and the KPCB

The pulp industry is extremely water-intensive and draws water from upstream of the Tungabhadra river, and lets out pollutants downstream that colour the river water even when the pollution level may be under control and meeting the stipulated standards. The by-product of the rayon pulp is waste liquor, which is very dark brown in colour due to its high biodegradable organic matter. This waste has a high PH value and cannot be discharged in the water body without treatment. Before it is discharged into the water body, it requires traditional treatment in anaerobic and aerobic lagoons, to treat the liquor rich in biodegradable matters. In 1985, research was initiated to set up a plant using state-of-the-art technology through the 'bio-methanation process'. The plant was set up in 1995 and is operating at 70 per cent efficiency. It produces methane as a by-product which can be used as a 'clean' fuel. The state-of-the-art technology to treat the waste liquor reduces the brightness of the liquor by 0.5 per cent and has received a special mention in the conference organized by UNDP under the Global Environmental Facility (Chaturvedi and Manjunath, 2004).

Continued pressure by the civil society has put the industry on the defensive and forced it to take an extreme position. It generates a high level of pollution and is a water-intensive industry and cannot help discharging the waste water in the river, for which it has permission from the state. Officially, the pollution control agency admits to pollution within permissible limits, by proposing a standard for discharging the water in the river within stipulated limits recommended by the pollution standards for such pollutants. People perceive this stand of the KPCB and the visible pollution in the form of coffee brown waters in the river as visible signs of collusion between the industry and the state agency, and continue to protest against it.

Genesis of the Protest Movement

A number of environmental NGOs currently claim to be active in the area. India Development Service (IDS) has been working in the Ranibennur *taluka* of Dharwad district since 1979, in a cluster of 21 villages, of which 11 are situated on the left bank of the river Tungabhadra. Two other NGOs called Transnational Centre for Non-violent Social Change (TNC) and Samaj Parivarthana Samudaya (SPS) are both from Dharwad and have published reports against the industrial pollution in this region. The inter-linkage between these is not very clear, though they seem to co-operate with each other.

There is a history of hostility against the polyfibre industry in that area and the local residents were organized to start protest movement by a local NGO, which dates back to over 20 years. The industry was given land to set up the factory by the state at subsidized rates. Then the raw material needed for the rayon fibre manufacturing was provided by the state, which created a captive plantation forest by consolidating and converting various village forests into eucalyptus plantations. The NGOs claimed that as these were village forests and therefore common lands on which the village poor depend for their subsistence needs, for fuel wood, fodder and small timber, the captive eucalyptus plantations resulted in the infringement of the customary rights of local people over these lands. According to the NGOs, the state appeared to be supporting the national interest of regional, economic and industrial development, at the cost of local subsistence rights of the communities (India Development Service et al., 1998).

Since it was not successful in protecting the common lands from a takeover by the state government, the movement shifted its focus to the adverse impacts of industrial pollution on the physical environment, fauna and flora, and people residing in the villages downstream of the industry. At that time, no environmental legislation was in place. But the leadership persisted in organizing and educating the local communities on the potentially adverse impacts of industrial pollution. The important activities that were undertaken towards this end are listed here:

1. An environmental education camp was organized in January 1984.
2. A skin disease detection and treatment camp was organized in two villages, one downstream, on 5 March 1985 and another upstream on 21 July 1985.
3. In July 1985, IDS conducted a 'survey' of abortion among sheep.
4. On 2 October 1986, SPS published its first report on 'Pollution and its effects caused by industries in Tungabahdra river at Kumarapatnam, Ranibennur *taluka*, Dharwad district, Karnataka state' (Kongovi and Markande, 1986).

The chronology of events indicates that the education camp and contact with the people may have motivated the NGOs to take on the other activities in order to substantiate the claims made by the people of the industrial pollution impacts. The camp and the 'survey' both quote absolute numbers of incidents at one time and no statistical analysis of longitudinal data is presented to substantiate the claim.

By 1986, the protest movement spearheaded by the NGO, had mobilized the local people, networked with experts and other likeminded NGOs, and had managed to get a lot of national level media attention. The discourse of environmental impacts of the Tungabhadra river water pollution is pegged on two main issues, that is, health impacts on humans and animals. The incidence of skin disease called 'superficial folliculitis' resulted in inflammation of hair follicles among fishermen and in fish kills in February 1985 and in the months of March and June in 1986. There has been no major fish kill since March 1994, though a small fish kill was reported on 11 June 1998.[7]

---

[7]Personal interview with the Assistant Director of Fisheries, Davangiri, December 1999.

Talking Claims

The social protest movement in this region is organized around two moral issues by a local NGO claiming to represent the local population. The first is the subsistence claims of the marginal groups, in this case, the claims of the fishermen to the fish, and of the grazers to graze their sheep and goats. The second claim concerns 'a quality of life issue'. The NGO (Parisar Sanwardhini, n.d.) claimed that the following environmental impacts could be directly attributed to the industry discharge:

1. Recurrent and major fish kill till 1994 (the one occurring in September 1994 led to a fisheries department investigation),
2. Major health impact on the cattle and goats living downstream of the industry, causing spontaneous abortions among them, and
3. Morbidity consequences for people living in downstream villages.

People have their own interpretations of social reality. They seek to make their versions credible through repetitive iteration, which helps in two ways: they begin to believe in their own stories, and to use these against the official version as legitimate counter-claims.

One man from the village said, 'The *Purana*s state that one should bathe in the Ganga and drink the waters of Tunga (Tungabhadra) as the river has the best tasting water in India. With this industry even the animals cannot drink this water now'. An agriculturist downstream of river stated, 'The coloured water that the factory lets out makes our paddy crops turn brown and lose their aroma'. A woman washing clothes in the river stated, 'We have stopped using white clothes. They lose colour within days of washing and bathing in the river'. A local villager stated, 'We used to fish in the river then, and we would get enough fish to consume and even take some to the market, now the fish we get is so small and tasteless that there is no point in fishing'. A resident from a downstream village complained that in summer, when the water in the river is less, the colour of the river becomes dark brown and it smells very bad, making it impossible for the people to use these waters when they need them the most.

Scientific Validity

Claims about environmental impacts by the NGOs are based on the alleged violation of pollution standards by the industry in that area, by discharging effluents into the Tungabhadra river. Pollution levels are claimed to be directly responsible for fish kills, abortions and deaths among animals, and increased morbidity among human population, including skin irritation and itching due to bathing in the river water. At this stage, the long-term impact of the low levels of pollution is a 'grey area' in scientific knowledge as it is not possible to conclusively prove that prolonged exposure to permitted levels of pollution causes disease, nor is it possible to prove the direct health impacts of pollutants on humans and animals. At best, one can only talk of possible explanation. The best epidemiological studies, even in the U.S., are able to prove that only a few chemicals like benzene have proven carcinogenic impacts on humans. Both the claims of violation of standards and direct health impacts on fish, animals and humans cannot be proved beyond reasonable doubt in a court of law.

None of the claims made by the NGOs are substantiated through in-depth scientific and longitudinal studies. Although some information collected through spot studies across two or more villages is mentioned above, it indicates a variation between upstream and downstream residents without stating if these variations were statistically significant (Kongovi and Markande, 1986).

Political leaders believe that if the factory puts the necessary chemicals in the water to clean it up, pollution is not a major threat to the people's health. On the other hand, industry provides decent wages to even labourers. Local scientific professionals like the Deputy Commissioner, Fisheries, and local medical and veterinary doctors, have never directly attributed the incidence of morbidity and mortality in fish, humans and animals exclusively to the discharge from the industry. They all claim that there could be other reasons and factors that may be causing the diseases. For example, the local medical practitioner reported that there was an increase in the upper respiratory tract infections in the past year or two and that the overall rate of these infections is higher than in Davangiri according to her experience but she hastened to add that it was difficult to isolate a single cause for these observations. The only fact beyond reasonable doubt was that people complain of itching and skin irritation when they wade through the water during the summer months.

In spite of the grey area in the claims made by the people, the industry has responded favourably to the social protest. Over the past few years, the industry is doing all it can to achieve the stipulated pollution control standards and is being closely monitored by the Davangiri pollution control board. In addition, it has set up a primary health centre with a medical practitioner, which provides treatment and medicines to people from the downstream villages free of cost. A private veterinary doctor is also available to the people if needed. The industry has constructed bore wells for the downstream towns and a village community hall in one of the villages. When Nadiarhalli village was said to have suffered the worst pollution, they even offered to relocate the village settlement. The social movement claims this as a major victory for itself and interprets all these actions as proof that the industry has been forced on the defensive.

Methodology

In order to validate the claims made by the movement, a systematic survey was conducted in the villages along the river bed. The focus of the survey was on the perceptions of the community about the quality of the Tungabhadra river water and the air surrounding their villages. It was assumed that the community perceptions about the river water pollution are real to them. This, however, does not make their perceptions right nor does one have to agree with them. But it is important to document the views of the community. Understanding the issue is the first step towards the implementation of any strategy.

The interview schedule was used as a tool to capture the social perceptions. A structured partially open-ended interview schedule was constructed for the purpose (KPCB, 2000). It was designed with the limited objective of understanding and documenting the social reality about the Tungabhadra river water pollution. The schedule is aimed at meeting the following objectives:

1. To reconstruct a socio-economic and demographic profile of the settlements both upstream and downstream of the river,
2. To document the current consumption patterns of the communities, pertaining to water, for various uses and from different sources,

3. To capture the perceived impacts of river water pollution on people, plants and animals, and to capture perceptions and attitudes related to air and river water pollution, and
4. Finally to capture the perception of people related to the industry and its pollution.

This social reality about the perception of pollution by the community is documented by using two interview schedules. Schedule I documents the general overview of reality through the interviews of significant locally residing individuals such as community leaders, local administrators, industry managers, and private medical practitioners. The information based on these schedules has already been used in the earlier part of the report. Schedule II was a partially structured interview schedule used to capture the social reality represented by individuals living in the villages along the river. The assumption is that the impacts of water pollution will be most severe for those who live along the banks of the river.

A total of eight villages including four upstream and four downstream of the industry discharge points, covering a total distance of 25 km downstream and 5 km upstream of the river, were selected. The villages located on either side of the river were selected and a 5 per cent sample of the total number of households as per the 1991 Census data was used. The households were selected randomly on the basis of the availability of the individual at the time of the interview. This method of sampling was adopted because the approach roads to the villages are mainly non-tar roads.

Findings of the Survey

A limited survey using an interview schedule was undertaken by the field staff, covering a total of 120 households of the total number of 3,501 households from nine villages, covering two *taluka*s of Harihar and Ranibennur, along the Tungabhadra river banks. The field staff were selected on the basis of their knowledge of the local language and the region; they were imparted training to conduct the interviews. A systematic sampling procedure was adopted for selecting the sample households to make them as representative of the population as possible.

Table 8.2
Sample Villages and Households along the Tungabhadra River

Name of the village	Sample/ households	Distance from discharge point
Halsabalu	7/141	5 km upstream
Kodiyal	11/994	4 km upstream
Nalwagal	7/229	1 km upstream
Guttur	34/655	1 km upstream
Nadiarhalli	15/307	2.4 km downstream
Dettur	12/224	5 km downstream
Pamenahalli	5/96	7.5 km downstream
Sarathi	19/385	10 km downstream
Airani	10/460	10 km downstream
Total	120/3,501	

Demographic profile

A total number of 240 individuals and 120 households of both sexes were covered in the survey. This included a total of 121 males, and 67 females, including 27 boys below 18 years of age and 25 girls below 18 years of age. Thus, the sex ratio in these villages is 621, which is far below the national average of 970. This is because a total of 88 households were reported to be single person households, wherein 22 females were single women and 66 males were single persons currently living in these houses. The females were between 35 to 75 years of age, with an average age of 42, and were widows or deserted women with no children and worked as labourers. The single males were between 35 and 50 years of age, with an average age of 38 years, and said that their families were in towns. It was observed that all the single persons gave their main occupation as agriculture or business. The average family size in the remaining households was five members. Only 32 households had most of their members living in the village. This indicates a very interesting profile wherein people recognize the better employment and education potential that a city or a town has to offer and therefore prefer to stay there than in a small village.

The education of the adult members was considered to decide the educational profile of the household. Except for 20 single persons, who were illiterate (and were agricultural labourers) and one family that was illiterate, everyone had had at least school education and 10 families had been educated up to the graduation level and above.

Socio-economic profile

Only 24 families owned between 1 and 9 acres of land. The average landholding is 3.1 acre of irrigated lands. In all, 73 households reported owning cattle, and the average number of cattle was 3.2 and the range was 1–7 animals. A total of 41 households reported to have sheep and goats but very few, only 18 households, had more than 10 animals and one had up to 60 animals. All the families which owned sheep and goats did not own cattle and vice versa. Thus a total of 114 families owned some animal.

Almost everyone owned a house in his name except 12 persons, some of whom were agricultural labourers. Only 20 households reported their occupation as agricultural labour. While 62 households were in business, 22 households had salaried incomes. The rest reported agriculture as their main occupation. Thus more than half the families were in business. The average household monthly income was reported to be Rs 1,892 and the range of income was reported to be Rs 1,000 to 15,000 per month, with the most frequently occurring income being Rs 900. Actual incomes were reported by the people and there could be a lot of under-reporting of the values.

This substantiates the earlier observations that the land is fertile and irrigated. A considerable number of households own animals, indicating the easy availability of fodder and/or pastures. Similarly, the principal occupation of more than half of the other households is reported to be business. This is also consistent with the earlier observation that Harihar and Davangiri are major commercial markets for agricultural products. Also, a large number of families prefer to stay in the nearby township because the quality of life, access to education, and employment opportunities offered by the town are better. However, they prefer to maintain and manage their ancestral homes and lands in their villages.

Perception of water

The aim of the survey was to gauge the perception about the water and air in the surrounding areas, which is why questions pertaining to the source and quality of water were asked.

Drinking water

The main source of drinking water is dug wells and all except 13 families identified it. Only seven households had a private piped supply of water, while only six families reported river water as their source of water. There was no seasonal variation in the drinking water source. Water was not treated domestically before consumption in any household. Only the six families that used river water reported that the water was not potable, and it had a brown colour and a foul smell. Twenty-six other households complained of a salty taste in the drinking water. The rest had no complaints about the drinking water.

Water used for washing, bathing, animals and agriculture

When the persons were interviewed about the source of water used for the washing of clothes, animals, vehicles and tractors, the reported sources varied considerably. Sixty-six households used the Tungabhadra river water, 42 used well water and seven families reported piped water supply as their source for washing. Forty-six households complained about the brown colour, 13 households complained about the taste, nine households said it tasted salty and four households said that it had an irritating taste.

A total of 102 households bathed in the river water. The others used well and piped water for bathing. Of these, 52 households complained of the brown colour and two households complained that it had a taste similar to that of a dye or a chemical, and an irritating, smell, while only seven households felt that it had a salty taste. River water and well water were given to the animals for drinking and bathing. All those who had lands used the water for irrigation by lifting the water directly from the river using pumps. A few others used canal irrigation water or well water. They all observed brown colour and salty taste in the water.

Perception of pollution and human impacts

This is one area wherein the NGOs have succeeded in convincing the local people about the health impacts. Fifty-seven households believed that the river water was polluted. A majority of the households, that is, 94, believed that the water was responsible for causing illnesses among their children, and 44 households had known of someone in the village who was ill because of the river water, while 32 persons had experienced some itching which they believed was caused by river water after they bathed in it during summers. Fourteen persons had personally sought treatment for it. The treatment was free.

Table 8.3
Perception about Impacts of Pollution

Perceptions	Households
Believe that water is polluted	57
Believe it to be harmful to children	94
Believe that others in the villages are affected	44
Personally experienced itching	32
Treatment sought	14
Cost of treatment	nil/free

Impact on plants and animals

A total of 105 out of 120 families did not believe that the water caused disease to animals. Among those who owned animals, six households believed that it causes diseases and abortions in animals, and that it prevented their proper growth and caused death. Fourteen persons attributed animal suffering in their community to the water they drink. Only seven persons said they had experienced their own animals falling ill and dying, which they attributed to river water. Only four households among those who owned lands believed that the plants were affected by the water, but only one person reported that the yields were low. No other household could specify the specific impact on plants.

Perception about industry

Only one out of 120 households believed that the shutting down of the industry was a solution to the pollution problem in the area. Of these, 114 households believed that a certain level of pollution has to be tolerated if there are industries, while six households did not believe this, and felt that there could be industry without pollution. Ninety-six households felt that industries are necessary for employment and the economic growth of the region. Only 45 households felt that air pollution caused health problems. Finally, these same 45 households were fairly knowledgeable about pollution and its abatement. They suggested that proper treatment of waste water at the effluent treatment plant for the industry and sewage treatment plant for the village sewage would reduce the pollution of the river. They blamed both the industry and the municipality for the present pollution, but how long a sustained political pressure of this kind can be maintained is anybody's guess. The bottom line is that the local community does not want the industry to shut down permanently.

Thus, to conclude, the survey confirms the preliminary observations of the villages being well organized, mobilized and knowledgeable about the water pollution problems in the Tungabhadra river as suggested by the local NGO. Their perception of the river water pollution and its impacts on human beings, animals and plants reflects this.

Future of the Movement

There has been a decline in the nature of local industry over the last few years. Although the rice mills and the brick making factories continue to operate, the cotton mills in Davangiri have shut down. Davangiri appears to be developing as a major educational centre and a marketplace for areca-nuts. Thus the whole region seems to be undergoing a social change in its occupational profile and economic development. The bottom line is that no one wants the industry to shut down but this is not a licence to pollute for the industry. It is also a signal to the NGOs that they can push their anti-pollution movement only so far and no further.

Conclusion

The community at this stage appears to have gained an upper hand over the industry in its battle against pollution. It is major victory for the movement at this stage. But how long a sustained political pressure of this kind can be maintained is anybody's guess. Sooner or later, the leaders of the movement will have to consolidate their gains through negotiations with the industry. Since the local community does not want the industry to shut down permanently, there are signs that the movement may not be able to sustain the pressure. Both the claims of violation of standards and direct health impacts on fish, animals and humans cannot be proved beyond reasonable doubt in a court. It is thus a good time for Pollution Control Board (PCB) to play the role of a mediator and bring about a negotiated settlement, otherwise, in the long run, it may adversely affect the economic development of the region. Social movements are good because they act as watchdogs over the pollution by industry and industry is good because it manages to bring development to the people. Thus both have an important role to play in the regional development. But a balance is essential or there will be only losers on both sides.

To summarize, within the theoretical framework, the predominantly irrigated agrarian community in the neighbourhood of a state-supported industrial area is an interesting site. The impetus for locating the industrial area came from national-level leaders and the techno-economic development resulted in visible pollution even though it was under control. The resultant popular perception could be used effectively to rally the original inhabitants who did not benefit from the industries through employment or otherwise. This resulted in an organized social protest movement that could continue to put pressure on the industry and force the PCB to monitor the industry closely. But all these efforts could not ensure subsistence-linked livelihood security for the fishing community in spite of sincere efforts by the NGOs and their attempts, as these claims were not considred to be 'valid' in terms of the scientific criteria.

Nine

Do Ideologies Matter in Urban Transport Projects?

Introduction

The assumption that the planned and time-bound implementation of a policy leads to desired outcomes is questionable even though that is the only choice a policy maker may have. One very important insight of this case study of the Mumbai (Bombay) Urban Transportation Project (MUTP, 1997) presented here is that the favourable outcome could not have been predicted. But the success of resettlement is increased if the process is carried out by involving all the stakeholders, albeit within the broad framework of policy. The stumbling block for the implementation of the urban transportation project was the clearance of railway tracks from encroachment by slums. The rehabilitation and resettlement of these slums was a major issue. A number of different social groups were involved in the project, each having a stake in a specific outcome. The various social groups involved in the project were the slum dwellers along the track, the Mumbai Metropolitan Regional Development Authority (MMRDA) or the authority responsible for implementing the rehabilitation action plan as part of the project, the World Bank, the train commuters (whose interest was represented by an NGO called Citizens for Just Society), the railway authority and the elected representatives of various political parties, including the leaders of the ruling party of the state government, and the state institutions like the judiciary, the police and the GMMC (Greater Mumbai Municipal Corporation). Each of these groups had their loosely or firmly defined ideology on the basis of which they chose a path of action. This led to a series of contestations and opportunistic decision-making, leading to a fairly successful resettlement of the PAPs.

By implication, the best way to avoid marginalizing the social groups disadvantaged by a development project coming into an area is to suggest that the resettlement and rehabilitation policy be well grounded in the specific context of social reality. Allowing a resettlement and rehabilitation policy to evolve as a result of suggestions and successful experiments, at the grassroots level is a good strategy for a comprehensive policy. Promoting transparency in entitlements and the procedures to be followed reduces the trauma of resettlement and rehabilitation for the PAPs.

Before the Project

The Mumbai (Bombay) Metropolitan Region is spread over an area of 4,350 sq km and has a population of 18 million and a population growth of 3 per cent per annum. The major population is concentrated in Brihan Mumbai, the island city with a population of 13 million in 2001. The city has seen a dramatic increase of 230 per cent in its population over the last 40 years. The city can be divided into four major catchments. These areas form the central area of Mumbai city and are bounded by five of the original seven islands. These also account for a majority of the jobs available in the city. The total number of jobs in the island city is 1.338 million and the figure is rising (Census, 1991). Members of the workforce commute to their place of work, with the average commuting time being about 45 minutes per trip. A dominant feature of passenger movement is the overwhelming dependence on the public transport system, mainly suburban railways and buses, which account for 88 per cent of the passenger trips. Therefore, improving the public transport efficiency constitutes a major thrust in the urban transport strategy for the metropolitan region. The Bombay Urban Transport Project I (BUTP I), a precursor to the Mumbai Urban Transport Project II (MUTP II), funded by the World Bank, focused on improving road transport. In order to facilitate commuter transport, the project provided a loan for the concretization of major roads in the city and its suburbs. Better roads reduce the maintenance needs and therefore ensure a more efficient and smooth flow of traffic.

The Transport Project

The Mumbai Urban Transportation Project II is the second phase of the continuing efforts to improve the transport of the metropolitan city. It is a multi-modal transport project, aimed at improving the efficiency of the existing transport system by promoting certain measures to increase speed and reduce congestion in the mass transit systems.

At the suggestion of the World Bank, a study for the development of a comprehensive transportation plan was undertaken by WS Atkins International, UK as consultants. The process began in 1996. The objective of the study was to provide a strategic planning framework within which various road and rail, public transport and traffic management schemes forwarded by various agencies could be prioritized. The MMRDA report (1994), produced by a British consultant, provided a strategic planning framework within which various railway, road, public transport and traffic management schemes forwarded by various agencies could be evaluated and prioritized. The report identified 52 projects that could be implemented during the next 5 to 10 years to rationalize the flow of traffic within the city and to improve transport efficiency (MMRDA, 1994). The Mumbai Urban Transport Project (MUTP) proposes to improve the urban transportation system in the city with its primary emphasis being on promoting mass transit systems and providing better connectivity between the north and south corridors of transportation in the city. This involves a more efficient use of public transport by developing and applying the rational principles of transport management. This involved a series of projects on grade separation and widening of road and rail corridors by taking into account population settlement trends in the city. The main thrust of the recommended policy was on improvement in railways to strengthen the mass transit systems. An environmental assessment study was commissioned by MMRDA (see MMRDA, 1997) to study the potential environmental impacts at the programmatic and sub-project levels in 1995. It was anticipated that a significant displacement of populations would take place. Therefore, a special study was commissioned with the help of three NGOs to create a baseline socio-economic profile of the PAPs for various projects. Finally, through this process, a total of 42 out of the original 52 projects related to roads and railways have been identified as priority projects within the framework, requiring an estimated investment of US$ 600 million.

Before the commissioning of the project, there was no comprehensive resettlement and rehabilitation policy for the displacement of PAPs in urban India. In the absence of such a policy for urban PAPs, the challenge before the implementing authorities, in this case the MMRDA, was to evolve a comprehensive rehabilitation action plan and implement it within a stipulated time frame for the project to be successful.

The major social environmental issues in promoting the railway improvement component of the MUTP II project is the encroachment of slum dwellers over lands owned by utilities. This involved a displacement and resettlement of 19,228 households or about 77,000 people. This would facilitate the transport of 6.2 million people using the railways. Given this social and economic justification for the project, MMRDA commissioned an Environmental Impact Assessment (EIA) of these comprehensive strategic options in 1995. An important component of the EIA was the social impact assessment of the resettlement of about 19,228 households, which had encroached on the railway tracks. The task of preparing a Rehabilitation Action Plan was given to three NGOs—Siddhi, the Slum Rehabilitation Society (SRS) and Society for Preservation and Resource Conservations (SPARC)/National Slum Dwellers' Federation (NSDF)—with each of them handling the slums on the harbour line (Mankhurd, Turbhe and Mandale), the western suburbs (Jogeshwari and Kurla) and the central suburbs (Kanjurmarg), respectively. Their primary task was to provide a baseline profile of the PAPs and their mandate was to come up with a comprehensive resettlement and rehabilitation plan acceptable to the PAPs, by 1998.

The Locale of Study

The land use in the city of Mumbai has been undergoing changes continually over the last 50 years. The city originally was a group of islands, which were mainly reclaimed to build industry and housing, including the major transport corridors as the port city of Bombay grew in size and population (Kosambi, 1986). The Greater Bombay population grew from 3 million in 1951 to 9.9 million in 1991 to 13 million in 2001. Thus, Bombay has registered an increase in population of 230 per cent during the last 40 years and of 433 per cent increase during the last 50 years.

Historically, the economic industrial development of Bombay city took place through a joining of the seven islands. These islands were joined and reclaimed by building *bunds* to prevent sea water from entering after the monsoons. Lands were initially used to cultivate paddy. As the population increased, these fields in low lying areas were taken over by industries and residential population. Roads, causeways and rail links were also created to establish communications. These transport corridors were either lands that were reclaimed from the sea or converted from agricultural use. As part of an urbanization strategy, government ownership was established over these lands which were left vacant. There are three main corridors that connect the island city with the rest of the suburban regions. All these corridors mainly run north–south and the commuter traffic is predominantly from north to south in the morning, and in the reverse direction in the evening. Once the planned road or railway infrastructure was put into place, the rest of the lands were left unused. As the population increased mainly through immigration from other rural areas, housing became a major problem. These lands, which were claimed by the government for developing the transport corridors, but were left vacant for the time being, were increasingly encroached upon by squatter settlements. These settlements tend to locate themselves near a regular colony where water supply is accessible. A settlement begins along the borders of the vacant lands and then moves towards the inner transport corridor. Thus the first settlers or the older settlement is farther away from the railway line or the operating road. As the population grows, the newer immigrants are closer to the roads or railway lines. It is important to understand this in the context of the relocation and resistance of the other inhabitants to it. There is a natural transition in the quality of housing as the slum colony grows in age. The older settlers 'develop' their dwelling units, build brick walls, get electricity and water connections nearer home, and provide services to the more 'formal colonies' in the form of domestic helpers, drivers and more recently, satellite cable service staff. Major encroachments on the railway line have occurred in the four major catchments. These areas form the central area of Mumbai city and are bounded by five of the original seven islands.

These areas are of special interest as they cause major flooding problems in Mumbai (Bapat, 1995a). Because of their vulnerability to flooding, these areas are occupied by the most marginal groups among immigrants to Mumbai. They also happen to be the transport corridors on which major encroachments have taken place, resulting in

Table 9.1
Major Catchment Areas from North to South Bombay Island City

Area in ha	Name of the region	Relocation site	Ward numbers/ catchment
487	Dadar, Mahim	Dharavi	F(N) &G(N)/C4
464	Dadar, Worli, Parel	Antophill	F(S)&G(S)/C3
504	Dadar, Ray Road, Matunga	Wadala	DE/C2
1,308	Bombay Central, Byculla	—	ABC/C1

the slowing down of transport, in general, and of local railway commuters on these routes, in particular. The houses in these areas are so close to the tracks that the inhabitants living in the house can actually easily reach out and touch a railway rake. The only exception is a site at Kanjurmarg, where the slum encroachment is not causing major obstructions on the transport line.

A total of 310,977 jobs are available in the D and E wards and a total of 452,879 jobs, in the formal sector, out of the total of 1,338,448 jobs that are available in the formal sector, in the A, B, C, D, E, F and G wards, as per the socio-economic and cultural tables in the 1981 Census.

Thus, two major points need to be made here. First, housing for the immigrants is a major issue. Immigrants first move from the boundary of the government lands towards the main corridors when they settle in Mumbai. Therefore, those closer to the tracks are more recent migrants to the city and are therefore poorer than the older migrants away from the tracks. Second, most of the people are employed in their immediate neighbourhood, which saves them commuting costs. If they own their dwelling units, they rent out part of the units or use them as commercial establishments, which become a source of supplementary income for the house owner. Both these points are relevant to the issue of rehabilitation of the PAPs considered for the MUTP II project.

Housing Issue

The Maharashtra Housing and Area Development Authority (MHADA) has been active in developing the housing needs of the people living in the Mumbai metropolitan region. It was set up as a separate authority for this purpose under the habitat funds from the

UNDP. The mandate was to build affordable housing for low, middle and high income groups of individuals living in the city. Capital assets were provided in the form of cheap long-term loans by the UNDP in the 1980s to cater to the housing needs of urban inhabitants. The categories of housing provided in Mumbai were LIG, HIG and MIG, respectively. Annual incomes were used as eligibility criteria for owning these houses. The earlier intention was to promote HIG houses with a profit margin as part of this project so that the LIG houses could be cross-subsidized. The eligibility criteria kept a majority of the people living in Mumbai and the surrounding regions out of these projects for two reasons, both linked with documentation. The groups were expected to form co-operative housing societies, which required a document such as a ration card as proof of residence. Second, a proof of income was needed to put them in one of the categories mentioned above, which is difficult to acquire for a recent migrant whose main income is from casual labour. Thus, over time only the HIG housing projects proved to be financially viable for MHADA, while the MIG and LIG housing projects proved to be financially non-viable (MEIP Project Report, 1993–94). Therefore, the dilemma before the MHADA authorities was to promote HIG projects and remain economically solvent, or to promote MIG and LIG projects and achieve social justice at the cost of financial insolvency. The MUTP II project provided an opportunity wherein the LIG projects could become viable as they would be paid for through the funding of the project. The MUTP II project funding considered resettlement and rehabilitation costs as part of the project. This is unlike most of the funding for infrastructure projects. The only exceptions are irrigation dam projects, wherein more recently the resettlement and rehabilitation component forms a part of the project costs.

Greater Good

In the meantime, a writ petition was lodged as a Public Interest Litigation (PIL) by an NGO called Citizens of Just Society in 1998, asking the court to intervene in clearing encroachments along the railway corridor. In response to the PIL, the Bombay High Court directed the Government of Maharashtra (GOM) to remove the people causing obstructions on the tracks of railway lines with or without resettlement. The GOM, on its own initiative and in response to the Bombay High Court's direction, has undertaken the resettlement of about 10,000 households to clear the 200-metre safety zone of railway tracks and to improve the operational efficiency of the local trains. The GOM proposed two options to shift the squatters, and to move them to already constructed tenements or to temporary transit houses. Subsequently, MMRDA purchased 4,000 already constructed houses from MHADA and undertook the construction of about 6,000 transit houses to shift all the squatters living within the safety zone from the railway track.

The directions of the court were to move the people within three months of the order commencing 28 February 2000. Thus, the initial displacement was done under emergency circumstances by using police force, and for the first 3,000 families, the demolition of their dwelling places was inevitable. The state then asked for an extension of three months and subsequently a further extension of three more months to complete the process of removing all persons residing along the safety zone of railway tracks.

Overall, the physical activities in the project are expected to move about 19,000 households or 77,000 persons, most of whom are squatters living dangerously close to the railway tracks to facilitate the 'right of way' of the proposed road widening corridors. During the implementation of the Mumbai Urban Transport Project (MUTP), a total of 3,935 households (20 per cent) have been relocated in 48

Table 9.2
Number of People Assigned to Temporary Tenements

S. No.	Site	Total no. of residential tenements available	Tenements distributed
1	Kanjurmarg	900	797
2	Mankhurd (S.No. 138 and 138B)	1,665	1,538
3	Turbhe-Mandale	835	809
4	Wadala (Kokari Agar)	3,600	2,981
	Total	7,000	6,125

Note: 103 from Kanjurmarg and 53 from Mankhurd site have been shifted to permanent sites. This information has been provided by MMRDA and has been validated for a few.
Source: MUTP, 2001.

multi-storeyed buildings consisting of seven to nine floors, in four different locations. In addition, 107 were also offered alternative shops to enable them to re-establish their livelihood. Another 6,125 (32 per cent) were shifted to transit houses, and will eventually be shifted to permanent houses within three years. The present status of permanent and temporary tenements and their distribution are given in Tables 9.2 and 9.3.

Table 9.3
Number of People Assigned to Permanent Tenements

S. No.	Site	Total no. of residential tenements available	Tenements distributed
1	Mankhurd	1,814	1,811
2	Wadala (Kokari Agar)	1,344	1,241
3	Antop Hill	395	395
4	Dharavi	576	530
	Total	4,129	3,977

Note: In addition to this provision is made in the form of units for shops in the Balwadi institutional and society office.
Source: MUTP, 20001.

The relocation to new housing involves several changes for the people concerned. People who were used to living in independent units now had to learn to live in multi-storeyed buildings with the urban culture, which was different from the culture they were used to. Among the advantages were access to improved infrastructure facilities, the contribution of fees for services, and the organizing in groups facilitated by local NGOs. A randomly selected sample of people were interviewed by using a partially structured interview schedule from each of the four permanent sites mentioned above. The overall perception of the people is reported in Table 9.4. As can be seen, a majority of the people believe that the amenities provided at the new site are better or at least as good as the ones they had in their original site. The disadvantage of the apartments is captured in the perception of the people. Most people perceived that the house was 'small' as they did not have much scope for increasing the living space in the small independent flats they received as compensation. This is in contrast to the living spaces they occupied in the original sites. These were mainly

Table 9.4
Infrastructure Amenities at Permanent Sites

	Worse	No change	Better
House	16	3	35
Drinking water	0	17	37
Toilet	0	0	54
Solid waste	0	1	53
Flooding	0	54	0
Electricity	1	25	28

single-storeyed rooms and they perceived that, in time, they would be able to construct an extra floor on top of these structures.

About 113 business shops were part of the site where the displacement took place. Of these, a total of 11 business owners were interviewed. All of them were licence holders. Three of the shop owners had their shops demolished and lost their goods from the shop. They feel that as compared with the old site, business in the new site here is low. The grocery shops do not share this perception but businesses providing services feel the difference. However, no major negative impacts were reported and they were all happy to have permanent sites. The relative isolation of the new settlements from the middle and high income groups is a major reason for this. Although the grocery shops located in the slums may cater exclusively to the slum dwelling residents, the services business catered to a richer clientele in the surrounding areas of the old settlement. Therefore, their losses due to the loss of clientele are more than those suffered by the grocery stores.

Challenge before the State

The Mumbai Metropolitan Regional Development Authority (MMRDA) was the co-ordinating agency responsible for the environmental impact mitigation related to the transport project. As a result of the Court order, the administrative authority responsible for vacation of the 'illegal encroachers' was the Greater Mumbai Municipal Corporation (GMMC), while their relocation and resettlement was the responsibility of MMRDA. These encroachers were part of the BUTP II project. The project negotiations had begun since 1995–96 and the dispute was over the status of the people who were to be displaced as a result of the expanding corridors for the railway and road widening projects. Therefore, the entitlement of these people had to be considered. The Railway authority in particular maintained that the lands belonged to the Railways and took a stand that these were illegal encroachers and they did not 'owe them anything by way of compensation'. When the Court orders were issued, the dilemma before the MMRDA was to decide the status of the displaced people. Since the Railways had refused to pay for the compensation of the displaced, the cost of resettlement of the displaced people was an issue for MMRDA if they chose to resettle them, and if they chose to ignore them, they would not get the loan from the World Bank, a major funding partner in the BUTP II project. When MMRDA approached the World Bank with this dilemma, the Bank authorities made the policy of 'no resettlement nor funding' clear. The destruction of the dwelling units as per the Court order was carried out by the GMMC, and the displaced people were shifted to alternate dwelling units over time by the MMRDA.

The site of relocation was a livelihood issue and had a political dimension. As mentioned earlier, the people who lived in the encroachments also worked within a radius of 5 km and they were usually casual or temporary labourers with no prospect of compensation or alternate jobs if they were moved very far from the site. The second issue was a demand from the local regional politics to ensure that the relocated 'vote banks' did not move out of their constituency. The ward boundaries determine the jurisdiction of the municipal corporators being elected from the wards. The political party which controlled a particular ward wanted to ensure that their constituents were protected. Even though both of these were local demands, they were very powerful as they were supported by the PAPs and the local politicians. Thus, the site of relocation had to satisfy the two criteria: it had to be within a 5 km radius to ensure economic sustainability, and had to be moved only within the municipal ward boundaries to ensure the socio-political sustainability of the rehabilitation.

The relocation of the PAPs was not easy because of the need to ensure that these two criteria were satisfied. The multi-storeyed LIG housing schemes available for occupation satisfied these two criteria. This ensured that at least the 'legal' owners, who were not necessarily the 'current occupants' of the dwelling units (as they are often rented out by the owners living in the vicinity), were given alternate dwelling units. But there was a lot of discontent among the settlers of original sites as the 'last in, first out' principle was applied to the selection of households to be resettled. As mentioned earlier, the encroachment begins at the outer periphery of these government-owned lands, and slowly moves towards the routes of transport. So the houses nearer the transport routes are occupied by the people who have come to the area last, as against those who live away from these routes. These sentiments were expressed with a feeling of guarded jealousy, as the 'illegal' occupation of these lands is made possible for the people initially because they happen to be casual labourers employed by the Railways, and subsequently, because their kith and kin move into the area.

Moving from a slum with inadequate infrastructure amenities to a multi-storeyed apartment complex involves a change in culture and in associated social and economic costs. Their neighbours in these apartments were not chosen but were assigned to them. So the social networks that existed in the original settlement were now spread over a larger geographical distance. Living in apartments involves a different discipline for garbage and waste disposal, and the use of electricity and other common spaces and amenities. Most of these buildings except the ones in Dharavi, were four over floors high and needed an elevator as per regulations. All this involved an additional economic and monetary cost to the residents. These costs were calculated and worked into the resettlement and rehabilitation compensation package. The idea was to provide sufficient capital in the form of 'development funds' that could be kept in an escrow account, so that the interest earned on it would be sufficient to pay for the additional common costs incurred by the residents due to the shifting to these sites. These costs include the cost of maintaining and operating elevators, electric bulbs in passages, the cost of garbage collection and the maintenance of common plumbing and sewage pipes. Eventually, these fairly large funds were to be managed by the members of the co-operative housing societies that would be formed by the members living in these buildings. Dealing with the transfer of 'management funds' is the most critical issue in the success of these resettlement efforts.

Ideologies of the NGOs

SPARC/NSDF, SRS and Siddhi were the three major NGOs which were initially identified to work on a rehabilitation action plan that was acceptable to the project promoters, funding agencies and the

PAPs. The former two organizations (SPARC/NSDF and SRS) had a history of creating successful housing projects for economically weaker sections. The Shiv Sena, the locally dominant political party, was an accidental party to the resettlement and rehabilitation programme in Dharavi.

The efforts of any successful resettlement and relocation programme require an organizational hierarchy from within the PAPs for its efficient implementation. In rural areas where villages are relocated, the village is characterized by a solidarity among its members as a community due to their shared common history. The political leaders within the PAPs act as a natural bridge between the project implementers and the PAPs. In an urban encroached land, however, the people living in the neighbourhood have not stayed long enough to develop a communal bond that cuts across the various ethnicities, or develop a natural hierarchy of leadership within them. This is a major challenge in an urban resettlement and rehabilitation programme. The success of this programme would depend on the ability to co-ordinate the project implementation efforts between the implementing officials and the PAPs through their leaders. These emergent leaders had to be embedded in the relocation sites and the amorphous transit colonies. The leaders had to be committed to dedicating a major part of their time to the welfare of the PAPs who lived with them. There had to be a considerable amount of trust and easy accessibility of the leader to the community. The ability of the leader to monitor the transit colonies and to carry all the PAPs together, more or less as a homogeneous group, was crucial to the success of the programme.

The fairly homogeneous group relocated in Dharavi had a political affiliation to the Shiv Sena, the party in power within the state. These PAPs were more or less homogeneous ethnically and by way of political affiliation. The political party was functional in this group and had a network of party workers and social workers. Being a predominantly local regional party, the political leaders had a vested interest in ensuring that the electoral constituency was intact and the resettlement and rehabilitation of the PAPs took place within the municipal ward boundaries. To ensure this, the political culture was used to relocate the PAPs to the new site directly. The allotment procedures and the relocation to the new site were fairly smooth.

The other organization that was successful in gaining the confidence of the PAPs was the SPARC/NSDF alliance. SRS, operating in Khar, helped in Jogeshwari as well, both located in the western suburbs of Mumbai. This was mainly because the SPARC (Society for Preservation and Resources Conservation), the NGO, and its associate organization, the NSDF (National Slum Dwellers Federation), which were mediating the process of resettlement, were actively involved in organizing and motivating the people settled along the railway tracks to seek safer and more permanent shelter since 1987 well before the advent of MUTP II. Their success is attributed to the sustained efforts and commitments of the NSDF president, Mr Jokin, for providing better housing to the people settled along the railway tracks near the Kanjurmarg station. But more importantly, the president, with his grounding in the trade union movement in Mumbai, had good organizational and motivational skills. He won the 1999 Magsaysay Award for his efforts there.

The 1980s was a decade of turmoil and crisis for the trade union movement in the city. The textile strike of 1982 was the longest and the biggest in the history of trade union movement in India, and was headed by an independent leader, Datta Samant. The strike lasted for 18 months from January 1982 onwards and was by not just one mill or shop floor or a few mills but by the entire textile industry. Regardless of the final impact of the strike on the industry, it brought about an anti-labour legislation that was passed during and after the strike. It prevented union growth in the service sector and educational institutions, thereby curtailing union solidarity across the industry sector. The new union leadership that emerged was more militant, firm-based and plant-based in nature. The rise of the employee-based union with no political party affiliation, was becoming a norm (Bhattacherjee, 1988). It therefore became difficult for the party-based 'career trade union leaders' to find work. The president of the NSDF was groomed to be a party-based career trade union leader. The industrial area of Ghatkopar–Kanjurmarg–Vikroli that surrounded the Kanjurmarg slum drew its labour force from there. This industrial area was a part of the advanced industrial sector in engineering and textiles, where the new individualized employee-based unions with no political party affiliation were emerging. Thus, while the conventional venue for union leadership was closing for leaders, the president of NSDF found a spatially concentrated labour force that could be mobilized on the issue of 'permanent housing'. This was very creative thinking on the part of the NSDF president who efficiently implemented his plans through dedicated work since the formation of his organization in 1987. That it happened to be the year for shelter, promoted by UNDP, facilitated his efforts.

All the training that the president had received through his past trade union activities, including recruiting and building a cadre of loyal cardholders generating funds to keep the operation functional, were the techniques used by him to create an efficiently functioning organizational structure that was overtly secular. There was no membership fee, but money was collected through *Mahila Milan* on a monthly basis as a saving account. Although individual passbooks were issued to the *Mahila Milan* account holders, the money collected was centrally deposited in one account. Thus, an organizational structure was instituted among the Kanjurmarg slum dwellers that could be replicated elsewhere, and could become the foundation of urban R&R policy.

The resultant process, arrived at through learning and experimentation at Kanjurmarg, was successfully applied in new tenements. Creating a local cadre among the amorphous newly relocated people in the temporary tenements was a challenge. The local leadership sometimes had to be 'appointed' or 'selected' by the president from among his loyalists in these new colonies. They had the dedication of the cardholders and the ideological motivation and commitment to work towards organizing people. This core leadership living among the PAPs was an essential backbone for the successful implementation of the project. This creation of the backbone was the greatest achievement of the NSDF, as it was very essential for success of the project. The 'two-stage' rehabilitation therefore helped. The temporary tenements and the hardship caused by the temporary nature of the settlement helped in building solidarity and a community feeling among the displaced, who constituted an amorphous group of people forced to live together, in the beginning. The formation of the societies and the regular meetings of the management committees helped in bringing together the future neighbours as a community. This solidarity, built on face-to-face relationships, and from facing hardships together and learning to trust their leaders, is the foundation for the success of future resettlement and rehabilitation programmes.

Process of Resettlement

A baseline survey of the PAPs at household levels was conducted by three NGOs. A total of 19,228 households have been identified for the entire BUTP II project. Of the 19,228 households, the data for

17,911 was ready by 2002. More than 99 per cent of the PAPs were squatters and did not have any tenurial rights on the land they occupied. The average monthly income of these households is Rs 2,601 and 26 per cent of the households fall below the poverty line of Rs 2,500 per household per month. Most of the PAPs obtain water through standposts and toilet facilities, even though these are inadequate. As indicated earlier, since these settlements occupy the low lying areas of the city, they are prone to monsoon flooding.

In the present case, due to the PIL, the total number of households that were displaced were 10,118 in June 2001 (6,261 in transit accommodation and 3,857 in permanent dwelling units). This is unprecedented. Even though the notice for displacement of the people was short, the process of resettlement and rehabilitation went off relatively smoothly. There was very good synchronization between the implementing authority, MMRDA and SPARC. In addition, there was adequate co-ordination and close communication between SPARC/NSDF and the PAPs. Given the emergency situation of the displacement due to Court orders, trauma of displacement was severe due to the demolition of settlements at very short notice. Information about the demolition was conveyed verbally and through mass media like newspapers. A smaller number of about 3,000 families had to undergo this trauma. But minimum the gap between the demolition and relocation was predominantly within eight days and never more than 90 days. The GOM also had to procure adequate resources to relocate people within Mumbai. At that time, the GOM, through its implementing agency, MMRDA, was able to purchase only 4,000 already constructed houses from the Maharashtra Housing and Area Development Authority (MHADA). It then undertook the construction of about 6,000 transit houses to shift all squatters living within the safety zone of the railway tracks. Thus emerged a two-stage resettlement plan whereby PAPs were first moved to a transit accommodation and were to be subsequently moved to permanent settlement sites. But not all the PAPs were resettled and some were moved directly to tenements that were ready, defying the two-stage plan in Dharavi from Mahim.

In hindsight what emerged was a new community of people with solidarity among themselves, before they moved to the new sites. This is essential for ensuring the success of a resettlement and rehabilitation programme as a whole, especially as it involves the handing over of a large sum of money for common resource management in the new tenements.

The Government of Maharashtra created the organizational

structure with associated responsibilities for this purpose. A steering committee, a project co-ordination committee and an independent monitoring committee were created for the effective monitoring and implementation of MUTP. The project co-ordinating agency for MUTP is MMRDA. Finally, a grievance committee to address the complaints of the PAPs was also created. The MMRDA faced a very difficult and uphill task. Since all the PAPs were illegal squatters, they had no documents of their tenure rights. It was thus difficult, to decide the legitimacy of the resettlement claims of one over the other in this situation of a 'boundary in flux'.

The organizational structure of the tenements is on the lines of registered co-operative societies, wherein there is management committee which is elected through a general body election of its members. The management committee then elects a chairman, a president and a treasurer, and deals with the day-to-day issues of managing the tenements.

Formation of societies

As stated earlier, the NSDF was actively involved in raising the consciousness of people about their right to dwelling as a fundamental right. It had encouraged these settlements to organize themselves into a more formal association where membership was voluntary. Different kinds of associations were encouraged such as youth clubs, women's association and housing residents' associations. Thus an array of semi-formal voluntary associations existed among the PAPs before relocation, which further facilitated the process of forming management committees and resident housing societies when they were shifted to relocation sites and started living together with the people they did not know before.

When people shifted to relocation sites, whether temporary or permanent, they were encouraged to organize along the societies they belonged to before the new site of relocation by SPARC. This allowed for a proportionate representation of interests of PAPs coming together from different locations on the basis of their area affiliations rather than caste, class or ethnicity, for the first time. Two members from each of the societies were selected by the members of those respective societies to represent their interest in the central management committee. This committee met once in three/four months. Then, a group of five/six members from this central management committee were selected to form a working committee that met more frequently or once a week as required (information extracted through a focused group discussion with the office bearers of the central management committee and representatives of other co-operative society members).

The procedure of setting up central management committees in the permanent sites was different. They were formed by selecting what SPARC/NSDF considered a proportionate representation of residents, two from each floor of the building.[1] For the day-to-day management of the issues of living, such as maintaining cleanliness and hygienic conditions in new sites, a working committee of five/seven members was selected from the central management committee, for ensuring that people change their habits in order to live harmoniously in multi-storeyed buildings. The challenges were several and the process is slow, but it is happening in most of the settlements.

Major Challenges and Achievements

There are three major challenges of resettlement. First, the occupants of tenements should have adequate incomes to take care of access to amenities like electricity and water supply. Second, they should be able to adopt new cultural practices that are more appropriate to apartment living. Finally, they should be able to manage large amounts of money to maintain the housing societies. Thus, all the three major challenges of resettlement are linked with the issue of poverty. The PAPs are the 'last in' on the encroached lands and at least one-quarter of them have incomes below the poverty line while 60 per cent of the others barely manage to survive. The relocation has imposed on them the direct additional cost of having to pay for the cost of public amenities. There is a loss of income or job opportunities due to the relocation and finally, there is the additional cost of maintaining the tenement. All these additional costs put a financial strain on the PAPs, who are quite poor. However, they have found an easy solution to getting an assured income. They rent part of the dwelling unit to someone else. The tenements are small and the owners continue to live there while a part of it is rented out. These

---

[1]Information provided by Mr Jokin, NSDF, 1 April 2002, MMRDA office.

illegal tenants living in the tenements add to the already stretched amenities, but it ensures guaranteed monetary income to the PAPs.

As stated earlier, the culture of apartment living is very different from slum living. At the minimum level, managing public spaces becomes important, especially when the neighbours are not known to each other. The formal association membership is to be used to create an atmosphere of mutual trust and friendship. Without the experience of living with each other and without the certainty of residence, with no input from the owner of the house in creating the trust fund, the management of a large trust becomes a major issue. There is tremendous temptation to collude among the management committee members to siphon off the capital funds. Hence the officials are very sceptical about the transfer of large sums of money to take care of amenities. At the same time, it is essential to take care of the additional cost of living for the residents if the resettlement and rehabilitation programme has to succeed, as one-quarter of the PAPs fall below the poverty line. Therefore, the authorities seem to drag their feet for the transfer of the money which adds to the problems.

The formation of a new organizational structure to manage the buildings has not been easy, due to the diversity of the PAPs' backgrounds. There have been instances wherein the central committee and management committee could not be formed due to internal conflicts, and an alternative to the central committee was created at the 138/B Mankhurd temporary site. The day-to-day management is taken care of by a SPARC employee.

The three major achievements of this resettlement and rehabilitation programme were a reasonable level of transparency about entitlements, efficiency of allotment, and a reasonable comfort level felt by the occupants of the tenements at the new sites. Focused group discussions with residents at each site indicated that overall they were satisfied with the fact that they had houses of reasonably good quality and close to their old place of residence. The allotments of tenements were based on random sampling to avoid any bias towards a particular group or community. This resulted in people having neighbours they did not know before. Most people made the necessary efforts to meet and know their fellow tenants. All the people interviewed were made aware of their entitlements after they vacated their old settlements, by SPARC, the NGO working on this project. Those who were allotted licensed shops were also fairly satisfied with the new allotment. But no one knew about cash compensation for relocation or resettlement needs. The cash compensation was a one-time payment for coping with the difficulty of accessing their old place of work and also for a loss of livelihood for all members of a family, who may have lost jobs due to relocation.

Everyone who was interviewed said that all their neighbours or people they knew from the old settlement had been given a house, either at a temporary or a permanent site. However, those who have been provided houses at temporary sites are unhappy and complain bitterly about a bias in allotments by SPARC (focused group discussion, Mankhurd temporary tenement owners, 28 March 2002).

A loosely defined criterion for the allotment of permanent housing was adopted by SPARC. Those who had a medical history, and those who were old or those who had a large family size were given permanent housing. Initially, in order to ensure that the cost of permanent housing was covered, only people who could afford to pay maintenance costs or those who had savings worth Rs 20,000 in the bank were given permanent dwelling units.

Perception of Benefits and Losses

Everyone stated the biggest benefit was that they had a permanent and safe roof over their heads. Overall, everyone believed that in the older settlements, the cost of living was much lower than at the new sites. A lot of people, mainly women, complained about the loss of jobs due to the need to commute a longer distance.

An objective comparison was made of access to infrastructure amenities like dwelling space, water, electricity, and toilet and garbage disposal before and after the resettlement. It clearly indicated that a majority of them (96 out of 106) were better off or at least as well off at the new site as at the old site. Just a few were worse off, mainly due to reasons of dwelling space. A majority of the people had to spend about 15 to 20 minutes more on travel to jobs, schools and health facilities. The travel distance to schools and to the doctor increased because a majority of the PAPs did not discontinue their old settlement linkages. But the quality and quantity of infrastructure services like water supply, drainage and garbage collection were not adequate. There were complaints of frequent water shortages, electricity failures and drain overflows. The water pressure during summer was especially low and only some taps in some areas (which could be low lying or nearer to the main source) in temporary settlements had water for five/six hours. In the permanent sites, the water pumped to overhead tanks is often inadequate. Although elevators are installed in the building, they are very expensive to operate and were therefore not operational. The operating cost of these additional expenditures is to be borne by a corpus fund that would be transferred to the housing society once the formalities were completed and the societies formally registered.

Talking claims

The trauma of displacement was very fresh and no one wanted to talk about it. The only accounts I have are from our meeting with the NGO head, and what he described was not very pleasant. The displacement was violent, brutal and quite inhuman with use of police force. My point of entry into this project was a major hindrance. The other thing that I was not informed about was the number of people who lived as tenants and were not given housing. Some did report that both the tenant and the house owner were given the tenements. There were other subjects on which people were willing to talk. They felt more safe and less harassed at the new site as compared to the old site. At the old site, the threat of demolition always existed and the perception of the trauma is very vivid in their narratives quoted below.

- 'The police hounded us all the time. If we sat down for dinner, they would pull away our plates, burn and destroy our belongings and there was no respite, come rain or sunshine.'
- 'We stayed for three months after demolition. We were not informed about the demolition. We had half an hour of notice to vacate our homes. Everything left inside was destroyed.'
- 'We were aware of the impending demolition due to the marking made by the Railways. We were given notice and our houses were demolished several times in the past. Since 1983, the Railways had given us notice to collect the cost of our houses and vacate premises. But without any viable alternative, where would we go? So when SPARC approached us two years ago, we agreed to shift to Dalda Colony, Kurla.'
- 'We stayed after the demolition. After 28 February till September 2000, there was no notice. There was sudden demolition. We had to bear the losses of our personal belongings as they were confiscated. We had to create a common kitchen, then

took a place on rent for six months. Many people lost jobs because of absenteeism due to demolition. Now we are safe.'
- 'All this (demolition) was done in such a hurry that we had no time to think; we had to take what we were given. I hope others will not be forced into similar situations like ours.'
- 'Only a few lucky ones were given the adequate notice and we were given keys of new houses 40 days before demolition, so the transition was smooth.'

All of them agreed that the new place was better than the old one as indicated by their narratives.

- 'There is no noise of the trains her; our house used to vibrate when a train passed.'
- 'It is safe for our children, where they can play in a colony; we are not scared of their meeting with accidents.'
- 'We have a decent living place with better sanitation facilities.'
- 'We have a better infrastructure. There is more open space, good ventilation and breeze.'
- 'It is cleaner and more peaceful.'

There were complaints of economic losses, increased household expenses, security concerns, and bad physical environment due to relocation. People who had leased shops from owners were losers. They stated:

- 'Everyone knew us, we could get shops on lease, customers came to us as regulars; now that we have moved away, they say, "Where have you gone? How can we give you a shop to run, who will go chasing you? I will find someone else to work for me"'.
- 'The old site had more business, here more people like us stay, how much can they buy? And our old customers wouldn't come to us here.'
- 'We had other sources of income there for which we didn't have to do very much like selling electricity or renting the *malas* (trinkets) easily got us Rs 2,000 per month and we did not have to pay out of our pockets.'
- 'There were more opportunities of work in Chembur (old site) than here.'
- 'Getting material for business is difficult due to the increased distance; there is more competition in business.'

In addition to the economic losses due to relocation, there were additional household expenses. These included one-time expenses due to shifting and recurring expenses due to the distance. These narratives are given below:

- 'All of us had to make arrangements of our own for transferring our goods.'
- 'Our ration cards are not transferred. We have to spend on transport every month when we get the ration from the old ration shop.'
- 'Schools are far for our children. From here we spend more.'

The other major concern at the new sites was individual safety, security and help available during emergencies:

- 'It is not safe here. Women cannot move after 7.30 p.m. here.'
- 'There is no police station nearby from where we can ask for help. There are no telephone lines. At the time of emergency, we are helpless.'
- 'Some of them have neither a ration card nor a voter's card, and are scared that they will never be getting any shelter.'
- 'There are no grills to the windows, that is an extra expense for us on the top floors.'
- For those 'staying in Dharavi, there is constant fear of that area since that is the first place which is targeted whenever there is any political problem.'

The maintenance cost of services available at the new site was a major expense that eveyone complained about. They said:

- 'Climbing up (the stairs in a permanent site) is a problem; the lift has not started as yet. Most of us do not have any earnings and it is difficult to pay for the maintenance.'
- 'Electricity cuts are frequent. It seems that the bills are not paid by the society. Asbestos sheets are very uncomfortable during summer.'
- 'The maintenance charges have increased and are unaffordable. We have to pay since there is no other alternative; we are scared that they will cut our electricity.'

Since most of these relocation sites were located on landfills that were mainly garbage dumps, everyone complained of bad smell and parasites in these lands. They stated:

- The dumping place is nearby. There are mosquitoes and rats. Drains are not cleaned regularly.'
- 'Children have started falling ill due to which the expenses on medicines have increased.'
- 'There is nuisance from the nearby chemical factory.'
- 'It has been three years since we are here but we are not able to get our sons married because this (Kanjurmarg) place is so unhealthy.'

Internal Battles

As stated earlier, the project has so far relocated only about 10,118 PAPs and about 9,000 more were yet to be relocated (as of April 2002). Although in principle, the rehabilitation was fairly straightforward, identifying the PAPs, removing them from their present sites and relocating them in new acceptable (to them) houses become very complicated when the implementation takes place. First, there is not enough land to allow people to build their own huts, so they have to be provided with houses acceptable to them. By implication, these new houses had to be much better than the ones they currently owned. Everyone who was displaced found the option of independent small apartments with all the modern amenities acceptable. As stated earlier, these are the 'last in' people. Given the dynamics of these informal settlements in Mumbai, the moral claim to the *pucca* housing with all modern amenities is the lowest among the informal settlers. They were therefore obvious targets of jealousy. The crisis of Kanjurmarg was therefore severe for NSDF which was trying to promote habitat as a fundamental right. It undermined the success and the path to success for the Kanjurmarg residents shown by NSDF. It is a sticky issue because unlike the commonsense knowledge of upward mobility of the immigrant culture, here are instances wherein there was instant improvement in the quality of life of people who came late, were the last in the queue and had jumped the queue. The insistence on formalizing the two-stage development on part of the NSDF has to be understood in this context. Since the project is only partially complete, and 9,000 families have yet to be relocated, the identification of new immigrants into the project sites and a cut-off date then become operationally important in promoting social justice. MMRDA resisted this two-stage resettlement proposed by NSDF, first to temporary shelters and then to permanent apartments, as a one-time move would complete the process faster and the loss-making MHADA could recover money from the funding agencies more quickly.

There is considerable unease within the MMRDA about the emergence of NSDF as the only mediating NGO between the PAPs and the MMRDA in the whole process. The management fund transfer is another battle between MMRDA and the NSDF which needs to be contextualized.

Also, the shock and surprise element ensured that there were no last minute free riders among the people who got identified as PAPs. In future, once the sites are known in advance, keeping records of the people to be resettled and keeping the free riders out will be a major problem, since the stakes are so high.

Conclusion

To sum up, in the absence of an urban resettlement policy, a comprehensive resettlement strategy evolved within the broad liberal policy framework as a result of the implementation of the urban transportation project that was based on the general principals of the resettlement and rehabilitation policy. It recognized the principle of the greatest good for the greatest number of people, at the same time as PAPs' rights to livelihood and housing as inalienable. Thus, the number of commuters affected by the encroachment were greater than the number of people who encroached the lands, and measures were taken to promote the benefit of the commuters first. The right to housing of the encroachers, even though they were illegal occupants of the lands, was accepted as an inalienable right. It was given due recognition and an alternate house was provided for the displaced. At the same time, the right to livelihood of the encroachers and the linkages between the location and livelihood were given due recognition in the resettlement efforts. Therefore, alternate housing was provided within a short distance from the original site of the residence. In order to make the relocation more acceptable to the displaced, a better quality of infrastructure and housing was provided to them. This strategy, implemented through appropriate mediating NGOs in urban infrastructure projects, has proven to be a great success, though all the problems have not yet been smoothened out.

This must be the only major development project in India in recent times, which has not resulted in an equally strong environmental protest movement against it. The situation and circumstances of the project forced different stakeholders with different ideologies to come to the same table and meet in an atmosphere of debate and dialogue. This negotiated bottoms-up approach allowed for the development of a successful resettlement of the PAPs, as well as a resettlement policy for an urban transportation project in India. This could set a precedent for similar projects in other cities.

Ten

Environmental Struggles, Protest and Survival

Analysis of the environmental impacts of development projects needs to begin with a comprehensive theory about the human–environmental relationship. Any development project goes through four distinct phases temporally: the planning stage, the implementation stage, the construction stage, and the operation stage, when the project starts production. The theory proposes that socio-political factors are responsible for locating the project at a particular site during the planning stage. These are partially beyond the control of the PAPs. All development projects in the tourism industry and infrastructure sector offer the promise of rapid economic development. This promise is fulfilled fairly quickly at the initiation stage. These projects, however, also have an adverse impact on the existing natural resources of that region. These impacts are particularly severe within a 5 km radius of the project. They start manifesting themselves during the construction phase of the project and continue through the operation stage. The EIA measures to control the adverse impacts of air and water pollution and even contractual labour for the project construction, within the project boundaries, are not discussed here. These solutions are technical and technological, and implemented by the project promoters without dispute.

Associated Impacts

There are other socio-economic impacts of the project, which are secondary. These are associated impacts that cannot be attributed to the project directly, and these continue through all the phases of the project. There is an increase in the local population due to migration, initially of labour and subsequently of related trades. There is increased money flowing in the local economy due to the transfer of lands and the monetization of services. The environmental impacts of the project affect the natural resources, particularly drinking water and bio-fuels adversely. Ecologically linked livelihoods of the region get adversely affected due to depletion and over-exploitation of natural resources, as new markets and growth in population increase their demand. As the local economy grows in size and diversity, the PAPs are left on the margins of development, as they have neither the skills nor the resources to take advantage of the economic boom. These adverse impacts on the PAPs may not be directly related to the project but they can be attributed to the accompanying socio-economic changes taking place due to the project. The sudden windfall due to changes in land use, from agriculture to commercial, industrial and residential does benefit some PAPs. This supports the development and economic growth rhetoric propagated by the project promoters and upheld by the local politicians, during the initiation stage. Very quickly, during the construction and operation stages of the project, the PAPs start facing the adverse, unintended consequences of the project.

Environmental Sustainability

Environmental specialists ensure environmental sustainability at techno-economic levels through environmental laws and pollution control procedures, while socio-cultural equilibrium is ignored. This forces the PAPs into reflexivity from which emerges new consciousness and new learning. Human beings, including the PAPs, by virtue of their 'universal ecological competence', have the ability to reflect on their past action, become environmental 'critics' and suggest remedial actions to restore environmental equilibrium in the socio-cultural sphere. Thus, the focus of critics shifts away from being specialists to being human beings affected by the development project. Their self-critique leads to enlightenment and new learning. The enlightenment is the realization that in order to ensure their socio-cultural survival as a distinct group, they do not have the choice of ignoring the project-related development taking place in their neighbourhood. They have to 'engage' with the project in order to ensure their socio-cultural survival, because however painful the engagement may be, the price of 'letting go' the project is much worse. The new learning is the realization by PAPs that there are as many realities as people and that they must therefore adopt a reality that is most favourable to restoring their socio-cultural equilibrium. They adopt appropriate action to change the reality in their favour. The actions they use are drawn from their unique social histories. But the underlying common thread that runs through these is the claim to moral ecology—a reality that is in their favour. The PAPs were there first and they have a right to survival as a distinct ethnic group with a unique socio-cultural adaptation to their physical environment. Historically, their physical and socio-cultural survival was linked with the natural resources of the lands. Due to the project operation, these resources have depleted and therefore the survival of the PAPs has become difficult, if not impossible. Therefore, they take appropriate actions to transform the social reality in their favour, in the form of protests, to ensure their survival. These actions are specific to their unique social histories. The fact that action occurs after the implementation of the project does not make it any less legitimate and therefore environmental policy should ensure ecological justice, based on the moral claim to 'survival first' made by the PAPs.

This paradigm provides the framework to understand the six different projects that were reviewed here. In each of the six projects, even though there is a diversity in the attitudes of PAPs, promoters and the government agencies, all the projects have a common underlying thread, even though the actual course of events is unique to each project. These projects can be categorized into three different types, namely, tourism projects, energy infrastructure development projects, and urban and industrial projects.

Project Location Decision

The decision to locate the project in specific region is a decision over which the PAPs do not have any direct control in all the six projects reviewed here. This decision follows the framework and procedures set up by the state for project approval. These procedures include clearances from various departments, including the Department of Environment and Forests.

The land in Gorai, Mumbai, was originally sanctioned for a prawn farming development project, to be set up by the project promoters. The decision to locate the amusement park on a small portion of this land came after the sanction for a prawn fishing project, as the promoters decided that the prawn project was not financially viable due to the falling international demand for prawns. The local city administration and state government gave the sanction for this project. In the case of the Sanjay Gandhi National Park at Borivali, the decision to convert the state forest lands into a protected wildlife sanctuary was a decision taken by the Ministry of Environment and Forests.

The decision to privatize the production in the power sector as part of the power sector reforms was a decision taken by the Ministry of Power. The location of the project in Guhagar, a coastal town in Ratnagiri district, was the result of a successful negotiation undertaken by the then chief minister of Maharashtra state. The decision to improve the efficiency of the coal washery of Moonidih at Dhanbad was also taken in Delhi by the Ministry of Coal after which the Central Government bureaucrats/technocrats went shopping for the best development aid package in international markets.

The decision to review the pollution levels in the Tungabhadra river was taken by the Karnataka Pollution Control Board (KPCB) prompted by the proactive judiciary within the state of Karnataka. The emphasis on Davangiri region of the river was a natural target as the pulp industries were located here. Similarly, the decision to improve urban transport in Mumbai city followed an earlier plan to improve road transport in Mumbai by the regional planners of the Mumbai Metropolitan Region Development Authority with the help of a consultant. They then approached the World Bank for a loan.

All these projects claimed to be using state-of-the-art technology that was environment, friendly, economically sustainable and capable of generating economic and social benefits for the local communities in the neighbouring regions.

Emergence of Crisis

Some attempt to inform the PAPs at the implementation stage was made by the promoters and government approvals based on standardized procedures provided legitimacy to the claims made by the promoters in each of the projects. The crisis in each case, however, emerged when the PAPs realized that the 'benefits' of the project were not in their favour and that the 'costs' of the project threatened their survival. Benefits resulting from the creation of new jobs and economic growth generated by the project were accruing to the 'outsiders' coming into the region who were able to benefit from the project more than the PAPs could. This was partially because the local people did not have either the technical competence to find skilled employment generated by the projects or the access to large finances needed to fully benefit from the sudden economic boom, and partially because the local government did not hold the project partially or fully responsible for any adverse impacts resulting due to a 'boom-town' effect that the project may have in that region. The socio-economic changes in their neighbourhood and the infrastructure deterioration that occurs due to the project, is beyond the control of the local inhabitants who have been living in the region 'before the project'. Thus, the local inhabitants find themselves marginalized in the economic growth resulting from the project. When the local communities in the neighbourhood of the project find that the natural resources that had ensured their subsistence in the past are eroding and that they are unable to tap the socio-economic benefits that occur due to the regional growth resulting from the project, it leads to a crisis of their survival. This realization makes the local communities into 'critics' that prompt the narratives of injustice and talking claims.

New Learning and Talking Claims

Land for the amusement park in Gorai was purchased as barren land from the state government and was thus dirt cheap for the promoters, who had adequate finances. None of the local landowners benefited as a result of the land transactions. But in Gorai, as a result of the compound wall set up around its estates by project promoters, some local landowners lost access to their own agricultural lands, as the park authorities granted no 'right of way' to these landowners. The latter lost access to the only sweet water well on that island and they could no longer collect dry wood from the mangroves in the 'barren' lands due to construction of the compound wall. Besides, the project did not provide them employment opportunities during construction or after the completion of the park. Finally, they had to face the harassment of tourists visiting the park. Thus, while the urban tourists benefited from the amusement park, local people suffered.

The decision to convert the state-owned forest lands in Borivali into a protected wildlife sanctuary did not entail any financial costs, just a change of ownership of land from the state revenue department to the state forest department. But the declaration of a 'protected area' meant that all human inhabitants living within its boundaries had to be relocated. These were tribal communities with no clear title to w*adi*s, the lands that they cultivated seasonally and to the minor forest produce. The physical relocation and displacement of tribal families led to a loss of access to the w*adi*s they cultivated and minor forest produce, like fruit, flower, leaves, firewood and small timber that had ensured their survival over the years. While the urban wildlife enthusiast benefited from the project, the tribal inhabitants suffered, as they had neither the skills nor the resources to adapt to the nearby city life where they were relocated.

The 'boom-town' effect that the power plant generated in the region led to a deterioration in the infrastructure services of the old town of Guhagar. There was deterioration in the water supply, sanitation, roads, housing and power supply of the existing town. On behalf of the project promoters, the Maharashtra State Electricity Board (MSEB) purchased the land needed for the project. Some of it was agricultural/horticultural land but most of it was barren. The compensation for the land was based on existing land use and not future land use. But anticipating the boom-town effect of the project, speculative land prices existed in the surrounding areas. Besides, the access to barren lands used by the fishing community to dry fish, or to collect fuel wood and fodder for domestic animals, was lost to them.

The decision to improve the efficiency of the coal washery at Moonidih in Dhanbad (as it was generating a loss of Rs 350 for every tonne of coal washed) was also taken in Delhi by the Coal Ministry. Bharat Coking Coal Limited (BCCL) officials posted to this washery were never consulted. The social and environmental component of the project would have severely affected the status quo. The effective implementation of technical improvements in addition to the new machines recommended by the development agency would have led to a disruption of the existing relationship between the coal 'mafia' and the washery officials, a situation that the officials perceived would be potentially life-threatening to themselves, given the history of the state. Thus, while the industries at large of both the countries stood to benefit in the long run, the local technocrats suffered.

Although the pollution levels caused by the industry, and particularly the fibre industry, met the norms of the Pollution Control Board, they caused the river water to change colour. While the industries generated jobs in the manufacturing and service sectors, the pollution levels affected the traditional paddy grown in the adjacent farms and farmers had to change their crops or give up farming.

The decision to improve urban transport efficiency in Mumbai caused displacement of people living too close to the project transport corridors. Since they were living on encroached lands, their status was unclear and it was doubtful if they would receive any compensation. So while improved transport efficiency helped the daily commuters in the metropolitan city, the future of the people living on the transport corridors was uncertain.

Thus the crisis faced by the original inhabitants was that while their traditional base of subsistence was eroded as a result of the growth and development in their region, they were not the sole or primary beneficiaries of the growth, and they neither had the skills nor access to finances to make the best use of the opportunity. This realization made the local communities into 'critics'. They examined what had gone wrong in their strategy to deal with the project authorities and what would be the best way to deal with this crisis. This self-critique led to the enlightenment that they needed to hold on to the project 'no matter what'. This enlightenment led to new learning, which included the realization that there are as many realities as people and that they must therefore adopt the one that is most favourable to them. The details of this more favourable reality as perceived by the PAPs or 'talking claims' have been elaborated in each of the chapters pertaining to these projects. These claims were moral ecological claims, and were specific to the project and the people who were affected by them. These essentially constituted subaltern rhetoric. But a common thread runs through these claims. These claims were for access to natural resources that had ensured their survival 'before the project'. Deterioration in the quality or volume of these resources was a major complaint. The second major complaint was of 'being left behind' in the changed social and economic environment caused by the project. The moral ecology claims, based on their notion of ecological justice, pertaining to each of the projects are now discussed.

Moral Claims and Ecological Justice

The moral claim of the PAPs was to safety, subsistence and socio-cultural survival of the group of people living in the area before the project at Gorai. The notion of ecological justice in Gorai was the PAPs' claim to drinking water—a limited commodity—electricity, 'right of way' to other properties, and their right to earlier economic activities such as tourism and fishing. The huge profits of the amusement park that were generated on their lands and the claim of government to sell lands were tolerated, but the monopoly over water, and violence against women and children, were intolerable.

In Borivali, ecological justice was conceptualized as the PAPs' right to their homes and survival based on their earlier economic activities, namely fishing for crabs, cultivating *wadis*, liquor making, hunting and basket weaving. The claim of the government to sell lands was tolerated, but the claim to their houses and their *wadis*, to drinking water, and access to forest resources, and taking away of the right of way to their housing was intolerable.

PAPs in Dhanbad sought justice in the right to maintain the status quo, disruption of which was life threatening in the enclave economy. Aid for improving the techno-economic system and the claim of the project promoter to technical efficiency were tolerated, but the claim to socio-cultural-political interventions to improve the efficiency of the techno-economic system was intolerable and perceived as life threatening by the public sector bureaucracy.

The notion of ecological justice in Guhagar was a right of the original inhabitants to maintain socio-political superiority over the town and the status quo by the public sector bureaucracy. Although, as in Dhanbad, PAPs initially accepted the idea of foreign funds being invested in the region and welcomed the promise of technical efficiency, public sector bureaucrats objected to the socio-cultural and political interventions associated with the project.

In Harihar and downstream of the Tungabhadra river basin, PAPs fought for their right to continue traditional agriculture, fishing and grazing activities. While the development of industrial estates through the growth of the techno-economic system and the claim of the project promoter to technical efficiency and economic growth were tolerated, the pollution of their river was perceived as life threatening to the agricultural and fishing communities and transhumance and therefore led to protest.

The notion of ecological justice in Mumbai was a right to housing. Aid for improving the transport system efficiency and the claim of the project promoter to improve the transport system were tolerated, but socio-cultural and political disruption due to resettlement was perceived as harmful, given the PAPs' illegal ownership status of their occupied lands.

Transformative Action

The actions taken to transform the social reality in their favour by the PAPs range from everyday forms of resistance to organized protest in the form of *morcha*s and *dharna*s and everything in between, depending on the social history of the PAPs. In case of the national park, the PAPs adopted the everyday forms of resistance, as they were a marginal tribal community. In the case of all the other five projects discussed here, the PAPs organized themselves to undertake collective action. The Gorai PAPs organized peaceful projects in the form of *dharna*s and *morcha*s, and so did the PAPs from Dabhol. The PAPs of Dhanbad, who were already organized public sector employees, successfully stalled the implementation of the project in Delhi. The PAPs from Harihar filed a public interest litigation (PIL) and held awareness camps. The PAPs of the urban transportation project in Mumbai organized themselves into pseudo-housing societies by adopting a formal organizational structure of housing societies under the Housing Societies Act.

During the lifetime of the project, the PAPs may change their forms of resistance depending on the time and resource mobilization ability of the organizers. This happened in the case of Gorai where the PAPs' action changed from active resistance against the project to passive resistance like pilferage. What was most striking was that the 'new players' or the public sector employees are now adopting the subaltern rhetoric that already exists in the context of any development project to resist change and to carry out their own agenda, as in the power and mining sector in Guhagar and Moonidih.

All these actions were taken after the project was initiated in the region and were not fully accepted as legitimate by the state or the project promoters. The realization of adverse impacts, the knowledge and the actions to resist the project always came after the fact, but this does not make it any less legitimate. The moral claim to ecological justice and survival because 'they were there first' cannot be denied. Thus, the present outcomes of all these projects are residual tension and resentment that persist between the project promoters and the original inhabitants many years after the project became operational. Given the nature of the impacts, ecological justice can be imparted to the PAPs only after the project is completed. Therefore, just as there is a mechanism to restore the techno-economic environmental equilibrium in the environmental policy, in the form of pollution abatement, there should be a mechanism in the environmental policy in order to restore equilibrium of the socio-cultural environment among the PAPs.

Thus, the critical theory framework proposed here offers a comprehensive framework to interpret the socio-environmental impacts of the development projects presented here. The measures taken to mitigate the adverse impacts of the project on the physical environment are not disputed, except in the case of the Tungabhadra river basin. Therefore, the measures adopted, such as an engineering and technical solution to reduce ambient air and water pollution, if any, are not elaborated here.

Who Won?

As stated earlier, the projects have been selected from among a range of others, because they include two each from the full range of environmental projects, amusement parks, industry and infrastructure projects. The resistance offered by the PAPs ranges from everyday forms of resistance to more systematic protests. The promoters of the project always use the development and modernization rhetoric to promote the project and do the minimum that is forced on them by the law, formally and informally, by the government agencies, towards the mitigation of the impacts of the projects.

The PAPs ranged from organized educated and urban city dwellers to illiterate, unorganized tribal communities. The leadership of the organized city dwellers came from within the community while the unorganized marginal groups had to depend on outside NGOs for help. Alternate discourse through 'talking claims' on the impacts of the project existed among the PAPs, irrespective of the nature of the PAPs. But the nature of resistance ranged from more active vocal protests to everyday forms of resistance, with organized groups having internal leadership more likely to use media and organized protest, and the marginal PAPs more likely to adopt passive resistance.

The promoters of the project were diverse. They included both public sector and private sector promoters. Among the private sector, there were multinationals or development aid agencies, while among the public sector, there were public sector companies and one government department promoting eco-tourism in the national park.

The government agencies that got involved included local governments like municipalities to the state level Department of Environment and even the Central Ministry of Environment and Forests. Every project involves three categories of social actors, loosely categorized into project promoters, PAPs and government agencies, who have the power to take policy decisions. The most important finding is typically that the outcomes of the projects work out in favour of the category of social actors whom the government agency, responsible for policy decision, chooses to support. This is true irrespective of the nature of the other two, and irrespective of whether the promoters are multinationals or local industries or global development funding agencies or whether the PAPs are marginal groups or organized public sector employees who choose to act as the PAPs. In three of the six cases, the PAPs, who were not supported by the policy makers, lost out in Gorai, Borivali and Harihar, while two of the project promoters lost out when not supported by the policy makers, in Dhanbad and Dabhol. Finally, when policy makers promoted co-operation, it was a 'win-win' situation in Mumbai. This is reflected in Table 10.1.

Thus, while PAPs are capable of learning and taking action to bring about social change, all their actions without the overt support of the government agency amount to 'water in sand', whereas with the latter's support, they always emerge as winners.

Thus, to conclude, government agencies responsible for implementing environmental policies should adopt a reconstructive adaptive strategy that should leave the physical environment better off, it should be sustained and strengthened by the social organizations within which it is practised and it should be (socially) just to all the human beings involved. Thus, it should result in a 'win-win' situation for both human beings and the environment, and the rules to arrive at it should be culturally incorporated. They should ensure both the survival of the PAPs and environmental sustainability simultaneously. The EIA methodologies developed as a tool to assess the impacts of development projects, in their present interpretation,

Table 10.1
Strategic Alliances and Outcomes of Projects.

	PAPs and leadership	Promoters	Funding	Alliance	Outcomes
Esselworld Amusement Park	PAPs formed NGO	Private Co.	National FIs	Project+Gov.− PAPs	PAPs lose
Sanjay Gandhi National Park	PAPs	Govt. Dept	Public	Project+Gov.− PAPs	PAPs lose
Moonidih Coal Washery	Public sector employees	International Aid	International Aid	PAP(PSU) +Gov.-Project	Project loses
Dabhol Power Plant	PAPs + Public sector employees	Private Co.	Multinational FIs	PAP(PSU)+Gov. +Pub−Project	Project loses
Harihar town and surrounding area	NGO representing PAPs	State Agency	Public	Gov.+Indiv.−PAPs	PAPs lose
Mumbai Urban Transport Project	PAPs formed NGO	International Aid	International Aid	Co-operative strategy	Win-win

are very limiting. The PAPs hold the new project responsible for the adverse impacts in their neighbourhood and there is substance to their claims. Therefore, it becomes extremely important for the government agency to be sympathetic towards the PAPs, if environmental equilibrium with social justice is to be established. The post-project scenario should leave the PAPs, especially those whose livelihoods were linked with the environmental resources before the project, at least as well off as they were without the project. Therefore, the policy makers should take the local discourse that emerges in relation to the project after the commissioning of the project, seriously. I have argued both at the theoretical level and the pragmatic level for the need to have a post-project evaluation as a mandatory policy with financial allocations promised by the project promoters to be set aside after the commissioning of the project in the form of a corpus fund or development fund. This fund could be used to augment physical and social infrastructure, with the PAPs being the primary beneficiaries. Thus, to conclude, the critical theory of environment provides a useful framework, and critical realism is an appropriate methodology with a practical intent to understand the environmental impacts of development projects more comprehensively.

References

Agarwal, A. and S. Narain, 1998. 'Post-Kyoto Politics, Creative Carbon Accounting', *Down to Earth*, 7(5): 27–37.

AIDAB (Australian International Development Aid Bureau), 1991a. *Social Analysis and Community Participation: Guidelines and Activity Cycle Checklist*, Canberra: Australia: Appraisals, Evaluation and Sectoral Studies Branch.

———, 1991b. Moonidih Coal Washery Project, *EIA Report*, submitted to the Department of Mining, Government of India.

———, 1992a. *Feasibility Study for the Coal Mines Benefication Project, Moonidih India*, Terms of Reference (TOR), 4 August, New Delhi.

———, 1992b. *Thailand Australia Lignite Mine Development Project Phase III*, Project Design Document, January, Canberra.

———, 1992c. *Moonidih Feasibility Design Study*, 6 November, Aide Memoir, Canberra.

Anderson, Benedict, 1983. *Imagined Community: Reflections on the Origin and Spread of Nationalism*, London: Verso.

Appadurai, A. and J. Holston, 1996. 'Cities and Citizenship', *Public Culture*, 8 (2): 187–204.

AusAid, 1997–98. *Socio-economic Profile of People Living in the Neighbourhood of the TSDF (Toxic Solid Waste Disposal Facility)*, Project Report for Andhra Pradesh Pollution Control Board, Hyderabad.

Balaram, Gunavanti, 1998. 'Government Plans to File Affidavit to De-notify Borivali National Park Land', *The Times of India* (Mumbai), 8 November.

Bapat, Jyotsna, 1995a. 'Impact of Infrastructure Development on Urban Communities: A Case Study of Bombay (Storm Water Drainage Project)', Paper presented at the UGC National Seminar on *Society and Environment: Interface and Tensions*, 27–29 March, Kolhapur, Maharashtra: Shivaji University.

———, 1995b. 'Comprehensive EIA Report: Social and Economic Impact', Mumbai: AIC Watson Pvt. Ltd.

———, 1997. 'Amusement Parks, Environment and Social Protest: A Case Study of Mumbai', Project report, 30 June, New Delhi: Indian Council of Social Science Research.

———, 1998. 'Scope of Environmental Sociology: Another View', *Sociological Bulletin*, 47(2): 229–32.

Barik, B.K. (ed.), 2000. *Rural Development and Human Rights Violation*, Jaipur: Rawat Publications.

Barney, G.O. (Study Director), 1981. The Global 2000 Report to the President, 'Entering the Twenty-first Century', Vol. I, Report by Council of Environmental Quality and the Department of State, New York: Michael Pister.

Barrow, C.J., 1997. *Environmental and Social Impact Assessment: An Introduction*, New York: John Wiley and Sons.
Baviskar, Amita, 1997. 'Ecology and Development in India: A Field and Its Future', *Sociological Bulletin*, 46(2): 193–207.
———, 1998. *In the Belly of the River*, New Delhi: Oxford University Press.
BCCL (Bharat Coking Coal Limited), 1992. 'Welfare Measures in Moonidih Area', 1 October, Dhanbad, Bihar: Bharat Coking Coal Ltd. (Mimeograph).
Bennett, John W., 1976. *The Ecological Transition*, New York: Pergamon.
Bharati, A.R., 1992. 'Brief Note on Sanjay Gandhi National Park—Borivali', June, Mumbai: Deputy Conservator of Forests, SGNP Borivali (Mimeograph).
Bhattacherjee, Debashis, 1988. 'Unions, State and Capital in Western India: Structural Determinants of the Bombay Textile Strike', in Roger Southall (ed.), *Labour and Unions in Asia and Africa: Contemporary Issues*, New York: St Martin's Press.
BNHS (Bombay Natural History Society), 1994. 'Conservation Education Project: Baseline Survey Report', August, Mumbai: Bombay Natural History Society.
Bulbus, Issac, 1982. *Marxism and Domination: A Neo-egalitarian, Feminist, Psychoanalytic Theory of Sexual, Political and Technological Liberation*, Princeton, NJ: Princeton University Press.
Business Standard, 2001a. 'Lenders Suspect DPC May Declare Itself Bankrupt: Loss-wary FIs Ask Government to Defuse Dabhol Crisis', 5 January.
———, 2001b. 'Dabhol Invokes Centre's Counter-guarantee', 7 February.
———, 2001c. 'Dabhol Power Play Continues, Maharashtra Throws Ball in PM's Court ... Centre Sends It Right Back', 8 February.
Buttel, Frederick H., 1986. 'Sociology and the Environment: The Winding Road towards Human Ecology', *Institute of Social Science Journal*, 106.
Carson, Rachel, 1962. *Silent Spring*, London: Penguin Books.
Census of India, 1991. *Socio-economic and Cultural Tables*, New Delhi: Government of India Press.
Chakraverty, C., 1996. *Environment for Everyone*, New Delhi: Augustan Publications and Distributors.
Chaturvedi, K.K. and S. Manjunath, 2004. 'Biomethanation of Waste Liquor from Rayon Grade Pulp Mill', May (www.undp.org.in/programme/GEF/June/p26-27.htm).
Clark, Tim and R.L.Wallace, 1998. 'Understanding the Human Face in Endangered Species Recovery: An Introduction to Human Social Process', *Endangered Species UPDATE*, 15(1): 2–9.
Cockerham, William C., 1998. *Medical Sociology*, Seventh edition, Princeton, NJ: Prentice-Hall.
Committed Communities Development (CCD) Trust, n.d. 'Know Our Organisation', Mumbai (Mimeograph).
Connerton, P., 1976. *Critical Socio!ogy*, London: Penguin Books Ltd.
Cooley, Charles H., 1964. *Human Nature and the Social Order*, New York: Schoken.
'Co-operative Societies in Harihar Taluka', 1999. Mimeograph prepared by the Tehsildar, Harihar Taluka.
Croswell, John W., 2002. *Research Design: Qualitative, Quantitative and Mixed Methods Approach*, Second edition, California, USA: Sage Publications.
Damale, Kedar, 2001. 'Enron is Responsible for the Bankruptcy of the MSEB', *Loksatta* (Marathi), 3 March.

Daniel, J.C. and J.S. Serao, 1990. *Conservation in Developing Countries: Problems and Prospects*, Proceedings of the Centenary Seminar of the BNHS, Bombay: Oxford University Press.

De, Arijit, S. Ravindran and Abraham Renni, 2001. 'Maharashtra Dithers on Dabhol Power but Reliance Allowed to Hawk Power from Patalganga to Third Parties', *Business Standard*, 6 May.

De Kadt, E., 1979. *Tourism—Passport to Development? Perspectives on the Social and Cultural Effects of Tourism in Developing Countries*, New York: Oxford University Press, for the World Bank and UNESCO.

Development Alternatives, 1989. *Environmental Restoration of Mines*, Tisco Study, New Delhi.

———, 1989–91. 'Integrated Rural Energy Planning for Sikkim, Phases I, II and III', North and South Sikkim and Sorang Division, New Delhi.

Dhaul, Harry, 2001. 'Power Play: Should We Persuade Enron to Stay on? Yes. Re-negotiate by All Means but Honour the Deal', *The Times of India*, 6 May.

Dobbin, F.R., 1994. 'Cultural Models of Organization: The Social Construction of Rational Organizing Principles', in Dianna Crane (ed.), *The Sociology of Culture: Emerging Theoretical Perspectives*, Malden, MA: Blackwell.

Dreyfus, H.L. and Paul Rabinow (eds), 1987. *Michel Foucault: Beyond Structuralism and Hermeneutics*, Illinois: The Harvest Press.

Drèze, J., M. Samson and S. Singh (eds), 1996. *The Dam and the Nation: Displacement and Resettlement and Rehabilitation in Narmada Valley*, New Delhi: Oxford University Press.

Dunlap, Riley E. and William R. Catton, Jr., 2002. 'Which Functions of the Environment Do We Study? A Comparison of Environmental and Natural Resource Sociology', *Society and Natural Resources*, 15, pp. 239–49.

Dwivedi, Ranajit, 1997. 'Parks People and Protest: The Mediating Role of Environmental Action Group', *Sociological Bulletin*, 46 (2): 209–44.

EIA Report, 1989. 'Environmental Impact Assessment of Esselworld Amusement Park', 24 December, Consent application and report submitted to the Ministry of Environment and Forests, New Delhi.

———, 1992a. 'Hyderabad Sewage Treatment Plant (STP) Part I', March, Associated Industrial Consultants and Brimstoward (UK) for Hyderabad Urban Development Corporation.

———, 1992b. 'Water Quality Monitoring for Rural Drinking Supply', Associated Industrial Consultants and Brimstoward (UK) for Jal Nigam, Uttar Pradesh and Karnataka Water Supply and Sewerage Board, Karnataka.

———, 1993. 'Dabhol Power Plant', Bombay: AIC Watson.

———, 1995. 'Poshir Dam Water Augmentation Project: EIA', Water and Power Corporation, Delhi for Maharashtra Water Supply and Sewerage Board.

Fay, Brian, 1987. *Critical Social Science: Liberation and its Limits*, Cambridge, Great Britain: Polity Press.

Ferguson, J., 1990. *The Anti-politics Machine: Development Depoliticization and Bureaucratic State Power in Lesotho*, New York: Cambridge University Press.

Forester, J.J., 1974. *World Dynamics*, London: Hutchinson.

Forrester, J.W., 1972. 'Alternatives to Catastrophe: Understanding the Counterintuitive Behaviour of Social Systems', in M.S. Gordon and M. Gorden (eds), *Environment, Management Science and Politics*, Boston: Allyn and Bacon Inc.

Fortmann, Lee, 1994. 'Talking Claims: Discursive Strategies in Contesting Property', Paper presented in the Colloquium Series, 14 January, New Haven: Program in Agrarian Studies, Yale University.

Gabor, D., U. Colombo, A. King and R. Galli, 1976. *Beyond the Age of Waste*, London: Hutchinson.

Gazetteer of Bombay Presidency, 1883. Vol. XV, Parts I and II, Kanara, Bombay: Government Press.

———, 1920, Bombay: Government Press.

Giddens, Anthony, 1977. *Studies in Social and Political Theory*, London: Hutchinson.

Gouldner, Alvin W., 1954. *Patterns of Industrial Bureaucracy: A Case Study of Modern Factory Administration*, New York: The Free Press.

———, 1970. *The Coming Crisis in Western Sociology*, London: Heinemann Educational Books Ltd.

Government of Maharashtra, 2002. 'Maharashtra Power Sector Reforms, White Paper', 28 August, Industries, Energy and Labour Department, Mantralaya, Mumbai.

Grove, R. and S. Sagwan (eds), 1997. *Environmental History of South and South-east Asia*, New Delhi and Boston: Cambridge University Press.

Guha, Ramachandra, 1989. *The Unquiet Woods: Ecological Change and Peasant Resistance in the Himalaya*, New Delhi: Oxford University Press.

Guha Ramachandra, and Juan Martinez-Alier, 1997. *Varieties of Environmentalism: Essays North and South*, London: Earth Scan Publications Ltd.

Habermas, Jürgen, 1971. *Knowledge and Human Interests*, trans. by Jeremy J. Shapiro, Boston, MA: Beacon Press.

———, 1988. *On the Logic of Social Science*, trans. by S.W. Nicholsen and J.A. Stark, MIT, USA: Polity Press.

Hanssen, Thomas Bloom, 1996. 'The Vernacularisation of Hindutva: The BJP and Shiv Sena in Rural Maharashtra', *Contributions to Indian Sociology*, 30(2): 175–214.

Hardin, G., 1968. 'The Tragedy of Commons', *Science*, 162: 1243–46.

———, 1974. 'Lifeboat Ethics', in L. Pojman (ed.), *Environmental Ethics: Readings in Theory and Application*, Stanford, CT: Wadsworth/Thomson Learning.

Harre, Rom, 1981. 'The Positive Empiricist Approach and Its Alternative', in P. Reason and J. Rowan (eds), *Human Enquiry: A Source Book of New Paradigm Research*, Chichester: John Wiley.

Held, David, 1980. *Introduction to Critical Theory: Hockheimer to Habermas*, London: Hutchinson and Company Ltd.

Heredia, R.C., 2000. 'Subaltern Alternative on Caste, Class and Ethnicity', *Contributions to Indian Sociology*, 34(1): 37–62.

Hindustan Times, New Delhi, 1984. 'Clergy Leads Kerala Fishermen Agitation', 4 June.

Huizenga, J., 1975. 'Cultural and Biological Adaptation in Man', in M. Salzano (ed.), *The Role of Natural Selection in Human Evolution*, Denmark: North Holland Publication Co.

India Development Service (IDS), Transnational Centre for Non-violent Social Change (TNC) and Samaj Parivathana Samudaya (SPS), 1998. Public Interest Litigation (PIL) filed in Karnataka State High Court, Bangalore.

Indian Express (Mumbai), 1989. 'Beach Development Top Priority', 31 March.

———, 1998. 'Karnatak Farmers Switching over to more Remunerative Crops', 23 July.

Iyer, Mani Shankar, 2001. 'Enroning of Maharashtra: How India's Most Prosperous State was Rendered Bankrupt', *The Indian Express*, New Delhi, 17 April.

Jarvie, I.C., 1972. *Concepts and Society*, London: Routledge and Kegan Paul.

———, 1976. *Revolution in Anthropology*, USA: Routledge and Kegan Paul.

Jenning, J.D. and E.A. Hobel (eds), 1958. *Reading in Anthropology*, New York: McGraw-Hill.

Kalberg, Stephen, 1994. *Max Weber's Comparative-Historical Sociology*, Chicago: University of Chicago Press.

Kant, Emmanuel, 2003 [1929]. *Critique of Pure Reason*, trans. by Norwan Kemp Smith, repr. with a new preface by Howard Caygill, Basingstoke and Hampshire: Palgrave Macmillan.

Karnataka Pollution Control Board (KPCB), 2000. 'Tungabhadra River Basin Project', Report compiled by Montgomery Watson India Pvt. Ltd., Mumbai, for Karnataka Pollution Control Board (KPCB), Bangalore.

King, A., 1975. 'The Club of Rome—An Insider's View', *Economic Impact*, No. 12.

Kongovi, Dandavatimath and L. Markande, 1986. 'Pollution and Its Effects Caused by Industries in Tungabahdra River at Kumarapatnam, Ranibennur *Taluka*, Dharwad District, Karnataka State', *Samaj Parivartana Samudaya*, Karnataka (Second revised edition was published in 1993).

Kosambi, Meera, 1986. *Bombay in Transition: The Growth and Social History of a Colonial City, 1880–1980*, Stockholm, Sweden: Almquist and Wiksell International.

Kothari, A., S. Singh and S. Suri (eds), 1996. *People and Protected Areas: Towards Participatory Conservation in India*, New Delhi: Sage Publications.

Ladden, David, 1990. *Peasant Hostory in South India*, New Delhi: Oxford University Press.

———, 1999. *An Agrarian History of South Asia*, New Cambridge History of India IV, UK: Cambridge University Press.

Maharashtra Times (Marathi), 2002. 'Annual Review of the Economy—Maharashtra State', 22 March.

Manohar, N.S., 1993. 'The Roller Coaster Ride', *The Independent*, Mumbai, 27 February.

Meadows, D.H., Dennis L. Meadows, Jorgen Randers and William W. Behrens III, 1972. *The Limits to Growth, A Report for the Club of Rome's Predicament of Mankind*, London: Pan Books Ltd

McKechnie, Alastair J., 2000. 'Transparency and Good Governance in Infrastructure Concessions', *Seminar on Building Knowledge and Expertise in Infrastructure Finance*, 7 July, Washington, DC: World Bank Development Institute.

Merton, R.K., 1968. *Social Theory and Social Structure*, New York: Amerind Publishing Co.

Mesorovic, M. and E. Pestel, 1975. *Mankind at Turning Point, The Second Report to the Club of Rome*, London: Hutchinson.

Metropolitan Environmental Improvement Plan (MEIP), 1993–94. Project Report, Mumbai: AIC Watson.

———, 1994. Umbrella Project, Mumbai: AIC and Cooper & Lybrand, UK, for World Bank.

Mills, C.W., 1960. *Images of Man*, New York: George Braziller Inc.

Morris, Peter and Riki Therivel (eds), 1995. *Methods of Environmental Impact Assessment*, Vancouver, Canada: University of British Columbia Press.

Mumbai Metropolitan Regional Development Authority (MMRDA), 1994. Report on *Transport Improvement Strategy for Mumbai Metropolitan Region*, A.K. Atkins Consultants, UK.

———, 1995. 'Bombay Urban Transportation Project II', AIC-Watson, Mumbai.

———, 1997. 'Environmental Impact Study of Urban Transportation Projects', AIC-Watson, Mumbai.

MUTP (Mumbai Urban Transport Project), 1997. 'Summary of the EIS Study', 2 June, prepared by AIC-Watson (Mimeograph).

———, 2001. 'Resettlement Action Plan', December, MMRDA, Mumbai (Mimeograph).

O' Connor, James, 1998. *Natural Causes: Essays in Ecological Marxism*, New York. The Guildford Press.

Omvedt, Gail. 1993. *Reinventing Revolution: New Social Movements and the Socialist Tradition in India*, New York: M.E. Sharpe Inc.

Pareikh, J.K., J.P. Painuly and Hemlata Rao 1985. 'A Rural Energy—Agriculture Interaction Model Applied to Karnataka State', Discussion Paper No. 3, Mumbai: Indira Gandhi Institute of Development Research.

Pareikh, J.K., J.P. Painuly and D.R. Shah, 1991. 'Rural Energy System and Agriculture: Alternative Scenarios for Gujarat', Discussion Paper No. 66, Mumbai: Indira Gandhi Institute of Development Research.

Pareikh, J.K. B.S. Panesar, Bhatnagar and J.P. Painuly, 1989. 'Modelling of Energy and Agriculture Interactions: A Case Study of Punjab State', Discussion Paper, Mumbai: Indira Gandhi Institute of Development Research.

Pareikh, J.K., R.P. Singh and J.P. Painuly, 1993. 'Rural Energy and Agricultural Interactions in 2000 AD: A Study of Uttar Pradesh', Discussion Paper No. 5, Mumbai: Indira Gandhi Institute of Development Research.

Pareikh, J.K., K.P. Pareikh, S.V. Gokarn, J.P. Painuly, B. Saha and V. Shukla, 1991. 'Consumption Patterns: The Driving Force of Environmental Stress', Discussion Paper No. 59, Mumbai: Indira Gandhi Institute of Development Research.

Parisar Sanwardhini, n.d. 'Environmental Impact of Industry Discharge in Tungabhadra River', Mimeograph.

Parsons, Talcott, 1967. *Social Theory and Modern Society*, New York: The Free Press.

Parsuraman, S., 1990. *Social Environment in Bolani*, Project Report, Kolkata: Steel Authority of India and BHP Kinhill Joint Venture.

———, 1991. *Involuntary Resettlement of People Displaced by Maharashtra II Irrigation Project*, Mumbai: Tata Institute of Social Sciences.

Peel, J.D.Y., 1972. *Herbert Spencer on Social Evolution*, Chicago: University of Chicago Press.

Polanyi, Karl, 1944. *The Great Transformation: The Political and Economic Origins of Our Times*, Boston: Beacon Press.

Punch, Keith C., 1978. *Introduction to Social Research: Quantitative and Qualitative Approaches*, California, USA: Sage Publications.

Ramachandran, Rajesh A., 2001a. 'A Power Failure Foretold', *The Times of India* (Mumbai), 13 February.

———, 2001b. 'Enron Counter-guarantee was Too Generous', *The Times of India* (Mumbai), 14 February.

Robson, Colin, 2002. *Real World Research: A Resource for Social Scientists and Practitioner-Researchers*, Second edition, Malden, MA: Blackwell Publishers.

Rothermund, D., 1978. 'The Coal Fields—An Enclave in the Backward Region', in D. Rothermund and D.C. Wadhawa (eds), *Zamindars, Mines and Peasants: Studies in the History of Indian Coal Fields and Its Rural Hinterlands*, New Delhi: Manohar.

Rothermund, I., 1983. 'Trade Unions and Trade Union Leadership in the Coal Fields', in J.P. Neelsen (ed.), *Social Inequality and Political Structures*, New Delhi: Manohar.

Rudel, Thomas, 2002. 'Sociologist in the Service of Sustainable Development?: NGOs and Environment—Society Studies in Developing World', *Society and Natural Resources*, 15: 263–68.

Savur, M., 1999. *Paper Industry*, IDPAD Project on the Paper Industry, New Delhi: Manohar.

Scheper-Hughes, Nancy, 1989. 'Death without Weeping: Has Poverty Ravaged Mother Love in the Shanty Towns of Brazil?', *Natural History*, 18 (October).

Schroyer, Trent, 1983. 'Critique of the Instrumental Interest in Nature', *Social Research*, 50(1): 158–84.

Schumacher, E.F., 1984. *Small is Beautiful: Economics as if People Mattered*, London: Penguin.

Schutt, Russel, 2001. *Investigating the Social World: The Process and Practice of Research*, California, USA: Pine Forge Press, Sage Publications Company.

Scott, Catherine V., 1995. *Gender and Development: Rethinking Modernization and Dependency Theory*, Boulder, Co: Lynn Rienner Publishers.

Scott, James C., 1976. *Moral Economy of the Peasant: Rebellion and Subsistence in South-east Asia*, New Haven: Yale University Press.

———, 1985. *Weapons of the Weak: Everyday Forms of Peasant Resistance*, New Haven, CT: Yale University Press.

Seidensticker, J., M.E. Sunquist and C. McDougal, 1990. 'Leopards Living at the Edge of the Royal Chitwan National Park, Nepal', in J.C. Daniel and J.S. Serao (eds), *Conservation in Developing Countries: Problems and Prospects, Proceedings of the Centenary Seminar of the Bombay Natural History Society*, Mumbai: Oxford University Press.

Shekhar, Nagothu Uday, 1998. 'Crop and Livestock Depredation Caused by Wild Animals in Protected Areas: The Case of Sariska Tiger Reserve', *Environmental Conservation*, 25 (2): 160–71.

Selltiz, C., K. Wrightsman and S. Cook, 1970. *Research Methods in Social Relations*, USA: Holt, Rinehart and Winston.

Singh, Satyajit, 1997. 'Introduction', in J. Drèze, M. Samson and S. Singh (eds), *The Dam and the Nation: Displacement and Resettlement in Narmada Valley*, New Delhi: Oxford University Press.

Steward, J.W., 1978. *Sociology, The Human Science*, New York: McGraw Hill Book Co.

Tak, Devendra, 1992. 'Setting a Fantasy', *Business India*, Mumbai, 12 October.

The Times of India (Mumbai), 1984. 'Church Dilemma over Fishermen's Stir', 4 June.

———, 1993. 'Esselworld Closed Indefinitely', 15 August.

———, 2002. 'Debt Ridden State—Banes of Reforms', 23 March.

Tinbergen, A., 1976. *Reshaping the International Order*, London: Hutchinson.

Tomas, W.I. and F. Zennenski, 1978. 'Three Types of Personality', in C.W. Mills (ed.), *Images of Man: The Classic Tradition in Sociological Thinking*, New York, George Braziller Inc.

Tulpule, B. and R.C. Dutta, 1995. 'New Technology, Productivity, Employment and Workers Response', in A.K. Bagchi (ed.), *New Technology and the Workers' Response: Microelectronics, Labour and Society*, New Delhi: Sage Publications.

United Nations, 1992. *Foreign Direct Investment and Technology Transfer in India*, New York: UN Centre on Transnational Corporations.

Volkart, E.H. (ed.), 1951. *Social Behaviour and Personality*, New York: Social Science Research Council.

Ward, B. and R. Dubois, 1972. *Only One Earth: The Care and Maintenance of a Small Planet*, New York: W.W. Norton.

Weber, Max, 1958. *The Protestant Ethic and the Spirit of Capitalism*, New York: Scribner's Press.

———, 1998 [1908]. *The Agrarian Sociology of Ancient Civlizations*, London and New York: Verso.

World Bank, 2001. 'Supply of Power to Agriculture, Haryana,' Report of World Bank Workshop, New Delhi, 7 February.

Index

Adaptive dynamics paradigm, 37–39, 43–45, 50, 57, 67
Adaptive strategies, biological adaptation, 51; definition of, 51; socio-cultural adaptation, 51
Agrarian sociology, 15
Amusement park, Gorai Islands, articulation of protest in environmental terms against, 94–95; case study on development of, 87–108, 218, 223; population of, and, 87–88; EIA, 89, 96, 101–02, 106; environmental changes due to, 93–94; environmental protest movement against, 87, 94–96; global influence, 101–03; impact of, on locale, 89–93, 107–08; other protest movements and protest movement against, 96–98; perceptions of local people about, 103–06; political battles over access to resources, 98–101; state response to protest movement, 96; local narratives about 103–06, 220–21
Anna Bari system, 29
Anti-caste movements, 29
Australian International Development Aid Bureau (AIDAB), 151, 153–54, 161, 165

Base–superstructure theorem, 43
Bechtel Power Corporation, 129
Bharat Coking Coal Limited (BCCL), 154, 160, 170, 221
Bombay Environmental Action Group (BEAG), 119
Bombay National Park Act, 1950, 112
Bombay Urban Transport Project-I (BUTP-I), 191, 199

Central Electricity Board (CEB), 136
Central Wage Board, 156
Change, origin to, 40, 44; resistance to, 62
Chipko Andalan, 29
Citizens for Just Society, 190, 196
Closed system, 83
Club of Rome, 16, 38
Coal India Limited (CIL), 154
Coastal Regulation Zone (CRZ), 100
Common property resources, access to, 63, 68; exploitation of, 62
Communication, theory of, 48–49, 70
Communicative competence, acquisition of, 48–49
Community participation, concept of, 163

Comparative sociology, 15
Constitutive interests, theory of, 49
Constructivist approach, 79
Contract Labour Abolition and Regulation Act, 156
Crisis and reflexivity, new learning emerging from, 59
Crisis, in environment, 44–47; Kantian, 55
Critical realism, emancipatory approach guided by, 80, 83, 85
Critical theory of environment, 37–38; amusement park and, 107; defence of universal values, 52–59; enlightenment, 44–47; lacuna in, 48–49; mode of combining the paradigms, 49–50; new learning, 59–64; paradigm, 39–41; points of disagreement, 41–44; reconstructive strategies, 50–52; research programme to develop, 36–37; theoretical development, 36–69; transformative action, 64–69
Critic, and the conception of environmental 'well-being', 46, 47; environmental, 44; role of, in development of project outcomes, 70

Dabhol Power Company (DPC), 129–30, 132, local narratives, 143–45; MSEB and, 135–38; protest movement, 145–46
Dabhol Power Project, Dabhol, ambivalence of local people about, 139; breach of social obligations by, 140–43; case study on, 129–50, 219; EIA of, 131–33; finances to, 130–31; locale of study on, 130–31; moral economy and, 139–43; power sector reforms and, 147–49; risk perceptions, 136–38; socioeconomic impact of, 132–33
Damodar Valley Project, 154
Data collection methods, 83
Department of Environment and Forests, 71

Dependency theory, 16, 19, 76
Devangiri district, Karnataka, 174–76
Development, environment theories and, 15–22; modernization theory, 16; sustainable, 16, 18, 20–22
Development projects, associated impacts, 216–17; construction stage, 14; definition, 36; delays in initiation due to protest, 73–74; ecological justice, 223–24; emergence of crisis, 219–20; environmental backlash against, 73–74; environmental impacts of, 15–16, 26–29, 58–59, 84; environmental protest and survival, 216–28; environmental sustainability, 217–18; essentializing the displaced and, 72–73; impacts on local communities, 55, 58, 217; impacts on subsistence economies, 62; Indian context, 26–28; initiation stage, 14; location decision, 218-19; moral claims, 223–24; new learning, 220–22; operational stage, 14; outcome of protest movements against, 225–28; planning and conceptualization stage, 14; pre-project socioeconomic impact assessment of, 28; reaction of PAPs to, 65–67, 74–76; resistance strategies, 64; scientific methodological approaches, 77–78; social environmental impact, 26, 29, 31–34; social protest movement and, 66; socio-cultural sphere context, 76–77, 84; sociopolitical consequences of, 21, 67–68, 84; stages of, 14, 27, 33; talking claims, 103–06, 121–22, 143–45, 220–22; transformative action, 224–25
Disequilibria, causes of, 40
Displaced people, human rights violation of, 72–73; resettlement and rehabilitation of, 72

Ecological carrying capacity model, 38
Ecological competence, features of, 52–53; general theory of, 48; universal value of, 52, 58, 84
Ecological paradigm, systems approach to, 39–40
Economic growth, concept of, 46; social justice and, 14
Eco-systemic models, 23
Emancipatory approach, guided by critical realism, 80
Enlightenment, 41, 44–47
Enron Virodhi Manch, 145, 147
Environment adaptation, theory of, 70
Environment development nexus, 37
Environment theories, critical theory, 24, 33; development and, 15–22; general theory of, 49
Environmental crisis, 44–47, 48, 54, 58
Environmental critique, 44–48, 53
Environmental Impact Assessment (EIA), 18, 25, 27, 58, 70, 74, 87, 131–33, 137, 139, 141, 193, 216
Environmental movements, 29–30
Environmental policy, pragmatic interest in, 31–32
Environmental protest movements, 20–21, 30–31; articulation of, 94–96; comparison with other movements, 96–98; national park at Borivali, 111–27; political battles and, 98–101, 124, 146–47; pollution in Tungabhadra river, 178–89; power generation project at Dabhol, 129–50; *see also*, Project-affected peoples (PAPs); state response to, 96, 118–21, 126, 147–49; technology transfer project, 151–71
Environmental sociology, 13–14, 24, 28, 36; trends in, 71–76
Environmental struggles, innovative alliances in, 73

Environmental well-being, 46
Esselworld Amusement Park; *see*, Amusement Park, Gorai Islands

Farmer's movement, 29
Fishworkers Co-operative Society, 93
Foreign direct investment (FDI), 152–53
Forest Conservation of Wildlife Act, 113
Forest Development Corporation, 112
Freedom, struggle for, 41

Gazetteer of Bombay Presidency, 87, 174
General Electric Company, 129–30
Global common resources, 17
Global environmental movement, 21
Godbole Committee report, 147
Gorai Islands, access to common property resources, 91–92, 95; before amusement park, 88; case study of development of amusement park at, 87–108; community, 87–88; impact of development of amusement park on locale, 89–95, 107–08; infrastructure facilities in, 93–94; *see also*, Amusement park, Gorai Islands
Greater Mumbai Municipal Corporation (GMMC), 178, 199–200
Green Revolution, 26

Habermas, communicative action, 57–58; crisis situation, 45; critic of knowledge, 56, 59; critical theory of 37, 45, 48–49; ecological issues, 48–49; general theory of communication, 70; methodology 53–54; new social movements, 29; synchronic approach, 42; universality of hermeneutics, 54, 59

Index 239

Harihar Polyfibres, 176
Harihar taluka, Karnataka; cooperative societies in, 175; locale of, 174–76; major players in development of, 176–77
Hermeneutics, 42, 54, 59
Human ecology, 22–26, 39–40; crisis faced by, 54; learning in, 57
Human–environment relationship, 22, 37, 48, 50, 53, 84
Human rights violation, 72–73
Human societies, problems faced by, 40
India Development Service (IDS), 178–79
Industrial and infrastructure development project, realities and challenges faced by, 14
Industrial estates, passive resistance by communities in, 71–72
Inner-self, 41, 44
Interpretative approach, 79

J.B. D'Souza Committee, 100
Jangal Mitra Bachao Rally, 111
Just and right, concept of, 46–47

Karnataka Pollution Control Board (KPCB), 173, 177–78, 219
Kerala Fishworkers' agitation, 95–98, 145
Keynesian welfare economics model, 19
Knowledge, about environment, 46; as science, 42, 54; constitutive interest, 42, 54–55, 59; creation of, 54; critique of, 56, 59, 61; forms of, 41; problem due to, 46; self-reflection of, 41
Krishnagiri National Park, 112

Labour union and coal mafia, 156–57
Learning, theory of, 44, 48
Lifeboat metaphor, 17
Limits to Growth, 16

Machimar Co-operative Society, Gorai, 97, 99

Maharashtra Housing and Area Development Authority (MHADA), housing needs, 195–97; construction of houses, 205; lossmaking, 214
Maharashtra Industrial Development Corporation (MIDC), 131, 139
Maharashtra State Electricity Board (MSEB), 129–31, 134–38, 146–50, 221; power sector reforms and, 147–49; risk perception by, 137–38
Mahila Milan, 204
Marxian sociology, 29
Marxian theories, 43, 57
Ministry of Environment and Forests (MOEF), 58, 71, 96, 100
Mississippi Valley Project, 154
Moonidih coal washery, audits, 162–63, 167–68; claims made by Aide Memoir, 162–65; coal mafia, 156–57; community, 157–58; contestation, 169; health and occupational safety audit, 167; historical background, 154–56; labour unions, 156–57; local narratives, 163–68; outcome of audit results, 169–70; perception of working conditions, 167; plant setting, 157; point of entry, 160–62; recommendations, 168–70; SWOT analysis, 166; sociological profile, 158–59; technical profile, 157–58; work culture at, 159–60
Moral ecology claims, 62–63, 75
Moral economy, 139–43; traditional agrarian system and, 62–65, 75
Mumbai Urban Transportation Project-II (MUTP-II), challenge before the state, 199–201; challenges and achievements of resettlement, 207–09; EIA of, 193; formation of societies by PAPs, 206–07; housing issue and, 195–96; ideologies of NGO and, 201–04; internal battles amongst

PAPs, 213–14; locale of, 193–95; Mumbai before the project, 191; perception of benefits and losses, 209–13; perception of PAPs resettled, 198–201; process, 192–93; resettlement of people obstructing, 196–99; resettlement process, 204–06; study on, 190–215, 219; talking claims, 210–13
Mumbai Metropolitan Regional Development Authority (MMRDA), 89, 100, 190, 192–93, 197, 199–200, 205–06, 213–14, 219
Mysore Kirloskar, 176

Narmada Bachao Andolan, 29–30, 71, 95–98, 118, 137, 145
National Alliance of People's Movement, 145
National Fishworkers Federation, Kerala, 96
National parks, as protected areas, 109–11, 114–15; formation, 112–13; see, Sanjay Gandhi National Park (SGNP), Borivali
National Slum Dwellers Federation (NSDF), 201, 203–05, 207, 213–14
Nationalist development model, 19
Natural resource sociology, 13, 39
Naturalistic approach, 79
New social movements, 29–30, 65
Non-violent protest, strategies of, 30

Peasant struggles, 29
Political ecology, 19
Political economic models, 19
Pollution Control Board (PCB), 168, 190, 222
Positivism, 78, 81–83
Positivistic view, concept of, 78–79
Preservation First! (PF!) principle, 19–21, 66
Production, structuralist theory of, 43

Project-affected persons (PAPs), 14–15, 20–21, 23–25, 32, 34, 50, 55–56, 62–69, 80, 83–85, 107–08; at amusement park, Gorai Islands, 87–108; at national parks, 111–27; at SGNP, Borivali, 111–27; breach of social obligations towards, 140–43; impact of development project on, 89–93, 107–08, 115–16, 126, 140–45, 206–14, 216; ownership rights, 56; perceptions of, about projects, 103–06, 140–43; political actions, 98–101, 124, 146–47; power generation project, 130–50; protests by, 94–96, 116–17, 145–46; resistance by, 94–98, 124–25, 127, 129; role in project implementation, 74–76; state response to, 96, 118–21, 126, 147–45; talking claims, 103–06, 111–24, 143–45; urban transportation project, 193–94, 198–215
Protected areas (PAs), crisis due to, 115–16; in India, 110; national parks as, 109–11; state action and, 118
Protected Areas Act, 1974, 116

Quality of life, concept of, 46

Real world research, plans for, 80–83
Realism, 80–83
Reciprocal social obligation, 64, 140–43
Reconstructive strategies, 50–52; primacy to life-world, 53
Recreational tourism, trend in, 102
Reduce, re-use and recycle (3Rs), of resources, 18
Relativism, 78, 81
Relativistic views, 78–79
Research methodology, backlash against projects, 73–74; bridge between theory and practice 76; constructionist currents, 79–80;

data collection methods, 83; emancipatory approach guided by critical realism, 80; essentializing the displaced, 72–73; inconsistencies, 74–76; innovative alliances in environmental struggles, 73; plans for realworld research, 80–83; positivistic view and its critique, 78; post-positivistic currents, 79–80; relativistic views and rejecting the extreme, 78; scientific, 77; theory and practice relations, 84–86; trends in environmental sociology and, 71–76

Research programme, 36–37; steps of, 37

Risk-averse behaviour, 61–62

Risk-taking behaviour, 61

SDCA, 193

SIDHI, 193, 201

Samaj Parivartana Samudaya (SPS), 173, 178–79

Sanjay Gandhi National Park (SGNP), Borivali; background, 111–12; case study, 111–27; crisis in tribal communities in, 115–16, 126; formation of, 112–13; harassment narratives about, 122–24; local community, 114, 126; non-benefit narratives about, 122–24; non-harmonious relations and self-help, 118; objectives of management of, 113, 125; passive resistance strategy, 127; perceptions about, 122–24; political action against eviction from, 124; resistance to, 124–25; state action against tribals in, 118–21, 126; talking claims about, 121–22, 220–21; transformative action of tribal communities, 116–17

Scientific methodology, 77

Self-knowledge, 41

Self-reflection, of knowledge, 41–42

Short-term equilibrium, maintenance of, 40

Silent Spring, 16

Slum Rehabilitation Society (SRS), 193, 201

Small is beautiful, doctrine of, 49

Social action, 60

Social evolution, theory of, 48

Social forestry projects, 29

Social Impact Assessment (SIA), 18, 25, 68, 74–75, 133

Social justice and economic growth, 14

Social obligation, breach of, 64

Social protest movement, 31, 65–66, 71; theoretical knowledge about, 28–31

Social situation, individual interpretations of, 61

Social systems, crises, 48; diachronic process of, 42

Socialist planning model, 19

Socialization, theory of, 48

Society, critical theory of, 45, 48; static image of, 42

Society for Preservation and Resource Conservation (SPARC), 193, 201, 203, 205–09

Socio-cultural models, of human interaction, 23

Socio-cultural systems, 38–39

Structural imbalance, 46–47

Survival, minimum security of, 62

Survival first principle, 63, 85, 218

Sustainable development, 16, 18, 20–22, 76

Sustainable resource exploitation, normative principle of, 46

System dynamics model, 38

Talcott Parsons, adaptation, 51; systems theory, 51

Talking claims, strategy of, 60–61, 75, 83, 103–06, 111–24, 143–45

Techno-economic systems, 53, 84

Technological development, logic of, 43

Technology transfer, historical background, 154–56; policy, 152–53; through aid, 151, 153; value-neutral, 153
Theory and practice, relationship, 84–86
Tourism, as green and nonpolluting industry, 102
Traditional agrarian system and moral economy, 62–63
Tragedy of commons doctrine, 17
Transformative action, 64–69
Transnational Centre for Nonviolent Social Change, 178
Tungabhadra Parisara Samiti (TPS), 173
Tungabhadra River Basin pollution, demographic profile of villages along the river, 184–85; drinking water, 186; environmental NGOs protest movement against in, 178–80; findings of survey, 183–84; future of protest movement, 189; human impacts of, 186–87; impact on plants and animals, 187; locale of study on, 174–76; major fish kill incident and, 172–73, 179–80; methodology to study on, 182–83; perception about industry, 187–88; perception of pollution, 186–87; perception of water, 185–86; protest movement against in, 178–79; risk perception by people, industry and KPCB, 177–78; scientific validity, 181; socio-economic profile of families along the river, 185; study on, 173–89, 219, 223; talking claims, 180; water used for washing, bathing, animals and agriculture, 186

United Nations Development Program (UNDP), 16
Universal ecological competence, 52, 58, 84

Vyavasai Sahakar Sangh Bank (VSSB), 175

WS Atkins International, UK, 192
Weber, Max, and environmental sociology, 15, 36; causal models 15, 24;
Well-being, conception of, 46
Wildlife Conservation Act, 1974, 110, 115
Women in development (WID), 163
Women's movement, 29

About the Author

Jyotsna Bapat is Senior Consultant at Feedback Ventures (P) Ltd, New Delhi. She was Substantive Faculty at the Department of Sociology, the University of Bombay (Mumbai), from 1991 to 2003. Her academic training in anthropology, along with her experiences at the National Council of Applied Economic Research (NCAER) and the Indian Institute of Technology (IIT), Bombay (from where she obtained her doctoral degree), provided her with both the theoretical and technical insight that have stood her in good stead in the numerous projects she has undertaken, concurrent with her responsibilities at Mumbai University. These projects were commissioned by bilateral and multilateral agencies, including the Overseas Development Agency (ODA), the Department for International Development (DFID), the Ford Foundation, AusAid and the World Bank.

Dr Bapat was Visiting Scholar at the Program in Agrarian Studies in Yale University (1997–98), and Fulbright Fellow under the Scholar in Residence Program at Macalester College in Minnesota, USA (2002–03). Besides an array of research and project reports, she has contributed articles to edited volumes and to journals like *Contributions to Indian Sociology, Sociological Bulletin, Journal of Indian Anthropological Society* and *Journal of Human Ecology*.